BOSTON

CAMERON SPERANCE

CONTENTS

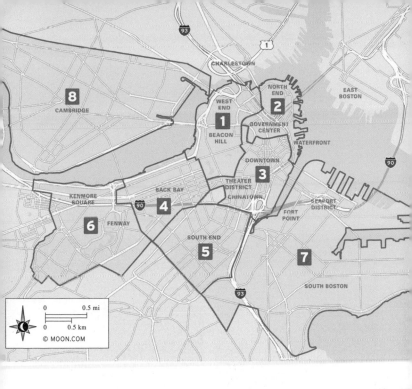

MAPS

Neighborhoods

Day Trips

DISCOVER
BOSTON

Welcome to Boston, a city on the cusp of its 400th birthday in 2030. While boldly looking forward to its future as the "new" Boston, it still warmly embraces its past—after all, this is the birthplace of the United States. Lace up a pair of comfortable shoes, grab a coffee, and meander the Freedom Trail to take in all 16 sites that commemorate the transformation of a rebellious group of colonies into a thriving global superpower.

History and higher education are Boston's backbone. The New England city's collegiate charm brings thousands of students to leafy campuses (and urban ones) around the metro area each fall. They are increasingly joined by a surge of new arrivals seeking employment in the region's booming technology and health-care industries. James Beard Award-winning restaurants seem to pop up on every cobblestoned corner. Bostonians flock downtown throughout the year for beer gardens, piping hot "lobstah" rolls, food trucks, and summer concerts in the same spot that once housed never-ending traffic.

Despite its progressive vision of the future, Boston wants you to remember where it came from. From the snowy, gaslit streets of Beacon Hill to the Italian Renaissance architecture of Copley Square—and even its glassy skyline on the rise—Boston is a walk through history.

10 TOP EXPERIENCES

1 **Walk the Freedom Trail:** Why read about history when you can walk through it? Follow the redbrick road and explore 16 key moments from the nation's past (page 65).

PUBLIC GARDEN
1837

2 **Catch a Game at Fenway Park:** Even if you don't root, root, root for the Red Sox, the country's oldest ballpark is worth a peek (page 74).

3 **Get Inspired at Harvard University:** You can't *pahk ya cah on the yahd*, but it's hard not to feel smarter after walking through the gates of the most esteemed university in the United States (page 78).

>>>

4 **Stroll the Boston Public Garden:** This array of seasonal plants and art installations is a must-see (page 64).

>>>

5 **Wander Faneuil Hall Marketplace:** The "Cradle of Liberty" is more like the cradle of shops and restaurants today. Enjoy the street performers and stick around for the nightlife (page 68).

>>>

6 **Check out the USS *Constitution* Museum:** Old Ironsides is alive and kicking—er, floating. See the ship that saved the United States (page 79).

<<<

7 **Shop on Newbury Street:** From vintage to couture and quirky to risqué, this street continues to be Boston's retail mecca for all tastes, shapes, and budgets (page 173).

8 **Gaze at Masterpieces at the Museum of Fine Arts:** Boston's most comprehensive museum spans French Impressionism and cutting-edge contemporary works—all under the same roof (page 75).

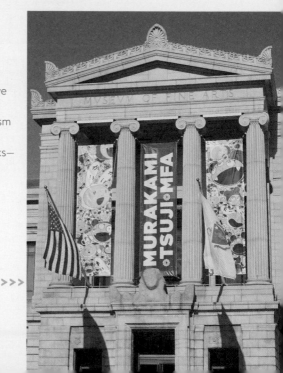

9 **Grab a Pint:** Home to Sam Adams and Cheers, not to mention numerous Irish pubs, sports bars, and new-school craft breweries, this city deserves a toast (page 123).

10 **Sample Boston's Classic Eats:** Lobster rolls and Boston cream pie, red sauce and Dunkin' Donuts . . . it's hard to label one dish as Boston's best, so try them all (page 85)!

<<<

EXPLORE
BOSTON

THE BEST OF BOSTON

>DAY 1:
BEACON HILL, GOVERNMENT CENTER, AND CHARLESTOWN

Any visit to Boston should start with the **Freedom Trail,** the city's most popular tourist attraction. Grab a coffee and breakfast on Charles Street in **Beacon Hill** and wander a few blocks up Beacon Street along **Boston Common,** the starting point of the 2.5-mile (4-km) trail. Continue up Beacon to the gold-domed Massachusetts State House.

Following the redbrick course of the Freedom Trail will take most of the day. Stops eight and nine (Old City Hall and the **Old South Meeting House**) are in **Downtown Crossing,** an area of countless restaurants, bars, and cafés that's a great spot to stop for lunch.

With some post-lunch pep in your step, head to the **Old State House** and the nearby monument to those who lost their lives in the Boston Massacre.

>> **PUBLIC TRANSIT:** If you want to skip some stops along the Freedom Trail, the Orange Line runs from State Station (below the

Old State House

BOSTON BY PUBLIC TRANSIT (THE "T")

Love it or hate it, Bostonians religiously rely on the MBTA, or the "T" as it is known to locals. The T is the oldest subway system in the United States, and because of that, it sometimes doesn't run as well as it should—but leaders say they're working hard to improve it. That being said, it is extremely convenient, comprehensive, and affordable compared to other systems around the country. Stop by South Station, North Station, Back Bay Station, or Downtown Crossing for on-site help with tickets and CharlieCards.

Old State House) to Haymarket Station and North Station, the most convenient access points for the North End.

After the dose of colonial history, head up Congress Street to Boston's City Hall. Marvel at the Brutalist architecture and then continue on the Freedom Trail into **Faneuil Hall Marketplace.**

After Faneuil Hall, head into the **North End** and **Charlestown** to round out the final portion of the Freedom Trail, a can't-miss section that includes **Paul Revere's House**

Paul Revere's House

and the **USS Constitution.** Be sure to save energy to return to the North End for dinner—**Neptune Oyster** is excellent for seafood, and any of the Hanover Street establishments are great for Italian. Dessert means making the decision between **Mike's Pastry** and **Modern Pastry** for cannoli.

> DAY 2: FENWAY, BACK BAY, AND SOUTH END

Hop on the Green Line to **Kenmore Station** and start your day with breakfast at **Eastern Standard,** conveniently located just above the station. Fueled up, head up Brookline Avenue to **Fenway Park** for an early tour of the country's oldest ballpark. Save time for **souvenir shopping** along Jersey Street and to enjoy an early beer at **Bleacher Bar** (built directly into the stadium!) on Lansdowne Street.

You can get back on the T, but if weather permits, walk the 10-15 minutes from Kenmore Square into Back Bay along the **Commonwealth Avenue Mall,** a leafy green space that runs the length of the neighborhood. Depending on your mood, the **Charles River Esplanade** is a great waterfront retreat where you can take a break from your morning strolling and touring. Veer one block to the south, and you'll be in the heart of shopping and dining mecca **Newbury Street.**

>> **PUBLIC TRANSIT:** Back Bay is accessible from Kenmore Square via any of the inbound Green Line trains. Take the train from Kenmore Station to Hynes, Copley, or Arlington Station.

Commonwealth Avenue eventually runs directly into the **Boston**

Commonwealth Avenue Mall

Public Garden, a picturesque spot filled with the fruits of some of the city's top greenhouses. If weather isn't ideal, grab a drink at the **Four Seasons Boston** to view the park from the dry indoors.

After the Public Garden, spend the afternoon visiting the attractions of nearby **Copley Square**. The **Boston Public Library** and **Trinity Church** are the most popular attractions in the neighborhood, while the **Prudential Skywalk Observatory** is literally the top view in town.

If you continue up Huntington Avenue, you can take a **Boston Duck Tour** departing from the Prudential Center. After you finish, walk down Dartmouth Street into the **South End** for eclectic dining and drinks in Boston's quirky, off-the-beaten-path neighborhood.

>> **PUBLIC TRANSIT:** You can also take an E-branch Green Line train from Copley Square to Prudential for an easier commute to the Prudential Center.

the Harborwalk

PRUDENTIAL SKYWALK OBSERVATORY
Boston's tallest observation deck, the Skywalk Observatory delivers the only 360-degree view in town, from the 50th floor of the Prudential Tower (page 73).

INSTITUTE OF CONTEMPORARY ART
While the art inside is breathtaking, the view of Boston Harbor, downtown, and Logan Airport from the ICA's glassy gallery is art in itself (page 77).

BUNKER HILL MONUMENT
Climb the 221 feet (67 m) to the top of this Charlestown memorial to the Revolutionary battle of the same name to get a breathtaking view of downtown (page 80).

HARBORWALK
This public walkway takes you along several piers and wharves as it winds along Boston Harbor. From jumbo jets landing at Logan Airport to a skyline backdrop to your selfie, the Harborwalk knows how to shake it up (page 163).

ARNOLD ARBORETUM
One of the largest links in Boston's Emerald Necklace, the Arnold Arboretum gives a one-of-a-kind view of the Boston skyline from its Peter's Hill (page 165).

>DAY 3: CAMBRIDGE AND SEAPORT

Start your day with a coffee—it's hard to avoid a **Dunkin' Donuts** while in town—and make your way to **South Station** (or any Red Line station). Take the train to **Harvard University**—it's time to see the "yahd."

An hour at **Harvard Yard** is enough to take in the architecture of the buildings on the university's main campus. If you're able to spend more time, the **Harvard Art Museums** and the **Harvard Museum of Natural History** can easily fill the rest of your morning.

Once you're done exploring campus, plan lunch in Harvard Square. **Alden & Harlow** is wonderful for weekend brunch, and **Harvest** is a great spot for lunch any day.

After getting some neighborhood bites, be sure to take time to explore Harvard Square's bookstores and other independent retailers. Afterward, hop back on the Red Line to South Station. Once you're back above ground, take a stroll along the **Rose Kennedy Greenway** and veer over to the **Harborwalk.** Take in the magnificent views of Boston Harbor, and as it gets closer to sundown, pop over to the **Seaport** neighborhood and enjoy drinks and dinner in Boston's newest dining destination.

WITH MORE TIME

PLYMOUTH

Just over 40 miles (64 km) south of Boston is Plymouth, where the pilgrims landed, and its famous eponymous rock.

Visit Plymouth Rock and take a walk back in time at Plimoth Plantation, a living-history facility that lets you experience life with the Wampanoag people and the early English colonists of the 1600s. Save time for waterfront dining at a local favorite, such as Anna's Harborside Grille, 1620 Wine Bar, or East Bay Grille.

PROVINCETOWN

In warmer months, hop on one of the Provincetown fast ferries (Bay State Cruises departs from the Seaport, and Boston Harbor Cruises leaves from Long Wharf downtown) in the morning and arrive on the Outer Cape in 90 minutes.

Enjoy the many galleries and eclectic shops along Commercial Street, including Cortile Gallery and Adam Peck for art, Henry & Co. for menswear, and Mate Provincetown Inc. for the best locally inspired souvenirs.

P-town has the best eating and drinking on the Cape. From dinner with a view at The Red Inn to high-end counter service on the beach at The Canteen (be sure to get a frozen rosé), you won't be disappointed by the gourmet offerings of this town at the end of the world.

BOSTON WITH KIDS

Boston may be a hub of history and higher education, but it's a great place to bring younger travelers, too. Stay at the **Hotel Marlowe** in Cambridge or the **Colonnade Hotel** on the Back Bay/South End border in Boston for kid-friendly accommodations. The latter has a rooftop pool that is great for all ages in warmer months.

>DAY 1

The **Boston Public Market** is a great foodie start to a day with children, as the numerous vendors at the food hall offer variety for all tastes and ages. After the morning nosh, stroll south down the **Rose Kennedy Greenway** and stop at the carousel near **Faneuil Hall Marketplace.** The carousel features animals native to Boston (such as the lobster and cod, as well as the skunk and harbor seal). Upon reaching Milk Street, turn left and enjoy time at Long Wharf, particularly at the **New England Aquarium.** The aquarium is a choose-your-own adventure attraction: You can pop in for a quick flick at the IMAX or spend a few hours watching the penguins and sea lions and vibrant marine life in the four-story Giant Ocean Tank. Take it into the wild and save time for one of the aquarium's whale-watches, which sail daily (except in winter) from Long Wharf.

Walk the **Harborwalk** along Boston Harbor from the aquarium to Congress Street and turn left and cross over the Fort Point Channel. A variety of restaurants

Boston Children's Museum

BEST PEOPLE-WATCHING

Faneuil Hall Marketplace

a street performer at Faneuil Hall

BOSTON COMMON
Whether it's a political rally, concert, Shakespeare play, or marijuana freedom rally, Boston Common draws a wide array of interests (page 67).

FANEUIL HALL MARKETPLACE
The "Cradle of Liberty" attracts people from around the world with its street performers, bars, restaurants, and history (page 68).

FENWAY PARK
Whether it's for the game or just to nosh on a Fenway Frank, fans of all ages head to the country's oldest ballpark to witness sports history (page 74).

HARVARD YARD
Prospective students and their enthusiastic parents pour through the gates each year to tour the university and rub the statue of John Harvard for good luck (page 78).

NEWBURY STREET
Millions of visitors (and their checking accounts) head to Boston's retail mecca each year to shop till they drop (page 173).

along the way are perfect for lunch, including a seasonal snack bar at the giant Hood Milk bottle outside the **Boston Children's**

Museum. Fueled up, you're ready for the museum—the interactive exhibits on all levels of the facility (the nation's second oldest of its kind) will easily take up an entire afternoon, so plan accordingly.

After wrapping up at the museum, stick around Fort Point and the Seaport for dinner, as seafood spots like **The Barking Crab** are fun options with outdoor seating.

>DAY 2
Grab a coffee near North Station and take the Green Line one stop up to the **Museum of Science.** The 700 exhibits at the museum on the Charles River keep many a scientific mind engaged for hours. After time indoors, head outside and hop aboard **Boston Duck Tours** for a ride through Boston that ultimately winds up in the Charles! These amphibious vehicles get you and your family up close to all of Boston's top attractions, including the river. Kids even get the opportunity to drive the boat while in the water.

Once you finish at the Museum of Science, you can wander

over to nearby Kendall Square in Cambridge for lunch. **Catalyst** is a local favorite for sandwiches and other lunch staples. Afterward, hop on the Red Line to Park Street and walk up to **Boston Common.** On nicer days, the Common is a great spot to relax and kill time. Keep walking along the trails across Charles Street and into the **Boston Public Garden.** There are many ways to spend your time in the BPG, but with kids, be sure to check out the *Make Way for Ducklings* statue, in honor of the children's book of the same name about a family of ducks who lived in the Public Garden. Also go on a ride on the Swan Boats, which have been city staples since 1877.

Hop on the Green Line afterward and head to Government Center. Once there, walk across City Hall Plaza to **Faneuil Hall Marketplace.** Stroll the cobblestones and take in the numerous street performers and vendors, which will entertain your whole brood. Afterward, do dinner in the North End. **The Original Regina Pizzeria** is particularly family friendly; afterward, be sure to stop by **Mike's Pastry** or **Modern Pastry** for cannoli.

>> **PUBLIC TRANSIT:** All inbound Green Line trains head from Arlington Station at the Boston Public Garden to Government Center. C- and E-branch Green Line trains will go one stop farther to Haymarket, if you want to skip Faneuil Hall and go directly to the North End.

GOOD TIMES IN BAD WEATHER

Inclement weather doesn't have to put a damper on your visit. Thanks to the MBTA, several of the city's top destinations are within short walks or are directly connected to the subway, preventing too much exposure to summer showers or winter blizzards.

MORNING

Start your day at the Museum of Fine Arts, where its New American Café offers lunch in the museum's expansive glass-enclosed courtyard. You can easily spend the entire morning (and well into the afternoon) exploring the special exhibitions and permanent, comprehensive collection of works ranging from the French Impressionists to profound contemporary pieces.

AFTERNOON

Grab an umbrella or your winter parka and walk three blocks to the Isabella Stewart Gardner Museum. The museum is home to the art collection of a 19th-century Boston socialite of the same name. The building's lush indoor courtyard is a great place to pass an afternoon and ponder the mystery surrounding a still-unsolved heist at the museum. The museum's Café G is also a fun spot for a bite before you take in more fine art.

EVENING

Head back to Back Bay from the MBTA E Line, which stops directly in front of the MFA. Take the train to Prudential Station, which is built directly into the Prudential Center. Head upstairs and stop into Eataly, a 45,000-square-foot emporium of all things from the boot-shaped country in the Mediterranean. It's a great way to shop and eat under a weatherproof roof.

WELCOME TO HIGHER ED AND "THE HUB OF THE UNIVERSE"

Many visitors to Boston are vying to get into one of the city's top institutions of higher education. While there are colleges spread across the city, most are found near a Green or Red Line T stop. Staying at a downtown hotel like the **Omni Parker House, Godfrey Hotel,** or **Ritz-Carlton Boston** puts you near Park Street, where the Green and Red Lines intersect.

> DAY 1

Get an early start and take the Green Line to **Boston College (BC).** By taking the B branch of the Green Line, you also go through **Boston University**'s more urban campus on a local-style service with multiple stops. For visitors wishing for express, take the D Line to Reservoir Station and take a BC shuttle from the station directly to Boston College's leafy, neo-Gothic campus.

Boston's hub-and-spoke design to its train system makes it difficult to quickly travel from BC to **Harvard.** The 86 bus runs from Reservoir Station to Harvard Station, but Uber is usually the most efficient way to travel between the two schools. Lunch options are more prevalent in Harvard Square and will fuel you up before exploring Harvard Yard, the square, and the school's picturesque swath of Charles River waterfront.

Take the Red Line from Harvard to Kendall Square Station. Catch a late-afternoon tour of the **Massachusetts Institute of Technology**

Massachusetts Institute of Technology campus

(MIT) and be sure to check out the Great Dome and Killian Court. While these areas are impressive on their own, they also offer an incredible view of Boston's Back Bay and downtown skyline from across the Charles. Having worked up an appetite, you should certainly afford time to explore Kendall Square, where a rapidly growing dining scene looks to catch the dollars of all the life science and tech companies in the area. **Café ArtScience** is great for the daring gourmand, while **Smoke Shop** proves Boston can do barbecue.

>DAY 2

Hop into a rental car or ride-share and head to **Brandeis University** in Waltham for a morning tour. Reserve extra time in your day to tour the school's **Rose Art Museum,** which features over 6,000 works from such names as Andy Warhol and Roy Lichtenstein. Waltham is on Route 128, and it's just a 12-minute jaunt north to the **Minute Man National Historical Park** in **Concord.** Add this historical detour to your college trip, and plan for lunch in the suburbs.

Head back toward the city and visit **Tufts University** in Medford. The research university is well regarded for its international relations programs as well as its medical school in the heart of downtown Boston. Tufts is also known for its undergraduate and graduate visual arts program affiliated with the Museum of Fine Arts in Boston. Walk to nearby Davis Square in Somerville for a variety of restaurant and bar options.

Take the Red Line from Davis (if you aren't using a car) to the JFK/

BEST GREEN SPACES

Swan Boats at Boston Public Garden

BOSTON PUBLIC GARDEN
Go for the Swan Boats and stay to enjoy the ever-changing flowers at the city's premier and historic green thumb hub (page 64).

BOSTON COMMON
The starting point for the Freedom Trail is also the oldest city park in the United States (page 67).

ROSE KENNEDY GREENWAY
What was once a congested Boston highway was buried and replaced by a linear park, the most expensive highway project in U.S. history (page 157).

WALDEN POND
Channel your inner Henry David Thoreau at this popular outdoor retreat in nearby Concord, Massachusetts (page 204).

UMass stop in Dorchester. Enjoy a late-afternoon tour of the **University of Massachusetts-Boston,** which shares a peninsula with the **John F. Kennedy Presidential Library and Museum.** The former commuter school is rapidly growing to include on-campus housing

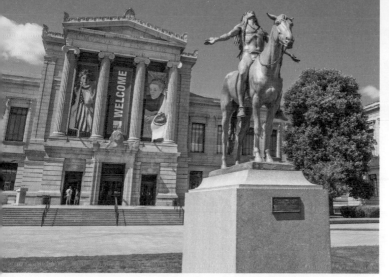

Appeal to the Great Spirt by Cyrus E. Dallin at the Museum of Fine Arts

and is now a notable landmark along Boston Harbor. Save room for dinner at a nearby Dorchester establishment, such as **Dbar.**

> DAY 3

Start your morning in the city's Fenway neighborhood exploring **Northeastern University,** a private school known for its co-op program, in which students spend two extra semesters over the span of a five-year program getting hands-on professional experience away from campus by working with an employer in their field of study. The urban campus flows into the **Museum of Fine Arts** and the nearby **Wentworth Institute of Technology** down Huntington Avenue.

Walk north through the **Emerald Necklace** to visit the **Colleges of the Fenway consortium:** Emmanuel College, Wentworth, MCPHS University, Massachusetts College of Art and Design, and Simmons College. The smaller colleges share resources to provide students with a more comprehensive education while retaining each of their unique strengths. The neighboring Longwood Medical and Academic Area is also home to Harvard Medical School.

Take a break from the college tours and enjoy the nearby Fenway neighborhood. Explore **Fenway Park** and take in the litany of bars and restaurants along Lansdowne Street, including **Bleacher Bar,** an all-ages favorite that offers the best view of the park without having to buy a ticket. Several family-friendly restaurants and stores are popping up amid new development along Boylston Street if you're looking to spend more time.

>> **PUBLIC TRANSIT:** The 60 bus runs along Brookline Avenue from several of the Colleges of the Fenway into Kenmore Square and by Fenway Park.

PLANNING YOUR TRIP

ENTRY REQUIREMENTS

A **passport** is a must for all **international visitors** to the United States. Depending on your home country, a visa may also be required. For a list of countries exempt from visa requirements, visit the State Department's website at http://travel.state.gov.

Canadians can visit sans visa, but a passport is still required. International guests arriving by car, train, or bus should expect questioning from border control agents regarding the purpose of their trip and their destination (including lodging). Transportation of fruit and plants may be prohibited, and there is a limit on the amount of alcohol and tobacco visitors may bring into the country.

More information regarding entry into the United States may be found at the Customs and Border Protection website at www.cbp.gov.

TRANSPORTATION

Most international and domestic travelers arrive via **Boston Logan International Airport.** Those visiting the city's northern suburbs also have the option of **Manchester-Boston Regional Airport,** and those visiting the southern suburbs sometimes travel

City Hall Plaza at the Government Center

DAILY REMINDERS

- **Monday:** The Institute of Contemporary Art is closed on Monday except for the holidays of Martin Luther King Jr. Day, Presidents' Day, Memorial Day, Labor Day, and Columbus Day.
- **Tuesday:** The Isabella Stewart Gardner Museum is closed on Tuesday; the Copley Square Farmers Market is open.
- **Wednesday:** Free summertime concerts often take place on Wednesday at the Hatch Memorial Shell on the Charles River Esplanade.
- **Thursday:** Copley Square Farmers Market is open.
- **Friday:** The Institute of Contemporary Art hosts First Friday events at the beginning of each month.
- **Saturday:** SoWa Market in the South End is open (May–Oct.).
- **Sunday:** SoWa Market in the South End is open (May–Oct.).

through **T. F. Green Airport** outside Providence, Rhode Island.

Road warriors arrive from the west on I-90 (the Massachusetts Turnpike), while those from the north and south usually take I-93 or I-95. Trains from the north terminate at **North Station** and those from the south at **South Station.**

Greater Boston transit comes in the form of the **Massachusetts Bay Transportation Authority**'s bus and bus rapid transit lines, subway lines, light rail lines, commuter rail services, and ferries. The bus, subway, and light rail accept the CharlieCard and CharlieTicket, a reloadable payment mode that can be acquired at any belowground train station, North and South Stations, Boston Logan International Airport, and many convenience stores near street-level light rail stations. Separate tickets are required for ferries and commuter rail. While the Silver Line bus rapid transit (BRT) operates efficiently through the core of the city, the regular bus is often confusing for visitors, so try to stick to BRT, the Green Line light rail, and traditional subway services. Cabs and ride-sharing platforms like Uber and Lyft are widely used throughout the city and for airport transportation.

Winding streets rule Boston (believed to be a holdover from the paths cows took in the early years of the city), and traffic is often congested and heated. Public transportation and ride-share are highly recommended when visiting sights in Boston proper and Cambridge. Rental car locations are spread throughout the city and at the airport if you need one for a day trip.

RESERVATIONS

Most Boston attractions have walk-up availability, but reservations can add peace of mind and convenience if you're looking for a set time. The **Boston Duck Tours, Fenway Park tours,** and **New England Aquarium whale-watching tours** are the three most likely tours to fill up; reservations are also wise for either company providing the **Provincetown fast ferry.**

Musicals and other performing arts acts in the Theater District and downtown tend to sell out, so contact the box office early if you wish to see a show.

Hotels are extremely hard to come by during college move-in (end of August into Labor Day) and

Boston Duck Tours take you to all the city's hot spots—by land *and* by sea.

graduation (staggered throughout May and June), so plan well ahead if you're visiting during those time frames.

It can be hard enough to find a table at Boston's restaurants in general, and this is especially true at exclusive establishments like **No. 9 Park.** Reservation websites like OpenTable can be your best friend, as it's often difficult to walk into any restaurant in town and expect to be seated immediately.

PASSES AND DISCOUNTS

The **Go Boston Card** (www. smartdestinations.com) starts at $78 and $53 for adults and children, respectively, for a three-attraction pass. Prices increase as high as $114 for adults on a five-attraction pass. Passes include admission to some of the city's most popular venues: Fenway Park tours, the Isabella Stewart Gardner Museum, the Museum of Fine Arts, and the New England Aquarium are but a few of the 41 attractions included. The three-, four-, and five-attraction passes include premium attractions like Boston Duck Tours, a New England Aquarium whale-watching tour, or a Boston Red Sox ticket.

The **Boston City Pass** (www. citypass.com/boston) gives 45 percent savings on admission to four top Boston attractions. The pass ($64 adults, $52 children) gets you into the New England Aquarium, Museum of Science, Skywalk Observatory, and either the Harvard Museum of Natural History or a Boston Harbor Cruises excursion.

The **USS *Constitution* Museum** in Charlestown is free, but donations are welcome. The **Isabella Stewart Gardner Museum** is free on your birthday, and the nearby **Museum of Fine Arts** is free (but donations encouraged) on Wednesdays after 4pm.

Free Tours by Foot (www.

freetoursbyfoot.com/boston-tours) offers guided walks through popular Boston areas like Chinatown, the North End, and the Freedom Trail, but tips (and reservations) are encouraged.

GUIDED TOURS

First time in the Hub of the Universe? Have no fear! There are plenty of guides willing to offer an expertly curated debut view of Boston. **Boston Duck Tours** delivers a quack-tastic excursion through the city from three pickup points. After getting tidbits of history even locals may not know, your World War II-inspired tour vehicle zooms into the Charles River for a jaunt where the kids (yes, adults, too) can take the wheel and feel like a captain.

The **Lessons on Liberty Tour** takes you along a significant stretch of the Freedom Trail with an "actual" colonial tour guide who delivers personal tidbits and factoids about some of the city's important historic sites.

Even if you come to town when the Red Sox aren't playing at Fenway Park, be sure to drop by the ballpark for a **Fenway Park tour,** a one-hour walking tour of the iconic venue known as the high church of Boston sports.

Looking for an Ivy League tour that isn't so stuffy? Book **The Hahvahd Tour** for a theatrical take on the Crimson campus. The guides are current students and are meant to perform for you on the 70-minute tour—so maybe book an official campus tour in addition if you're deciding whether to apply.

retired players' numbers outside of Fenway Park

WHEN TO GO

CALENDAR OF EVENTS

MARCH

In March it seems like all of New England flocks to South Boston (the city's historically Irish enclave) for the annual **St. Patrick's Day** parade. Arrive early and expect to pay steep cover charges for bars up and down Broadway—it's the price one pays for the luck of the (Boston) Irish.

APRIL

Patriots' Day, the third Monday in April, commemorates the Battles of Lexington and Concord. The two towns celebrate with remembrances and battle reenactments, but the biggest celebration happens in Boston proper, where the holiday is also known as **Marathon Monday.** The city hosts the **Boston Marathon** the same day.

MAY

The **Boston Calling** music festival held each Memorial Day weekend has quickly won critical acclaim. A wide variety of musical acts have performed at this relatively new three-day concert series on Harvard's athletic fields in Boston's Allston neighborhood.

JUNE

Boston Pride (www.bostonpride. org) is more than a week of celebrations in honor of the LGBTQ community. The Boston Pride

Boston Marathon

WHAT'S NEW?

- **Encore Boston Harbor:** This five-star resort opened in 2018 just north of downtown Boston, offering a casino, restaurants, and bars.
- **Food Halls:** From Fenway to downtown, it's hard these days to find a Boston neighborhood without a food hall. The **Boston Public Market** kicked things off in 2015, and the local food hall scene has expanded to include **Eataly, Time Out Market,** and **High Street Place.**
- **Seaport Shopping:** Even the Seaport's staunchest critics agree the waterfront neighborhood is evolving into a true destination. With the arrival of early phases of Seaport Square, more retail and restaurants have added more street-level vibrancy to what was just a sea of parking lots not long ago.

parade happens on the second Saturday of Pride Week and weaves through Back Bay, the South End (the city's historically LGBTQ neighborhood), and downtown before wrapping up in a celebration at City Hall Plaza. There are also block parties in Back Bay and the South End.

JULY

The annual **Boston Pops Fireworks Spectacular** is an evening with headlining musical acts performing alongside the Boston Pops from the Charles River Esplanade, culminating in a pyrotechnic show over the river basin between Cambridge and Boston.

SEPTEMBER

Labor Day weekend is normally marked by insane traffic from U-Hauls galore as the city's hundreds of thousands of students return to campus for **move-in day(s).**

OCTOBER

The second-to-last weekend of October might be peak foliage season, but it's also time for thousands of elite rowers and even more New England prepsters to flock to Boston for the **Head of the Charles,** the world's largest two-day regatta. Even if you don't race, it's a festive event, with vendors and grandstands dotting the banks from the basin past Harvard Square.

DECEMBER

Rather than a ball drop, Boston celebrates the end of the year and the start of a new one with **First Night/First Day** (www.firstnightboston.org), a free celebration with performances, ice sculptures, and light displays at multiple locations across the city, including a 7pm fireworks display.

NEIGHBORHOODS

BEACON HILL AND THE WEST END

Beacon Hill and the West End

Map 1

Boston's most **exclusive** neighborhood is also one of the country's most **historic.** Be it the golden dome of the **Massachusetts State House** or the glow of gaslights upon Louisburg Square's townhomes, the magnificent **Museum of Science** or the bustling activity of shoppers and diners along **Charles Street,** Beacon Hill and the West End have hours of entertainment.

The residential neighborhood still bustles with politicians working at the State House. In the West End, residences and retail are beginning to emerge in the blocks surrounding the **TD Garden.** Nearby, **Boston Common** and the start of the **Freedom Trail** bring a steady stream of visitors to the neighborhood's compact streets and brick sidewalks.

TOP SIGHTS
- Boston Public Garden (page 64)
- Freedom Trail (page 65)
- Museum of Science (page 66)

TOP RESTAURANTS
- J. P. Licks (page 86)
- Savenor's Market (page 87)

TOP SHOPS
- December Thieves (page 169)

TOP HOTELS
- Liberty Hotel (page 184)

GETTING THERE AND AROUND
- Metro lines: Red Line, Green Line
- Metro stations: Charles/MGH, North Station

Government Center, North End, and Waterfront   Map 2

Be it **City Hall** (the Brutalist building Bostonians love to hate), the glass towers along **Atlantic Avenue,** or the cozy European feel of the **North End,** the buildings in this part of town are as varied as the residents. **Faneuil Hall Marketplace,** one of the most popular tourist destinations in the country, got its start as the "Cradle of Liberty" and is today a retail hub in the middle of a reinvention. The **Rose Kennedy Greenway,** a former highway turned into a linear park, is both an artist showcase and leafy retreat. Perhaps the most European of Boston's neighborhoods, the North End is an Italian enclave known for its carb-heavy **eateries** and **cozy bars.**

TOP SIGHTS
- Faneuil Hall Marketplace (page 68)
- New England Aquarium (page 69)

TOP RESTAURANTS
- Neptune Oyster (page 87)

TOP NIGHTLIFE
- Improv Asylum (page 125)

TOP RECREATION
- Rose Kennedy Greenway (page 157)

TOP HOTELS
- Boston Harbor Hotel (page 185)

GETTING THERE AND AROUND
- Metro lines: Green Line, Orange Line
- Metro stations: Government Center, Haymarket, North Station

FREEDOM TRAIL FOR FOODIES WALK

TOTAL DISTANCE: 2 miles (3.2 km)
WALKING TIME: 1 hour

The Freedom Trail guides you through Boston's Revolutionary history along its red path, and the trail's back half passes through some of the city's newer foodie attractions as well as established dining destinations in the North End, Boston's Little Italy. This walk converges with and diverges from the Freedom Trail at various points, pairing it with recommendations for nearby food and drink along the way.

Ideal for an early or midafternoon start, this walk will take you by great options for lunch or an early dinner and culminate along the Charlestown waterfront. History buffs may want to start the Freedom Trail at Boston Common in the morning in order to pick up this walk at the midpoint and reach the Boston Public Market or North End in time for lunch. Those less interested in stopping along the way to tour the numerous historic sites can set out from Government Center in late afternoon to pass through the North End for an early dinner and arrive in Charlestown for a nightcap.

GOVERNMENT CENTER, NORTH END, AND WATERFRONT

A convenient starting point is the Government Center MBTA station—served by the Green and Blue lines—at Boston's City Hall Plaza. Depending on the time of year, you might be able to enjoy seasonal programming as part of the city's ongoing initiative to bring more fun to the plaza, like a pop-up beer garden in summer.

1 From the station, walk to the right of city hall's main entrance, heading east and down the brick stairs to Congress Street. Cross the street and kick off your walk with a pint at the new **Sam Adams Downtown Boston Taproom,** home to Boston's biggest craft brewer, which has until recently only operated from its brewery miles away in the Jamaica Plain neighborhood. It's just south of the bronze *Samuel Adams* statue.

2 From the taproom, head east a short way on the Freedom Trail and continue east on Market Street to find the South Market entrance of **Faneuil Hall Marketplace.** The Revolutionary-era meeting space is now a lively place to wander, home to numerous shops, restaurants, and street performers.

3 Exit the way you entered, at the South Market entrance, heading back in the direction you came from and turning right onto

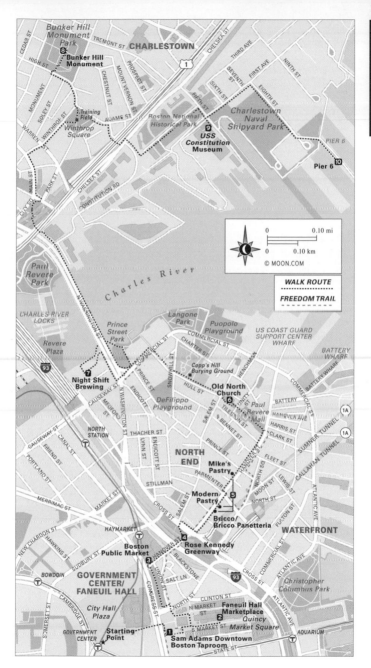

Bunker Hill
Monument
Park
8 Bunker Hill Monument

TREMONT ST
CHARLESTOWN

CEDAR ST
HIGH ST

CHELSEA ST

THIRD AVE

SECOND AVE
FIRST AVE
NINTH ST

PROSPECT ST
MOUNT VERNON ST
CHESTNUT ST
MONUMENT
SOLEY ST
WINTHROP ST

SIXTH ST
FIFTH ST
SEVENTH ST

ADAMS ST

Training
Field
Winthrop
Square

WARREN ST
PARK ST

Boston National
Historical Park

EIGHTH ST

Charlestown
Naval
Shipyard Park

PIER 6

9 USS Constitution Museum

O TO MAIN ST
PARK ST

CONSTITUTION RD

Pier 6 10

Paul
Revere
Park

CHARLES RIVER
LOCKS

Charles River

Revere
Plaza

Prince
Street
Park

Langone
Park

Puopolo
Playground

US COAST GUARD
SUPPORT CENTER
WHARF

BATTERY
WHARF

93

N WASHINGTON ST

COMMERCIAL ST
CHARTER ST

HENCHMAN

COMMERCIAL ST

CAUSEWAY ST
MEDFORD ST
ENDICOTT ST
PRINCE ST

Copp's Hill
Burying Ground

7 Night Shift Brewing

HULL ST

UNITY
SALEM ST
TILESTON ST

Paul
Revere
Mall

BATTERY

HANOVER AVE

1A

DeFilippo
Playground

Old North Church 6

BENNET ST

HARRIS ST

COMMERCIAL ST
BATTERY WHARF

N WASHINGTON ST

THACHER ST

CLARK ST

1A

NORTH
STATION

T

LYNN ST
ENDICOTT ST

PRINCE ST

FLEET ST

SUMNER TUNNEL

CAUSEWAY ST

STILLMAN

NORTH
END

HANOVER ST

MOON ST

CALLAHAN TUNNEL

FRIEND ST
CANAL ST

**Mike's
Pastry**

NORTH SQ

ATLANTIC AVE

PORTLAND ST

PARMENTER

NORTH ST

WATERFRONT

MERRIMAC ST

MARKET ST

CROSS ST
SALEM ST

**Modern
Pastry 5**

**Bricco/
Bricco Panetteria**

COMMERCIAL ST

NEW CHARDON ST
HAWKINS ST

HAYMARKET

T

Christopher
Columbus Park

BOWDOIN

SUDBURY ST

**Boston
Public Market 3**

HANOVER ST
BLACKSTONE

**Rose Kennedy
Greenway 4**

93

ATLANTIC AVE

CROSS ST

T

GOVERNMENT
CENTER/
FANEUIL HALL

UNION ST
CONGRESS ST

City Hall
Plaza

SOMERSET ST

CAMBRIDGE ST

SALT LN

NORTH ST
N MARKET ST

CLINTON ST

**Faneuil Hall
Marketplace 2**
*Quincy
Market Square*

ATLANTIC AVE

**Starting
Point**

GOVERNMENT
CENTER

T

S MARKET ST

**1 Sam Adams Downtown
Boston Taproom**

STATE ST

AQUARIUM

T

0   0.10 mi

0   0.10 km

© MOON.COM

WALK ROUTE
· · · · · · · · · · · · ·

FREEDOM TRAIL
- - - - - - - - - - - -

Merchants Row for less than a block before turning left onto the Freedom Trail (between the Faneuil Hall building and Sephora). Follow it west and then north until Union Park. Break off the trail, heading left to continue north through the park and, at its northeast end at the intersection of Congress and Hanover Streets, enter the **Boston Public Market,** one of the city's newer food halls. The market features nearly 40 local vendors under the same roof, from doughnuts to banh mi, making it a convenient way to get a taste of Boston. Despite all the delectable temptations, try to eat lightly or share a treat with a friend—even more delicious must-have dishes are just around the corner in the North End. You might also save your treats for the next stop, which makes a fine picnicking spot.

4 Head out of the market at its southeast exit, at Hanover Street and John F. Fitzgerald Surface Road. Cross Fitzgerald Surface Road to head into the **Rose Kennedy Greenway.** This linear park is a great spot to picnic with your purchases from the Boston Public Market or take in views of the city's skyline, particularly under the metal sculptures where Hanover Street meets Cross Street. When you're ready, pick up the Freedom Trail from here, continuing east on Hanover Street, the official gateway into the North End.

5 Boston's North End isn't just for tourists; the neighborhood is constantly finding ways to reinvent itself and menus at even the longest-running dining rooms. The two-block stretch of Hanover Street between Cross and Prince Streets (you'll lose the Freedom Trail for one block on this stretch, but it's worth it to see all these hot spots) hosts some of the neighborhood's finest foodie options, including establishments like **Bricco,** offering red-sauce masterpieces for dinner, and its bakery, **Bricco Panetteria,** where you can pick up fresh artisan bread, as well as **Modern Pastry** and **Mike's Pastry,** dueling for the city's best cannoli title.

6 Continue down Hanover Street on the Freedom Trail, past numerous other North End bakeries and cafés, turning left to continue on the trail through Paul Revere Mall. Meander west through the brick-paved park, home to a statue of Revere and the **Old North Church,** the launch point of his Midnight Ride to warn Bostonians the "Redcoats" were coming. At the end of the mall you'll hit Salem Street. Continue to follow the Freedom Trail, crossing Salem Street onto Hull Street, heading north. You'll pass **Copp's Hill Burying Ground,** a historic cemetery that dates to 1659, on your right. When you reach Commercial Street, take a left and walk a block and a half until you hit the intersection with Washington Street bridge.

BEACON HILL AND THE WEST END

7 If you're ready for a drink break, cross Washington Street and make an immediate right to walk along the western side of the bridge, and then turn left down the steps at Lovejoy Wharf to stop in at **Night Shift Brewing**'s taproom, complete with a waterfront view of the TD Garden and Zakim Bridge.

CHARLESTOWN AND GREATER BOSTON

8 Exiting Night Shift, head back east to cross under the Washington Street bridge on the Harborwalk. Take your first right along the path once you cross under the bridge to return to Commercial Street and the Washington Street bridge intersection, rejoining the Freedom Trail. Cross the bridge and then continue two blocks to Chelsea Street, and cross the street into City Square Park. Head diagonally northeast across the park along the trail and up on Main Street for two blocks before following the trail right on Winthrop Street. Head two blocks up, passing Charlestown's **Training Field** park, a former militia training ground used ahead of the Battle of Bunker Hill and the Civil War, before veering left on Winthrop where it intersects with Adams Street. About a block and a half up, you'll reach Monument Square, home to the **Bunker Hill Monument.** More dog park than battleground these days, this is a great area to relax and take in Boston skyline views or, for those needing an extra dose of cardio, climb the 221-foot obelisk free of charge when weather permits.

9 Head back the way you came down Winthrop Street, then turn left on Adams Street once you reach the Training Field again. You'll follow the Freedom Trail back to the waterfront in a different direction, proceeding on Adams Street for two blocks before taking a right at Chestnut Street. Continue on the trail along Chestnut and under the Tobin Bridge overpass to arrive at Boston National Historical Park, a waterfront park in the Charlestown Navy Yard that includes the **USS Constitution Museum** and Old Ironsides herself. Head into the museum if you like, or just spend some time exploring the park.

10 Take a left and head east on 1st Avenue until you reach the intersection with 8th Street, where you'll make a right. You'll shortly reach a rotary roadway with Tuffy's Garden, a small park, on your left. Follow the signs to **Pier 6** and grab another bite to eat or a drink on the outdoor patio, which has some of the best views across Boston Harbor of the downtown skyline. Water taxis stop nearby and make a return trip easy.

Downtown, Chinatown, and the Theater District Map 3

Downtown Boston is undergoing a radical transformation from 9-to-5 financial hub to 24-hour neighborhood. New condominium towers, **boutique hotels,** and **chic eateries** atop some of the city's busiest transit stations have led to **bustling streets** every day of the week. The **Downtown Crossing** area, formerly the city's historic shopping district, is today more known more for its numerous places to grab a bite. Broadway shows and local treasures keep the marquees lit and after-show restaurant business in the Theater Dis-

trict booming. While gentrification is rampant elsewhere in the city, officials have made great efforts to keep **Chinatown** affordable and true to its origins—ensuring some of the city's most authentic Asian culture and cuisine remain mainstays.

TOP RESTAURANTS

- Yvonne's (page 91)
- No. 9 Park (page 92)

TOP NIGHTLIFE

- Mr. Dooley's Boston (page 127)
- Royale (page 127)

TOP ARTS AND CULTURE

- Wang Theatre (page 144)

TOP HOTELS

- Four Seasons Boston (page 186)
- InterContinental Boston (page 186)
- XV Beacon (page 186)
- HI Boston Hostel (page 188)

GETTING THERE AND AROUND

- Metro lines: Red Line, Orange Line
- Metro stations: Downtown Crossing, Park Street, Chinatown, State
- Major bus routes: Silver Line 4, Silver Line 5

Back Bay

Map 4

By Boston standards, Back Bay is fairly young, as it actually rose from a Charles River tidal basin during a mammoth 19th-century filling project. Known today for its lush **green spaces,** fashionable **shopping,** and **historic buildings,** scenic Back Bay is what many envision when they picture Boston. Stand in awe of the **architecture** of the Boston Public Library and Trinity Church. Bring your wallet: There's no better way to close out a good shopping session on **Newbury Street** than with a glass of wine at one of Back Bay's numerous tony restaurants and bars.

TOP SIGHTS
- Boston Public Library (page 72)

TOP RESTAURANTS
- Stephanie's on Newbury (page 98)

TOP ARTS AND CULTURE
- Galerie d'Orsay (page 146)

TOP RECREATION
- Charles River Esplanade (page 160)

TOP SHOPS
- RH Boston (page 172)
- Topdrawer (page 172)
- Trident Booksellers and Café (page 172)
- Marathon Sports (page 173)
- G2O Spa and Salon (page 173)

TOP HOTELS
- Mandarin Oriental (page 189)
- The Newbury (page 190)

GETTING THERE AND AROUND
- Metro lines: Green Line
- Metro stations: Hynes, Copley, Arlington
- Major bus routes: 1, 39

BACK BAY

BACK BAY WALK

TOTAL DISTANCE: 1.5 miles (2.4 km)
WALKING TIME: 1 hour

Whether you're a history buff or a gleeful user of your credit card, Back Bay has it all. Begin this walk a little before noon, as all Newbury Street stores will be open no matter the day of the week. Be sure to coordinate times for brunch at Stephanie's on Newbury or lunch at places like Select Oyster Bar earlier in the walk. The winding path will take you past some of the city's toniest residential and retail enclaves as well as some of Boston's best-known architecture.

Hop off the MBTA Green Line at the Hynes Convention Center stop. Head out the Newbury Street exit from the station, and you'll be at the intersection of Massachusetts Avenue and Newbury Street. Newbury is Boston's retail boulevard. Closer to Massachusetts Avenue, the stores verge on the eclectic and edgy: Independent booksellers and athletic companies mingle with smoke shops and high-end adult entertainment stores on this stretch.

1 Head away from Massachusetts Avenue (east) on Newbury Street and you'll see a variety of cafés and restaurants for refreshments. **Trident Booksellers and Café** should be on your right; stop in to browse and grab a coffee, a smoothie, or a light snack (leave room for brunch at the next stop). This is a favorite among the city's students and young professionals.

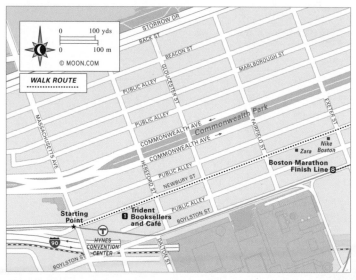

2 Keep moving east. As you cross Gloucester Street, you'll notice more spas and bigger chain retailers like **Zara** and **Nike Boston.** At the intersection of Exeter and Newbury, brunch spots abound, and the retail starts getting pricey! **Stephanie's on Newbury,** on the southeast corner of Newbury and Exeter, is a must for mimosas and dining alfresco.

3 After you've filled up on brunch, continue east on Newbury until you hit the intersection with Berkeley Street. On your left is the **Church of the Covenant.** Completed in 1867, the Gothic Revival building is home to a Presbyterian congregation as well as **Gallery NAGA,** a very popular collection featuring New England artists. If you're walking Tuesday-Saturday, stop in the gallery and take your time viewing the beautiful art.

4 Across Newbury from the church is **RH Boston,** Restoration Hardware's gallery at the former Museum of Natural History. This expansive home decor showroom spans several floors of what used to be Boston's natural history museum. Today, it's an excellent spot to browse and take a quiet breather from the sometimes loud Back Bay streets.

5 Newbury's final block between Berkeley and Arlington is also its most exclusive. From **Valentino** to **Chanel,** this is a see-and-be-seen stretch where plenty of damage can be done to your checking account. After shopping till you drop, or just admiring the storefronts, take a right on Arlington. The **Boston Public Garden** will be on your left; it's a welcoming place to read, picnic, or just lounge.

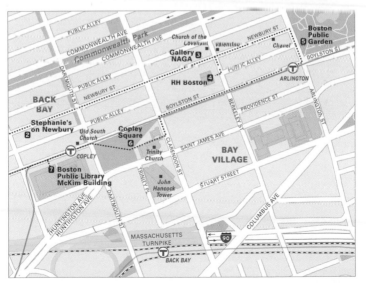

6 From the garden, continue on Arlington toward Boylston Street. When you reach Boylston Street, turn right and keep walking until you get to Clarendon Street. Cross Clarendon and turn left so you are by the **Trinity Church.** You're now in the heart of **Copley Square,** where you should take time to explore the architecture. Trinity Church and the Boston Public Library are locked in a Romanesque-versus-Renaissance battle as they face each other

Trinity Church on Copley Square

head-on from the opposite sides of the square. Towering above it all is the blue-hued 200 Clarendon Street Tower (formerly and best known as the **John Hancock Tower**). If you're walking on a Tuesday or Friday afternoon, you'll notice this stretch becomes a twice-weekly farmers market.

7 Head to the northwest corner of Copley Square and the intersection of Boylston and Dartmouth Streets. Be sure to snap photos in front of the impressive **Boston Public Library**'s **McKim Building** before crossing Boylston. You'll be in front of the **Old South Church,** another Gothic Revival structure that was completed in 1873. Its focus on an

Boston Public Garden

John Hancock Tower

urban ministry has made the Old South Church particularly popular with the city's largely liberal and diverse population.

8 Take a left on Boylston and head west, keeping an eye on the street. When you see a blue streak stretching across Boylston from your side of the street over to the library, you will be where the beloved **Boston Marathon** finishes each year—and where this walk ends, too!

South End

Map 5

The **South End** gets high marks for all things trendy. With the largest concentration of Victorian row houses in the country and arguably the city's greatest stock of **bars** and restaurants, the South End knows how to mix historic and hip and serve it with a twist. While it can easily be paired with sightseeing in neighboring areas like Back Bay or the Theater District, it's worth a full day to explore its **charming cafés,** boutiques, galleries, bars, and **award-winning restaurants.** Weekends tend to be the best time to visit, as large crowds at the **SoWa Market** and Harrison Avenue **art galleries** keep things busy.

TOP RESTAURANTS

- B&G Oysters (page 100)
- SRV (page 100)
- The Beehive (page 101)

TOP NIGHTLIFE

- Wink & Nod (page 130)
- Wally's Café (page 133)

TOP SHOPS

- Sault New England (page 174)
- Follain (page 176)

GETTING THERE AND AROUND

- Metro lines: Orange Line, Silver Line
- Metro stations: Back Bay/
  South End, Union Park
- Major bus routes: 1, 9, 43

Fenway and Kenmore Square

Map 6

The ballpark may have taken its name from this neighborhood, but this is far from just a one-trick-pony kind of place. Home to some of the city's best **museums, parks, music venues,** and—yes—**spectator sports,** Fenway and Kenmore Square are rapidly growing to encompass more than home runs.

TOP SIGHTS

- Fenway Park (page 74)
- Museum of Fine Arts (page 75)

TOP NIGHTLIFE

- Bleacher Bar (page 133)
- The Hawthorne (page 134)

TOP ARTS AND CULTURE

- House of Blues (page 148)

TOP RECREATION

- Boston Red Sox (page 162)

TOP HOTELS

- Hotel Commonwealth (page 191)
- The Verb (page 191)

GETTING THERE AND AROUND

- Metro lines: Green Line
- Metro stations: Fenway, Kenmore, Symphony
- Major bus routes: 1, 39

South Boston

Map 7

Home to **chic restaurants, iconic museums** like the Institute of Contemporary Art, and luxury residences, the **Seaport, Fort Point,** and South Boston area is the poster child for the **new Boston.** South Boston (aka "Southie"), the source of the infamous "*pahk the cah in Hahvahd Yahd*" accent, has evolved from true grit in the era of Whitey Bulger to a desirable area for young professionals as well as major corporations looking to relocate. Originally an **artists' community** (which it remains to a lesser extent these days), Fort Point is bustling with tech and startup companies, becoming the de facto hub of Boston's innovation economy.

TOP RESTAURANTS
- The Barking Crab (page 109)
- Legal Harborside (page 110)

TOP NIGHTLIFE
- Drink (page 134)
- Lookout Rooftop and Bar (page 134)
- Harpoon Brewery and Beer Hall (page 135)

TOP RECREATION
- Harborwalk (page 163)

GETTING THERE AND AROUND
- Metro lines: Red Line, Silver Line
- Metro stations: Broadway, Andrew, Courthouse, World Trade Center
- Major bus routes: 7, 9, 10, 11

HARBORWALK

TOTAL DISTANCE: 2 miles (3.2 km)
WALKING TIME: 1.5 hours

Boston Harbor has played an instrumental role in the city's history since before the American Revolution—but it hasn't always been so pristine. Ever since legal fights forced regional leaders to clean it up, the harbor has become a treasured part of the city, with many parks built to connect Bostonians with the water. Start this walk later in the morning to check off a few items on your itinerary before stopping for lunch in the Seaport or Fort Point neighborhood. By the time you reach the end, you will have earned a local libation from Harpoon Brewery and Beer Hall.

1 Start outside South Station's main entrance. Facing the Federal Reserve Bank of Boston tower across Summer Street, turn right (heading east) and walk toward **Fort Point Channel,** a waterway separating South Boston from downtown. Before crossing the bridge into the Fort Point neighborhood, take a left (north) on Dorchester Avenue and walk a block up to Congress Street. Take a right (east) onto the Congress

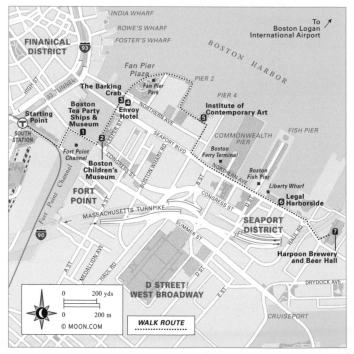

Boston Tea Party Ships & Museum

Street bridge and into Fort Point. Halfway across the bridge, you will reach the **Boston Tea Party Ships & Museum.** This is a great spot to stop and enjoy a dose of history and channel your inner colonist by dumping replica tea chests into Boston Harbor!

2 Once you reach the other side of Fort Point Channel, you're officially in the Fort Point neighborhood of South Boston. With the channel on your left, head down Harborwalk and locate the **Boston Children's Museum** on your right (Arthur the aardvark will be waving from the roof). Fun for all ages, the museum is an easy way to spend hours, so plan your time accordingly.

3 Continue along the waterfront boardwalk under the Seaport Boulevard bridge and you'll find yourself sandwiched between two of the Seaport's hot spots: **The Barking Crab** and the Envoy Hotel. If you time things well, lunch at The Barking Crab is highly entertaining and filling, with a fun waitstaff and huge portions of shellfish at the waterfront picnic tables (don't forget to order an oyster shooter).

4 After filling up on shellfish, pop over to the **Envoy Hotel** for late-afternoon/early-evening

Fan Pier Park

The Barking Crab seafood restaurant

cocktails at the rooftop bar. Warning: There's typically a long line to get in.

5 Keep walking north on the Harborwalk, which will begin to curve to the east as you round the front of the John Joseph Moakley United States Courthouse. As you pass the green **Fan Pier Park** on your right, turn around and look at the downtown skyline a short distance across Boston Harbor. This vantage point is seen in numerous postcards of Boston, so be sure to snap a photo to make one of your own. Continue east to enjoy this view of Boston Harbor, which will give you glimpses of just how active this water is with ferries, container ships, and cruise ships. Across the harbor is the bustling **Boston Logan International Airport,** where you'll see airplanes from around the world flying in and out around the clock. The Harborwalk eventually banks south. To your left will be a cantilevered building reaching out toward Boston Harbor. This is Boston's **Institute of Contemporary Art** (the ICA). With architecture just as impressive as the works hanging inside, you'll feel just as cultured observing from the outside as you will in the galleries.

6 Once you reach Seaport Boulevard, head east. You will pass the World Trade Center on your left, which includes the **Boston Ferry Terminal.** (When you're feeling like a day trip, this is one of two options for a fast ferry to eclectic Provincetown on the outer reaches of Cape Cod.) Continue walking east on Seaport Boulevard and you'll pass the active **Boston Fish Pier,** home to several fisheries (don't mind the fishy smell in warmer months!). Eventually, you will reach **Liberty Wharf,** a sprawling waterfront dining mecca. Home to **Legal Harborside,** the

Legal Harborside

flagship of the Legal Sea Foods restaurant group, Liberty Wharf is a place best visited on an empty stomach. Stop in for a delicious meal.

7 Continue east on Seaport Boulevard, and it will begin to get a little less congested—but no less entertaining. Hopefully you've saved room for a pint, because a few blocks up you'll conclude your walk with the top prize: a local craft brew at **Harpoon Brewery and Beer Hall.**

Cambridge

Map 8

The hallowed halls of learning don't get any more prestigious than those of **Harvard University** and **MIT,** located in Cambridge, a separate city across the Charles River from Boston. From MIT's Great Dome to the Georgian buildings lining leafy Harvard Yard, Cambridge knows a thing or two about education. An influx of international students and growth of the tech community in Kendall Square keep things innovative and diverse, while Central Square is a hipster hotbed with a trove of **live music venues** and **vegetarian eateries.**

TOP SIGHTS

- Harvard University (page 78)

TOP RESTAURANTS

- Veggie Galaxy (page 117)

TOP NIGHTLIFE

- The Sinclair (page 138)

TOP ARTS AND CULTURE

- American Repertory Theater (page 150)
- Kendall Square Cinema (page 150)

TOP RECREATION

- North Point Park (page 163)

GETTING THERE AND AROUND

- Metro lines: Red Line
- Metro stations: Harvard, Central, Kendall/MIT
- Major bus routes: 1, 66

CRIMSON TOUR

TOTAL DISTANCE: 1.6 miles (2.6 km)
WALKING TIME: 1.5 hours

Across the Charles River, Cambridge beckons visitors with its tech scene and esteemed institutes of higher education. Harvard Square gets the most attention, and this walk is best enjoyed in midafternoon, when crowded morning campus tours have cleared out and you can arrive back in the heart of the square for dinner. Start your tour outside the Harvard MBTA station, as public transportation is the best way to get to this notoriously parking-devoid stretch of town.

1 Head southwest on Brattle Street to enjoy some of Harvard Square's quaint stores and bookshops, like **The Coop.** The official bookstore for Harvard, The Coop is also a go-to spot for all things Crimson. Grab a T-shirt, a mug, or even a Harvard-branded rocking chair to take home.

2 Turn right on Brattle Street for more of the neighborhood's independent shopping and dining destinations. Weekend afternoon

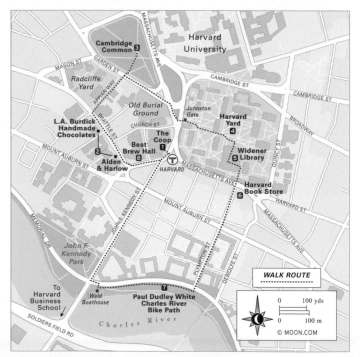

Alden & Harlow

strollers will pass by **Alden & Harlow** just in time for a late brunch (otherwise it opens at 5pm for dinner), while those looking for sweet treats to take home should pop into **L. A. Burdick Handmade Chocolates,** on the left just past the Brattle Theatre.

3 Turn right when you reach Appian Way, which dead-ends at **Cambridge Common.** This green space is where George Washington gathered troops during the Revolutionary War, but these days it's mainly used for sports and as a quiet place to read in nice weather. Wander around the park before heading east on Garden Street. Take a right onto Massachusetts Avenue for a short stint until you see the ornate **Johnston Gate** on your left.

4 Pass through the Johnston Gate and into **Harvard Yard,** arguably the best-known college campus in the world and the pinnacle of the neighborhood's collegiate culture. Explore the Federal and Georgian architecture of the buildings lining the leafy yard. Directly in front of you as you enter the gate is the famous statue of John Harvard, believed to be a good-luck charm for admittance if you rub the toe of his left shoe.

5 Head farther into the yard, and you'll reach **Widener Library** on your right. Named for a Harvard graduate who died in the sinking of the Titanic, the library is not open to the public, but the columned building's exterior is still a marvel (and the steps a great spot to take a midwalk break).

Harvard Yard

6 Round the library by heading to the right, and you'll eventually exit onto Massachusetts Avenue in front of another of the neighborhood's leading bookstores, the **Harvard Book Store.** Pop inside to peruse the vast collection of new and used books, or wander into any of the nearby cafés and restaurants for a snack. Otherwise, head down Plympton Street to the right of the bookstore.

Harvard Book Store

7 You'll pass Harvard dorms like Quincy House on your left as you walk along Plympton toward the Charles River. Upon reaching Memorial Drive, cross the road to Riverbend Park, which includes the **Paul Dudley White Charles River Bike Path** and amazing views of the winding river. The area is an ideal spectator spot during October's Head of the Charles regatta.

8 Turn right (west) and walk along the waterfront, and you'll enjoy the views of **Harvard Business School** across the river in Allston and Harvard dorms on the right. Tucked at the corner of where the Anderson Memorial Bridge meets Memorial Drive is the **Weld Boathouse,** home to Harvard's women's rowing team. Upon reaching John F. Kennedy Street, turn right and head back into Harvard Square. You'll pass

Harvard Business School

the Harvard Kennedy School of Government on your left before getting back into the thick of the eateries, shops, and cafés. Dinner is approaching, so pop into one of the square's popular restaurants, like **Beat Brew Hall,** or any of the cozy bars to unwind after your tour.

Greater Boston   **Map 9**

Like most of Boston's neighborhoods, **Charlestown** has shed its seedy past to become home to some of the city's priciest real estate. The hilly enclave ranges from waterfront parks to trendy eateries tucked among the townhomes and the final steps of the Freedom Trail. From the deck at Pier 6 to the peak of the **Bunker Hill Monument,** Charlestown offers several vantage points for the best views of the Boston skyline, as well as the **USS *Constitution* Museum.**

It's also worth your while to hop on a train or into an Uber and explore life beyond the Freedom Trail. The **John F. Kennedy Presidential Library and Museum** offers an immersive look into America's Camelot, while rock clubs in Brighton lure some of the top local and touring music acts. Student life is situated predominantly in **Allston/Brighton,** while a young and diverse scene is found increasingly in **Dorchester.**

TOP SIGHTS

- USS *Constitution* Museum (page 79)
- John F. Kennedy Presidential Library and Museum (page 80)

GETTING THERE AND AROUND

- Metro lines: Orange Line, Blue Line, Red Line, Green Line
- Metro stations: Community College, Sullivan Square, JFK/UMass, Maverick, Forest Hills
- Major bus routes: 57, 66, 86, 93, 111

SIGHTS

Be it the water, the history, or the culture, Boston has more than enough sights to provide visitors with an exhaustive itinerary. From the Freedom Trail's lesson in the country's foundation to the most daring pieces displayed in the Museum of Fine Arts' contemporary wing, the streets of Boston are filled with attractions for all interests.

Grab a gourmet doughnut or lobster roll (it's never too early . . . we won't tell) and begin your path through this historic and rapidly growing city. Whether you're more inclined to study Paul Revere's midnight ride or want to see New England marine life and maybe learn about the country's biggest unsolved art heist, the sights of Boston captivate their audience with reflection, engagement, and even mystery.

Faneuil Hall Marketplace

HIGHLIGHTS

✪ **BEST GREEN SPACE:** Accomplished and aspiring green thumbs will delight at the ever-changing flowers in Boston Public Garden, Boston's premier botanic space (page 64).

✪ **BEST WALK THROUGH HISTORY:** Why read about history when you can walk through it on the 2.5-mile (4 km) Freedom Trail (page 65)?

✪ **BEST PLACE TO EMULATE EINSTEIN:** Live like Zeus and cast lightning; then see how the world works with the innovative collection at the Museum of Science (page 66).

✪ **BEST SHOPS WITH A REVOLUTIONARY START:** It began as a gathering place for revolutionary thought, but Faneuil Hall Marketplace is now a gathering place to shop (and eat) till you drop (page 68).

✪ **THE CLOSEST YOU'LL GET TO *THE LITTLE MERMAID*:** Imagine life under the sea, catch a sea lion pup feeding, and embark on a whale-watch cruise from the bustling New England Aquarium at Boston Harbor (page 69).

✪ **BEST SPOT TO RUB ELBOWS WITH THE CLASSICS:** Brush against some of the finest literature, art, and architecture in the entire city at the Boston Public Library (page 72).

✪ **BEST HOME RUN:** The cathedral of Major League Baseball (sorry, Yankees fans), Fenway Park, the country's oldest ballpark, makes it hard to not root, root, root for the Red Sox (page 74).

✪ **BEST BRUSH WITH GENIUS:** From Monet to Murakami, the Museum of Fine Arts has a canvas for every artistic interest (page 75).

✪ **BEST SCHOOL FOR PERFECT SAT SCORES:** The Ivy League may have eight members, but there's only one Harvard University. The Crimson campus is a must-see even if you didn't get a perfect SAT score (page 78).

✪ **BEST PLACE TO SEA HISTORY:** Old Ironsides may be getting up in age, but she's still an active military ship and welcomes visitors to her home port in Charlestown at the USS *Constitution* Museum (page 79).

✪ **BEST PRESIDENTIAL LIBRARY:** Camelot and the Kennedy legacy are alive and well at the waterfront John F. Kennedy Presidential Library and Museum south of the city (page 80).

Beacon Hill and the West End

Map 1

✪ Boston Public Garden

The land that is now the Boston Public Garden was the first to rise from the early 1800s filling project that created the Back Bay neighborhood. Landfill material from what was Mount Vernon in nearby Beacon Hill was used to birth a new neighborhood from the tidal basin. After an early proposal to make the land a graveyard was defeated, philanthropist Horace Gray and 16 other Bostonians petitioned the city in 1837 to establish what would become the country's first botanic garden. The city leased 20 acres to these "Proprietors of the Botanic Garden in Boston," and the Public Garden was officially born in 1838.

The organization fought the city several times against plans to sell off the land to developers, and in 1859, it was put into law that the Public Garden would forever be preserved as Boston's botanical mecca. Features like the pond, fountains, George Washington statue, and Swan Boats have been added over the decades. While it faced a period of decline during the height of 1970s urban renewal, the Public Garden today is treasured and viewed as the more groomed and formal cousin to the adjacent Boston Common. A key link in the Emerald Necklace, this park is a lush retreat any time of the year. Featuring the plantings of 14 city greenhouses, the gardens are dotted with tulips, roses, and flowering shrubs that can be enjoyed while cruising the lagoon.

MAP 1: 4 Charles St., 617/635-4505, http://friendsofthepublicgarden.com; 6:30am-11pm daily (open 24 hours for pedestrian use)

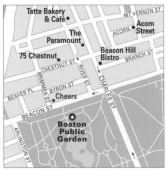

Boston Public Garden

NEARBY:

- Stroll down **Acorn Street,** the country's most photographed street (page 67).
- **The Paramount** serves delicious food cafeteria style (page 84).
- Local gem **75 Chestnut** is cooking tasty classics (page 85).
- **Beacon Hill Bistro** features

seasonal ingredients and cozy ambience (page 86).

- People-watch with a homemade pastry at **Tatte Bakery & Café** (page 86).
- Head to **Cheers,** a TV show-made-famous popular bar where everyone knows your name (page 122).

TOP EXPERIENCE

✪ Freedom Trail

Boston is such a walkable city that you can stroll through its revolutionary beginnings. As the city began a building spree in the mid-20th century, local preservationists grew concerned that its historic sites were being lost to soaring skyscrapers. Bill Schofield, a writer for the paper that ultimately became the *Boston Herald,* collaborated with Bob Winn, a member of the Old North Church, and floated an idea for a "Puritan Path," "Liberty Loop," or "Freedom's Way" in one of his "Have You Heard?" columns in March of 1951. The idea reached city hall, and mayor John Hynes dedicated the Freedom Trail, which was originally a series of painted signs pointing out Boston's most popular historic sites, in June of the same year.

The path went through several routes before reaching its current 2.5-mile (4 km) form in 1972. In 1974, the National Park Service established the Boston National Historical Park, which includes seven sites connected by the Freedom Trail. More than four million people each year traverse the trail's 16 stops, including iconic spots like Boston Common, the USS *Constitution,* and Paul Revere House. Be sure to visit the National Park Service's visitors center at the Faneuil Hall stop to get free guides, or stop at the Boston Common Visitor Center at

on the Freedom Trail in Charlestown

the beginning of the trail (139 Tremont St., near the Boston Common and State House stops) for a free map. The trail is marked by red brick or paint.

While it is free to walk the Freedom Trail, some of the stops charge admission. The Old State House, Old South Meeting House, and Paul Revere House all require paid tickets, while King's Chapel, the Old North Church, and USS *Constitution* have suggested amounts for optional donations. While each of the stops on the trail is historically significant, travelers in a rush should try to at least visit Boston Common, the Massachusetts State House, Granary Burying Ground, the Old South Meeting House, the Old State House and site of the Boston Massacre, Faneuil Hall, Paul Revere House, the Bunker Hill Monument, and the USS *Constitution.*

The National Park Service tours are excellent, economical ways to gain more insight into the trail, but paid tours through the Freedom Trail Foundation (617/357-8300, www.thefreedomtrail.org) are great, entertaining ways to spend 90 minutes with

REVOLUTIONARY TIMELINE

As visitors walk along the Freedom Trail, they get the opportunity to learn about Boston's role in the American Revolution. The following is an overview of what throttled the city and colonies forward in the quest for independence. A series of taxes, viewed as unjust by colonists and warranted by the British, rubbed new Americans the wrong way. The way the taxes were enforced and debated pushed the region toward revolution, which finally sparked in fields outside Boston.

- **April 1764:** The British government passes the Sugar Act as a tax to pay for defense of the American colonies and force colonial exports through British customs. The measure was heavily protested, including by colonists outside Boston's Faneuil Hall.

- **March 1765:** British Parliament passes the Stamp Act, taxing most legal documents, newspapers, and pamphlets.

- **June 1767:** Britain passes the Townshend Revenue Act, which placed a tax on tea, paint, glass, lead, and paper to fund administrative duties of the colonies. Colonists assemble to protest with the mantra "no taxation without representation," used by local Boston politician James Otis.

- **October 1768:** British troops arrive in Boston to quell political unrest.

- **March 1770:** Bostonians confront a group of British soldiers outside the city's customs house (near the State MBTA station today), stemming from colonial anger at their presence. One soldier's musket was fired into the crowd after he was knocked into snow. Fighting escalated, and more shots were fired into the crowd, killing five.

- **May 1773:** Parliament passes the Tea Act and exempts the East India Company from the import levies, which colonists angrily viewed as a subsidy to a British company.

- **December 1773:** Angered by the tea taxes, American Sons of Liberty disguised as Mohawk Indians storm a British ship in Boston Harbor and dump barrels of East India Tea Company tea into the harbor in protest in what is known today as the Boston Tea Party.

- **May/June 1774:** Britain strips Massachusetts of self-government and judicial independence via the Intolerable Acts in response to the Boston Tea Party.

- **September 1774:** Colonial delegates convene a Continental Congress to discuss opposition to the Intolerable Acts.

- **April 1775:** Shots are fired at the Battles of Lexington and Concord, the initial fight of the American Revolution.

- **June 1775:** The Battle of Bunker Hill gives colonial troops a morale boost after they cause significant damage to British military forces, despite losing the battle.

- **September 1783:** The Treaty of Paris formally ends the American Revolution.

an "actual" colonist (or at least a very convincing actor) to learn more about how each of the sites came to play a role in the nation's history.

Or DIY, and combine some of the back half of the trail's highlights with food and drink (page 32).

MAP 1: www.thefreedomtrail.org

✪ Museum of Science

The Boston Society of Natural History originated in 1830 when a group of men wished to collaborate on their varied interests in science. Home to 700 exhibits, the museum draws schoolchildren from across the region to its planetarium, while nighttime events like the "Beyonce Experience" draw a decidedly more adult crowd to the same venue. Also an accredited zoo, the museum is home to over 100 animals—many of them rescued from precarious living situations. The museum is a regular beneficiary of former New York City mayor Michael Bloomberg, whose $50 million donation in 2016 was the largest gift in the history of the museum.

MAP 1: 1 Science Park, 617/723-2500, www.mos.org; daily 9am-5pm; $29 adults, $25 seniors, $24 children

Boston Common

Dating back to 1634, Boston Common is the oldest city park in the United States (take that, Central Park!). Whether hosting the 2017 Women's March, summer Shakespeare in the Park, or winter ice-skating on its Frog Pond, Boston Common has been every Bostonian's favorite playground and an activist hub for centuries. Everyone from Martin Luther King Jr. to Barack Obama has rallied New Englanders on the Common to do better, which is why you can't help but feel moved while passing along its historical green lawn.

MAP 1: 139 Tremont St., 617/635-4305; 6:30am-11pm daily (open 24 hours for pedestrian use)

Acorn Street

Known as the most photographed street in America, Acorn Street has modest roots in relation to Beacon Hill's otherwise luxurious beginnings. The cobblestoned street was home to many coachmen who worked for families living in mansions on nearby Mt. Vernon and Chestnut Streets. Today, tourists from around the world flock to take photos of its Federal-style townhomes accessorized by the American flag—colonial chic at its finest.

Museum of Science

MAP 1: At the intersection of Acorn St. and Willow St., two blocks off Charles St. in Beacon Hill

Massachusetts State House

It's hard to miss the seat of government for the Commonwealth of Massachusetts: It's under the enormous gold dome on Beacon Hill. Home to the governor and Massachusetts General Court (what the state calls its legislative body), the redbrick State House is the oldest building in Beacon Hill and was designed by famed Boston architect Charles Bulfinch. The gold dome is a significant landmark early on the Freedom Trail, but it was painted over in dark coloring during World War II to protect the area in case of bombings. Today, the Federal-style building is open to the public, with guided and self-instructed walking tours provided. If you choose the latter, the state has brochures outside the State House to direct you to all the building's top spots and historical tidbits.

MAP 1: 24 Beacon St., 617/727-3676, www. malegislature.gov; Mon.-Fri. 8am-6pm; free

Government Center, North End, and Waterfront   Map 2

TOP EXPERIENCE

✪ Faneuil Hall Marketplace

One of the country's most visited tourist sites, Faneuil Hall has been a marketplace, meeting hall, and political hotbed since 1742. Boston had tried to build a public market for much of the early 18th century, but nothing ever materialized. Peter Faneuil, the city's most affluent merchant, offered to build one as a personal gift to the city in 1740, and he constructed it over the course of 1742. The market did not gain its current title until Peter Faneuil passed away in 1743. From its opening, Faneuil Hall served as a bustling commerce center, marketplace, and meeting hall leading up to and after the American Revolution. Patriots like Samuel Adams and other Sons of Liberty delivered impassioned speeches against "taxation without representation" from Faneuil Hall, which gave the marketplace its "Cradle of Liberty" nickname.

While a fire destroyed it in 1761, it was rebuilt the following year and greatly expanded in the 1800s thanks to renowned architect Charles Bulfinch, who designed new galleries, increased its height, and enclosed certain open areas. The building was named a National Historic Landmark

Faneuil Hall Marketplace

in 1960 and added to the National Register of Historic Places in 1966. While it still gets the occasional political platform, Faneuil is now largely a shopping, dining, and drinking destination. It sees 18 million visitors a year, according to the market's current operator. Whether you're looking for a cocktail or Crocs, almost anything can be found here.

MAP 2: 4 South Market St., 617/523-1300, www.faneuilhallmarketplace.com; spring-fall Mon.-Sat. 10am-9pm, Sun. 11am 7pm, winter Mon. Thurs. 10am 7pm, Fri.-Sat. 10am-9pm, Sun. noon-6pm

NEARBY:

- Learn more about the tragic events of the holocaust at the **New England Holocaust Memorial** (page 70).
- Browse some of the region's most popular culinary spots in **Boston Public Market** (page 89).
- **Haymarket** is one of the country's oldest open-air markets and has drawn people for its fresh food for many years (page 90).
- **Durty Nelly's** is a friendly Irish dive bar with cheap, cold beer (page 125).
- **Bell in Hand** is a cozy Irish pub, popular with Boston's many college students (page 125).
- **The Black Rose** boasts Irish pride with a food and drink menu to match (page 125).
- Live music and DJ-hosted events keep **Ned Devine's Pub** alive (page 125).

✪ New England Aquarium

Aptly located on prime property on Boston's waterfront, the New England Aquarium has welcomed millions of visitors since it opened in 1969. While the building's concrete and steel exterior might not be the most inviting, it's a welcoming and friendly place of aquatic life and education as soon as you step inside its doors. Whether it's a brutally cold New England day or the peak of summer, it's never a bad time to visit the aquarium. Over a million visitors stream in each year to see the four-story Giant Ocean Tank, which once held the crown as the largest circular ocean tank in the world. A replica of a Caribbean coral reef and hundreds of fish populate the tank and will be sure to pique interests of all ages, though those under the age of 12 seem to be the most prevalent!

An on-site IMAX theater features a variety of ocean-themed films and gives the most lifelike experience short of walking outside and jumping into Boston Harbor. Be sure to save time for sea lions and penguin feedings. Longer visits between late March and mid-November should also include a **whale-watching cruise** ($55 adults, $47 seniors, $35 ages 3-11, $18 children under 3, $150 family four-pack), which sails from neighboring Long Wharf to the Stellwagen Bank marine sanctuary and lasts 3.5-4 hours. If you don't see a whale on your excursion, the aquarium will give you a free ticket for another cruise.

New England Aquarium

MAP 2: 1 Central Wharf, 617/973-5200, www.neaq.org; Mon.-Fri. 9am-5pm, Sat.-Sun. 9am-6pm (hours may vary seasonally); $31 adults, $29 seniors, $22 children

New England Holocaust Memorial

The six glass towers just outside Boston's City Hall and Faneuil Hall represent the six million Jewish people killed in the Holocaust. The New England Holocaust Memorial was built in 1995, and visitors can walk through it and see quotes from survivors of each camp. Each tower also represents a major concentration camp as well as the six years from 1939 to 1945 that the mass killings took place.

MAP 2: 98 Union St., 617/457-8755, www. nehm.org; daily 24 hours; free

Paul Revere House

Away from bustling Hanover Street, this gray wood house on a quiet cobblestone square was the home of midnight rider Paul Revere at the time of the American Revolution. The home, built around 1680, is the oldest building in downtown Boston. The Revere family lived in the building from 1770 to 1800; the building's chimney was an addition made during their occupancy. The building became one of the first historic home museums when it opened its doors to the public in 1908. Today, exhibits cover the Midnight Ride and Revere's work both before and after the Revolution.

MAP 2: 19 North Square, 617/523-2338, www.paulreverehouse.org; mid-Apr.-Oct. daily 9:30am-5:15pm, Nov.-Dec. and early Apr.-mid-Apr. daily 9:30am-4:15pm, Jan.-Mar. Tues.-Sun. 9:30am-4:15pm; $5 adults, $4.50 students/seniors, $1 children

Old North Church

"One if by land, two if by sea," was Paul Revere's warning signal at the start of the American Revolution, and he sent it from the steeple of the Old North Church in the North End. Built in 1723, the church is the oldest standing building of its kind in the city. President Gerald Ford delivered a bicentennial address from the church in 1975, and even Queen Elizabeth II got in on the celebration the following year to honor its place in history. Today, the church still has Episcopal services and is an important stop on the Freedom Trail.

MAP 2: 193 Salem St., 617/523-6676, www.oldnorth.com; Apr.-Oct. 9am-6pm daily, Nov.-Mar. 10am-4pm daily; $8 adults, $6 students/seniors, $4 children

Downtown, Chinatown, and the Theater District   Map 3

Black Heritage Trail

Largely out of gratitude for black service in the American Revolution, in 1793 Massachusetts became the first state to abolish slavery. As a result, a sizable population of escaped slaves and freed black people settled in Beacon Hill and the nearby North End. Today, the Black Heritage Trail links 15 sites exploring this community that led the movement for equality. From Underground Railroad stops to houses of worship and schools, the Black Heritage Trail documents the early road to achieving civil rights. The Robert Gould Shaw and Massachusetts 54th Regiment Memorial at Beacon and Park Streets is the start of this trail. The trail is intermittently signed, and you can find a map online (www.maah.org/bostoncampus).

MAP 3: 14 Beacon St., 617/725-0022, www.maah.org or www.nps.gov/boaf

Granary Burying Ground

Boston's third-oldest cemetery (founded in 1660) is the resting place for some of the city's most historic names. Paul Revere, Samuel Adams, and John Hancock are all buried here, and the ashes of those killed in the Boston Massacre are interred near the cemetery's entrance along Tremont Street. This can't-miss spot is a stop on Boston's Freedom Trail.

MAP 3: Tremont St. (between Park St. and School St.), www.thefreedomtrail.org; daily 9am-5pm

King's Chapel Burying Ground

Boston's oldest cemetery is a stop on the Freedom Trail and was the city's only burial ground from its founding in 1630 until 1660. Among the burial ground's more famous interred is Elizabeth Pain, whose headstone is said to have inspired Nathaniel Hawthorne to write Hester Prynne's character in *The Scarlet Letter.* The father of Ralph Waldo Emerson is also buried here.

Granary Burying Ground

71

MAP 3: 58 Tremont St., 617/523-1749, www.thefreedomtrail.org; Mon.-Sat. 10am-4:30pm, Sun. 1:30pm-midnight

Old South Meeting House

The Old South Meeting House, which originated as a Congregational church at Milk and Washington Streets downtown, is where church and state mixed. Angry colonists met outside the building in December of 1773 to protest unpopular taxes thrust upon them by Britain. The protests grew into the Boston Tea Party. Today it's a museum and still attracts politicians who wish to speak about hot-button issues amid a historical backdrop.

MAP 3: 310 Washington St., 617/482-6439, www.osmh.org; Apr.-Oct. daily 9:30am-5pm, Nov.-Mar. daily 9am-5pm; $6 adults, $5 seniors/students, $1 children

Old State House

Boston's Old State House was—you guessed it—the original seat of Massachusetts government. In 1770, the Boston Massacre occurred in front of this building; six years later, the Sons of Liberty arrived at the same location to read the Declaration of Independence. Today, the Old State House serves as a museum, a stop on the Freedom Trail, and a station for the MBTA. While the museum itself is small, every 30 minutes an in-character colonial "guest speaker" provides the audience with details of his or her life in early Boston and answers questions.

MAP 3: 206 Washington St., 617/720-1713, www.bostonhistory.org; daily 9am-5pm; $12 adults, $10 seniors/students, free for children

Back Bay

Map 4

✪ Boston Public Library

Copley Square's "Palace for the People" is a sanctuary for readers, art lovers, and architecture buffs. The ornate, Renaissance-influenced McKim Building atrium features murals by John Singer Sargent. Upstairs, the Bates Hall reading room is the perfect hushed spot to pen the next great American novel. The newer Johnson Building underwent a $78 million renovation in 2016 to include an NPR radio studio and café, making this an excellent spot for a Back Bay break.

MAP 4: 700 Boylston St., 617/536-5400, www.bpl.org; Mon.-Thurs. 9am-9pm, Fri.-Sat. 9am-5pm, Sun. 1pm-5pm

Copley Square

Boston's most popular public square is also the hub for some of the city's most iconic cultural institutions. Lined by the Boston Public Library, Trinity Church, and John Hancock Tower (to name a few), Copley Square serves as a daily gathering place for lunchgoers and those simply looking to rest and take in the fountain. It is also a key landmark for annual events like First Night (Boston's New Year's celebration) and the Boston Marathon. Architecture buffs will fawn over the different building styles, while bibliophiles flock to the square's annual book festival.

MAP 4: 560 Boylston St. (between Dartmouth St. and Clarendon St.)

Boston Public Library

Trinity Church

While the glassy, 790-foot John Hancock Tower might lord over Copley Square, Trinity Church holds its architectural own with its Romanesque towers and arches. Open since 1877, the Episcopal church was built to feel like you are walking into a painting—an effect achieved by the 20,000 square feet of murals that are found throughout the building. The church is also known for its choirs, which perform in its five Sunday services. Daily guided and self-guided tours are offered.

MAP 4: 206 Clarendon St., 617/536-0944, http://trinitychurchboston.org; open for prayers and tours Sun. 12:15pm-4:30pm, Wed.-Sat. 10am-4:30pm

Prudential Skywalk Observatory

Head to the 50th floor of Boston's Prudential Tower, the highest observation deck in New England, for the city's only public 360-degree view from the clouds. Audio tours point visitors to the city's top sights below. The city is compact enough that you can see it all from the Skywalk, while the Blue Hills and other topographical features in the distance show just how impressive New England's natural beauty really is.

MAP 4: 800 Boylston St., 617/859-0648, http://skywalkboston.com; spring-fall daily 10am-10pm, winter daily 10am-8pm; $21 adults, $17 seniors/students, $15 children

Trinity Church

South End
Map 5

SoWa Market

There's no better sign of warmer weather than when Harrison Avenue is crowded with weekend visitors to the SoWa (South of Washington) Market. Home to over 150 artisan vendors, food trucks, galleries, and farmers, SoWa is open every Saturday and Sunday from the end of April through October. It's the one spot in the city where you can walk away with hand-blown glass bowls, a banh mi sandwich, and a new statement piece for over the mantel after a single visit. Just be sure to save room—and time—for the highly popular beer tent (and maybe an ice cream sandwich from the food truck out front).

Map 5: 530 Harrison Ave., www.sowaboston.com; hours vary

Fenway and Kenmore Square
Map 6

TOP EXPERIENCE

✪ Fenway Park

Fenway Park, Major League Baseball's oldest ballpark, has been in the heart of the Fenway/Kenmore neighborhood since 1912 and was added to the National Register of Historic Places during its centennial celebration. Host to 10 World Series—the Boston Red Sox have won five and the old Boston Braves won one—Fenway is also one of MLB's smallest ballparks due to the dense neighborhood surrounding the park.

Fenway has been renovated numerous times in its long life to stay modern with bigger scoreboards and features like the Green Monster, the 37-foot left field wall with terraced seating. Whether you're there to root for the Red Sox, jam at a summer concert, or just to grab a delicious Fenway Frank, nobody leaves disappointed. Daily hour-long tours (Apr.-Oct. daily 9am-5pm and Nov.-Mar. daily 10am-5pm depending on game schedule; $21 adults, children 12 and under $15) leave on the hour and take you through this cathedral of Boston sports, providing a detailed history of how this storied team overcame the "Curse of the Bambino."

Despite efforts in 1999 to build a new Fenway Park and later to move

Fenway Park

it entirely to a sports megaplex in South Boston, the Fenway between Lansdowne Street and Jersey Street is here to stay. The Red Sox ownership announced in early 2017 that the stadium is usable for another 30-50 years. **MAP 6:** 4 Jersey St., 877/733-7699, www.boston.redsox.mlb.com

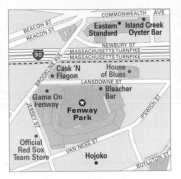

NEARBY:

- **Island Creek Oyster Bar** boasts a sea-to-table experience with its own oyster farm nearby (page 106).

- The Japanese gastropub **Hojoko** serves small plates with unique flair (page 107).

- Elegance, fine dining, and romantic ambience can be found at **Eastern Standard** (page 108).

- If you don't have tickets for the game, head to the **Bleacher Bar**, which is built right into the outfield wall at Fenway Park (page 133).

- **Cask 'N Flagon** is one of the most popular sports bars in Boston (page 133).

- **Game on Fenway** makes it impossible to miss any sporting event by offering patrons 30 TVs to choose from (page 133).

- **Official Red Sox Team Store** offers tons of festive merchandise for Red Sox fans (page 177).

✪ Museum of Fine Arts

Home to Mario Testino's first U.S. photography exhibit and a permanent collection featuring the likes of Renoir and Van Gogh, the Museum of Fine Arts is one of the world's top museums. Over a million visitors pass through the neoclassical space each year to see contemporary, Egyptian, and Asian art—to name a few.

The contemporary wing houses works that push the envelope just enough in this famously provincial city. The Art of the Americas wing is accented by a glass-enclosed courtyard featuring the museum's **New American Café**—one of four on-site dining options—and weddings when the museum closes for the evening. Plan to visit on a nicer day, as the Japanese gardens are serene spots to reflect on the MFA's masterpieces.

Admission after 4pm on Wednesday is free, and your ticket gets you $2 off at the nearby Isabella Stewart Gardner Museum within two days of your visit.

Museum of Fine Arts

ISABELLA STEWART GARDNER AND THE UNSOLVED HEIST

Very early on March 18, 1990, thieves disguised as Boston police officers gained admission into the Gardner Museum, tied up the guards, and stole 13 works of art by the likes of Vermeer, Rembrandt, and Degas. In total, the art was worth $500 million; the heist ranks as the largest private property theft in the history of the world. The art is believed to have been offered for sale on the black market periodically since the theft, but most leads have come up short and the case remains unsolved. Today, you'll see vestiges of the works in the form of the left-behind gold frames in the galleries (and enhanced security). The museum is offering a $10 million reward for any information that would result in the return of all 13 pieces in good condition.

MAP 6: 465 Huntington Ave., 617/267-9300, www.mfa.org; Mon.-Tues. 10am-5pm, Wed.-Fri. 10am-10pm, Sat.-Sun. 10am-5pm; $25 adults, $23 seniors/students, $10 children

Isabella Stewart Gardner Museum

One would be hard-pressed to find a greater story and character than the late Isabella Stewart Gardner and her eponymous museum. Housing art collected by the socialite and her husband from their 19th-century travels around the world, the Gardner Museum was built to look like a Venetian palace. Its three floors of galleries and lush courtyard have become Boston's nod to idiosyncrasy, as none of the collection can be rearranged or added to—or everything (including the building) goes to Harvard, per Mrs. Gardner's will. Home to the empty gold frames from the largest art heist in history, the gallery also houses works by John Singer Sargent, Titian, and Rembrandt. Because of Mrs. Gardner's affinity for the Red Sox, anyone wearing team memorabilia will get a discount on admission. Those named Isabella or visiting on their birthday get in for free!

Café G, the sleek, glass-enclosed museum café features views of the gardens and is a great way to refuel before or after spending some time viewing masterpieces.

MAP 6: 25 Evans Way, 617/566-1401, www.gardnermuseum.org; Wed. and Fri.-Sun. 11am-5pm, Thurs. 11am-9pm; $15 adults, $12 seniors, $10 students

Citgo Sign

The saying around town goes, "London has Big Ben, Paris has the Eiffel Tower, and Boston has the Citgo sign." Kenmore Square's 60-foot LED Citgo sign is a mainstay in Red Sox telecasts, as it lords over the Green Monster. Visible for miles when lit up at night, the sign has made enough of a cultural impact that many Little League fields across the country have replicas to give their "turf" some added authenticity. The Boston Landmarks Commission gave it preliminary landmark status in 2016 when its fate was uncertain after the building beneath it gained a new owner.

MAP 6: 660 Beacon St.; available for a photo 24/7, but the lights go out at midnight; free

South Boston

Map 7

SIGHTS

SOUTH BOSTON

Institute of Contemporary Art

Come for the thought-proving art and stay for the view. Boston's ICA is talked about as much for its architecture as for the installations inside the building's galleries. Home to galleries and performance space, the museum features a permanent collection of contemporary works as well as exhibitions. The cantilevered top of the building affords visitors the greatest art of all: Boston Harbor. Plan for the busy but fun First Friday and Free Thursday events.

MAP 7: 25 Harbor Shore Dr., 617/478-3100, www.icaboston.org; Tues.-Wed. and Sat.-Sun. 10am-5pm, Thurs.-Fri. 10am-9pm; $15 adults, $13 seniors, $10 students, free for children

Harpoon Brewery

Sam Adams might be the Boston brew found nationwide, but Harpoon has become the local craft favorite thanks in part to its Seaport brewery and beer hall (not to mention its tasting events throughout the year). Head to the industrial edge of the neighborhood for a guided tour as well as samples of all that Harpoon brews. The beer hall features homemade pretzels and dipping sauces to pair with its lineup of IPAs and seasonal offerings.

MAP 7: 306 Northern Ave., 617/456-2322, www.harpoonbrewery.com; Sun.-Thurs. 11am-8pm, Fri.-Sat. 11am-11pm; tours $5

Boston Tea Party Ships & Museum

No taxation without representation! Maybe it's the historical reenactments and full-sized replica of an 18th-century ship, or maybe it's the fact that you get to cathartically dump barrels of tea into Boston Harbor, but this museum feels like a true taste of revolutionary America. It offers an immersive take on the events leading up to the Boston Tea Party, with engaging actors playing parts of those involved in the event, and even houses one of the surviving tea chests from the actual day. Take time after for tea and refreshments in the tea room, which includes samples of the most popular tea at the time of the Boston Tea Party.

MAP 7: 306 Congress St., 617/338-1773, www.bostonteapartyship.com; daily 10am-5pm; $29.95 adults, $21.95 children

Boston Children's Museum

Find Arthur the aardvark waving from a rooftop along Fort Point Channel, and you'll have reached the Boston Children's Museum. This facility for the young and young-at-heart is the second oldest of its kind in the United States. From learning the inner workings of heavy construction to interactive exhibits like the bubble room and a real two-story town house from Kyoto, Boston's sister city, the museum is a fine place to spend an afternoon indoors. Visit on Friday evening after 5pm for Target Friday Nights and enjoy $1 admission. Be sure to check out the adjacent Martin's Park, built to honor Boston Marathon bombing victim Martin Richards; it features an expansive playground.

MAP 7: 308 Congress St., 617/426-6500, www.bostonchildrensmuseum.org; Sat.-Thurs. 10am-5pm, Fri. 10am-9pm; $18 all ages, children under 1 free

TOP EXPERIENCE

✪ Harvard University

Southerners say the Mississippi Delta begins in the lobby of Memphis's Peabody Hotel. Northerners could say New England begins in Harvard Yard. College rankings fluctuate depending on the periodical, but there's only one that remains firmly number one in the minds of many around the world: Harvard. Established in 1636, this crown jewel of the Ivy League is the country's oldest university. Its alumni include 32 heads of state (including eight U.S. presidents), 48 Nobel laureates, and 48 Pulitzer Prize winners.

Harvard Yard is the nucleus of the 209-acre main campus in Cambridge, and, no, you can't pahk ya cah on it. It is, however, the oldest part of the university. It contains most of the freshman residential halls, several academic buildings, and multiple branches of the Harvard Library, the largest academic library system in the world; noteworthy is **Widener Library**, which isn't open to the public, but whose columned exterior is a marvel. Pass through **Johnston Gate**, the main gate to the yard off Massachusetts Avenue, and you'll be greeted with redbrick Georgian buildings and many a plaid-dressed collegiate to satisfy your preconceived image of New England.

MAP 8: 1465 Massachusetts Ave., Cambridge, www.harvard.edu

NEARBY:

- **Harvest** offers seasonal fare with an upscale twist (page 114).
- Visit **Alden & Harlow** for surprisingly delicious flavor combinations in small plates (page 114).

Harvard University

■ Get your Harvard memorabilia at The Coop (page 178).

MIT

Cambridge's other esteemed institute of higher learning is a global leader in the sciences, and its presence has drawn many tech companies to its adjacent Kendall Square neighborhood. The Grand Dome at Killian Court, the landmark of the 168-acre campus, is easily recognizable from across the Charles River in Boston. MIT is rapidly growing: In 2017, the college won the rights to pursue a $750 million project in Kendall Square that would bring Cambridge its new tallest building. Trademark Tours (www.trademarktours.com) offers MIT student-led tours of the campus featuring wildly entertaining stories of the school's history and the students' own experiences on campus. Tours are $14 for adults and $11.50 for children and seniors.

MAP 8: 77 Massachusetts Ave., Cambridge, www.web.mit.edu

■ Innovative cuisine lures patrons to Beat Brew Hall (page 114).

■ Hong Kong Restaurant has both an upstairs dance floor and reliably delicious Chinese food (page 137).

■ Enjoy gastropub food and drinks with lively music that'll please any hipster at The Sinclair (page 138).

■ Mint Julep is a chic women's boutique with a wide selection of clothing and accessories (page 178).

■ Harvard Book Store is a charming independent book shop with an excellent used selection (page 178).

Greater Boston

Map 9

GREATER BOSTON

✪ USS *Constitution* Museum

The USS *Constitution* launched in 1797 as one of the original six ships commissioned for the then-infant United States Navy. The ship won over the hearts of the American people after defeating five British war ships and repelling countless enemy shells during a battle in the War of 1812, and its strength left many to wonder if it really was just wood making up the powerful frigate's hull. A British sailor during a battle in the War of 1812 reportedly yelled, "... her sides are made of iron!" after watching 18-pound cannonballs bounce off the *Constitution*'s hull, giving the oak-hulled ship the nickname "Old Ironsides." The ship has been spared from scrapping due to her everlasting popularity, and she is now the oldest commissioned vessel in the world. You can see her at the Charlestown Navy Yard museum (one of the last stops on the Freedom Trail), where, after a three-year restoration completed in 2017, the *Constitution* is back on water and ready for visitors. The on-site museum offers an interactive exhibit showing what life at sea entailed during the ship's famous fights, while other exhibits detail the ship's history and life in early America. Because of the navy yard's out-of-the-way location, water taxi from Long Wharf (near the New England Aquarium) is an efficient, enjoyable way to get to the museum if you don't feel like walking the Freedom Trail.

MAP 9: Building 22, Charlestown Navy Yard, Charlestown, 617/426-1812, http://ussconstitutionmuseum.org; Apr.-Oct. daily 9am-6pm, Nov.-Mar. daily 10am-5pm; suggested donation $10-15 adults, $5-10 children (any amount is appreciated)

✪ John F. Kennedy Presidential Library and Museum

In an interview at the Kennedy compound after her husband's assassination in Dallas, Jacqueline Kennedy mused to a reporter, "There will be great presidents again, but there will never be another Camelot." John F. Kennedy and his family have been viewed as the closest thing to an American royal family, and nowhere is it more apparent than Boston. Born in the suburb of Brookline, JFK served in World War II before entering politics. After representing Massachusetts in both the House and Senate, Kennedy became president in 1960. His brief presidency was marked by the Cuban Missile Crisis, criticism of communism, and the drive to get the United States in the lead in the space race.

While the Kennedy brand isn't a major political machine anymore, Camelot roars on at the John F. Kennedy Presidential Library and Museum in Dorchester. Designed by star architect I. M. Pei, the Columbia Point complex was built after Cambridge residents opposed the project opening in Harvard Square due to the projected heavy volume of tourists. Seven permanent exhibits walk visitors through the Kennedy years at 1600 Pennsylvania Avenue. The library is also home to a collection of Ernest Hemmingway artifacts donated by his widow, Mary; President Kennedy had permitted her to travel to Cuba (despite a travel ban) to claim her husband's belongings after his death in 1961. There isn't much nearby the museum, but it's worth the detour.

MAP 9: Columbia Point, Boston, 617/514-1600, http://jfklibrary.org; daily 9am-5pm; $14 adults, $12 students/seniors, $10 children

John F. Kennedy Presidential Library and Museum

Bunker Hill Monument

Offering no-filter-needed views of the Boston skyline, the 221-foot Bunker Hill Monument honors the revolutionary battle that took place on then-neighboring Breed's Hill in 1775 (but Bunker Hill is what still stands and somehow got the naming rights). The granite obelisk was constructed over several decades of the mid-1800s and is the final stop on the Freedom Trail. Climb the 294 steps to the top and—apart from working off your lunch—take in the incredible views

BATTLE OF BUNKER HILL

At the time of the American Revolution, Boston's geography was different than it is today, with the city being siphoned from the mainland via the Boston Neck isthmus and surrounded by several hills that have since been shaved down. Colonial troops learned in June of 1775 that the British military intended to occupy these hills to control Boston Harbor and hastily moved to Breed's and Bunker Hills in Charlestown. The British got wind of the maneuver and attacked the colonial troops on June 17. The **Battle of Bunker Hill** (largely fought on Breed's Hill) ensued, with American colonel William Prescott telling his men, "Don't fire until you see the whites of their eyes!"

When the Redcoats were in close range, the Americans fired, causing the British to retreat. They attacked again, and the colonial troops responded in the same manner. When the Americans ran low on ammunition, they retreated, giving the British the win. However, while there were around 450 American casualties and losses, the Redcoats had more than 1,000. The battle served as a morale boost to the Yanks, who realized victory in the war was attainable.

of surrounding Charlestown and beyond. The adjacent Bunker Hill Museum on Monument Square offers small exhibits on the American Revolution. Four-legged friends can enjoy the area around the monument, as Monument Square is extremely dog friendly.

MAP 9: Monument Square, Charlestown, 617/242-7275, www.nps.gov/bost; daily 10am-5pm; free

Edward M. Kennedy Institute for the United States Senate

The longtime liberal lion of the Senate gets a shining spot at Columbia Point next to his brother's presidential library. For nearly 47 years, Ted Kennedy served as a Massachusetts senator. Despite his embrace of liberal policies, Kennedy was known for striking deals with Republicans across the aisle. The Kennedy Institute opened in 2015 with the goal of restoring respect for congress. Home to a full-scale replica of the U.S. Senate Chamber, the institute features innovative exhibits calling for visitors to craft and cast votes on legislation with

ideally more ease than it takes these days down in Washington.

MAP 9: 210 Morrissey Blvd., Boston, 617/740-7000, http://emkinstitute.org; Tues.-Sun. 10am-5pm; $16 adults, $14 seniors/students, $8 children

Sam Adams Brewery

The Sam Adams name belongs to more than just a Founding Father in these parts. Named in honor of the legendary statesman, Sam Adams is the quintessential Boston brew. Its test brewery in Jamaica Plain offers free tours to visitors interested in the backstory of one of America's largest craft brewers. Taste malts, smell the specialty hops used to make Boston Lager, and, yes, even sample the Sam Adams lineup of brews—even a few not seen on menus quite yet. Only guests 21 and older are allowed, so don't forget your ID. More extensive tours are available for a fee.

MAP 9: 30 Germania St., Boston, 617/368-5080, http://samueladams.com; Mon.-Sat. 11am-8pm, Sun. noon-6pm; tours (21+ only) free-$20

RESTAURANTS

Island Creek Oyster Bar

As Boston's economy roars, so does its restaurant scene. The city has gone from chowder to Julia Child and churning out annual James Beard Award-winning chefs and establishments. Buttery (or mayonnaise-y) lobster rolls and briny Wellfleet oysters are a must while in town, particularly at one of the many waterfront seafood hot spots. The North End's Hanover Street is still the nucleus of Boston's Italian dining scene. Cambridge is increasingly known for its experimental kitchens and daring food scene just as much as it is for being the hub of higher learning. Whether you're hankering for a lobster roll on the run or want to splurge on an eight-course tasting menu, this city has a dish for you.

HIGHLIGHTS

✪ **BEST ICE CREAM:** Boston loves its ice cream, and it really loves the flavors from local chain **J. P. Licks** (page 86).

✪ **BEST SHOP TO SPICE UP A DIY MEAL:** If **Savenor's Market** was good enough for Julia Child, it is certainly good enough for the rest of us gourmands-in-training (page 87).

✪ **BEST LOBSTER ROLL:** Grab a book and line up early to have a chance for a seat at **Neptune Oyster,** where the warm, chunky lobster on a buttery roll is worth the time commitment (page 87).

✪ **BEST DATE SPOT:** Kinda-speakeasy, kinda-hipster haven, **Yvonne's** is the city's current too-cool-for-school gourmet dining room (page 91).

✪ **BEST WAY TO BLOW A PAYCHECK:** Chef Barbara Lynch is a local celebrity who has expanded her empire, but it's hard to beat a night at her original restaurant and the pinnacle of Boston fine dining, **No. 9 Park** (page 92).

✪ **BEST SCENE:** Tourists, über-rich college students, and celebrities all jockey for a patio table at **Stephanie's on Newbury** (page 98).

✪ **BEST INLAND SPOT FOR SEAFOOD:** Just because it doesn't have a view of Boston Harbor doesn't mean what's served on the half shell in the back garden of **B&G Oysters**—one of the city's finest seafood restaurants—is anything less than perfect (page 100).

✪ **BEST ITALIAN:** California cool meets *la dolce vita* at **SRV,** a South End Italian spot known for homemade pastas and small plates (page 100).

✪ **BEST MUSICAL BRUNCH:** Eggs *shakshuka* and a sidecar go well with trombone and piano at **The Beehive,** the South End's go-to for jazz brunch (page 101).

✪ **BEST CLASSIC SEAFOOD:** It's always a circus under the carnival tent at Seaport's **The Barking Crab,** where enormous platters of steamers, crab, and fried seafood come with friendly service (page 109).

✪ **BEST CHOWDER:** Legal Sea Foods' clam chowder was served at every presidential inauguration from Ronald Reagan to Barack Obama. There's no better place to have a creamy, piping-hot bowl than **Legal Harborside** (page 110).

✪ **BEST WAY TO GO GREEN:** **Veggie Galaxy** is a reliable go-to for vegetarians on the hunt for a diner experience—and absurdly delicious potato salad (page 117).

PRICE KEY

$	Entrées less than $15
$$	Entrées $15-25
$$$	Entrées more than $25

Beacon Hill and the West End

Map 1

ITALIAN

Scampo $$$

Chef Lydia Shire is known for her fiery hair and personality, and the intensity permeates each of the dishes at her Italian restaurant in Boston's Liberty Hotel. Scampo's dark dining room is a cozy winter retreat, while its outdoor patio is ideal for pizza and wine in warmer months. Gluten-free lunch offerings mean anyone can enjoy Italian comfort classics.

MAP 1: 215 Charles St., 617/536-2100, www.scampoboston.com; Sun.-Wed. 11:30-2:30pm and 5:30pm-10pm, Thurs.-Sat. 11:30am-2:30pm and 5:30pm-11pm

Toscano $$$

If you take a seat at Toscano's bar and just observe who walks through the front door, it can often feel like the punch line to a joke. Whether it's the priest at the local parish, a well-heeled couple dressed in something more expensive than a month's rent, or a doctor from nearby Mass General, everyone seems to stumble their way into Toscano for its carb-laden Italian staples. The menu has extensive offerings of pasta, fish, and charcoal-grilled meats.

MAP 1: 47 Charles St., 617/723-4090, www.toscanoboston.com; daily 11:30am-10pm

AMERICAN

A&B Burgers $$

Local burgers, boozy milk shakes, and amazing views of Boston's Zakim Bridge are enough to turn anyone into a regular at A&B Burgers. Located downstairs in one of the neighborhood's countless new towers, the burger spot exclusively uses beef from grass-fed cows raised in Maine. Dishes range from a basic cheeseburger to Mediterranean-style lamb burgers.

MAP 1: 115 Beverly St., 857/449-2251, http://anbburgers.com; Mon.-Fri. 11am-midnight, Sat.-Sun. 10:30am-midnight

The Paramount $$

Just because you thought you left your cafeteria line days behind you doesn't mean you should skip a trip to the Paramount. Since 1937, diners have lined up for American classics, from hearty omelets in the morning to white truffle fries and other comfort food for dinner. Be warned: You can't grab a seat before you've checked out and been given your food, but don't

CLASSIC BOSTON EATS

From the raw bar to dessert, Boston is known for its bites. It's typically with the first taste of a toasted hot dog-style bun packed with chunks of lobster salad (hot or cold is an entirely different conversation depending on the kitchen) that visitors realize this city's cuisine is an attraction in itself. Not all lobster rolls are made the same. Chefs often disagree on whether the filling should be created from a mayonnaise or butter base and if chips or fries should be the paired side item. For the best, head to Neptune Oyster (page 87).

Omni Parker House

The city's menus are also populated by other offerings from the sea, namely cod, scallops, clams, and oysters. New England clam chowder is as much a part of the city as the Red Sox (and it was here first!). Legal Sea Foods is the most prevalent source of Boston seafood dishes today, with numerous locations throughout Greater Boston—check out the Harborside location (page 110)—serving chowder, fish-and-chips, oysters, and more. It was tradition to serve Legal's clam chowder at every U.S. presidential inauguration from President Ronald Reagan's in 1981 through President Barack Obama's second inauguration in 2013.

As for dessert, the Parker House Hotel (the precursor to today's Omni Parker House) is said to have created the Boston cream pie, a yellow butter cake filled with cream or custard and topped with a chocolate glaze, in the 1800s. Today, it can be sampled in doughnut form at some of the city's top spots, like Blackbird Doughnuts (page 104). Dunkin' Donuts also got its start here, in the suburb of Quincy in 1950, and has since become a morning staple in the city and country. With hundreds of locations in Boston, you won't go far without seeing one.

fret. The system hasn't broken down and left anyone standing looking for a table since the place first opened.

MAP 1: 44 Charles St., 617/720-1152, www.paramountboston.com; Mon.-Fri. 7am-10pm, Sat.-Sun. 8am-10pm

75 Chestnut $$

Maybe it's the bronze and dark wood accents, the dim lighting and red wine, or just the cozy setting on Charles Street, but 75 Chestnut is a local gem just off the beaten path enough to make any visitor feel like a native. Since 1997, the team here has served American classics like Nantucket seafood stew, steaks, and whitefish that are reliable and perfect when you're wanting a hearty meal on a cold night. Allow yourself time to sidle up to the rustic bar and hear stories from the neighborhood over the years.

BOSTON'S ICE CREAM OBSESSION

New England winters may pack a punch, but that doesn't keep Bostonians from screaming for ice cream all year long. Boston is one of the top ice cream-consuming cities in the country. Award-wining **J. P. Licks** has everything from raspberry hot chocolate, house-roasted coffees, and their signature Lixwiches (aka ice cream sandwiches) to keep crowds coming back for more. **Toscanini's**, equally beloved and oft-awarded, has creative flavor combinations that are sure to please.

MAP 1: 75 Chestnut St., 617/227-2175, www.75chestnut.com; Mon.-Thurs. 5pm-11pm, Fri. 5pm-midnight, Sat. 10:30am-3pm and 5pm-midnight, Sun. 10:30am-2:30pm and 5pm-11pm

GASTROPUBS
Tip Tap Room $$

If you wander far enough over the incline, you'll find one of Boston's top craft beer bars on the back side of Beacon Hill. Tip Tap Room features more than 35 rotating beers on draft, ranging from sour to fruity to local IPAs. For the hungry, chef Brian Poe offers a variety of "tips" like chicken, beef, and tofu to go with whatever you order on "tap." Weekends are usually packed at the bar, but twentysomething singles will likely take solace in such.

MAP 1: 138 Cambridge St., 857/350-3344, www.thetiptaproom.com; Mon.-Fri. 11:30am-1:30am, Sat.-Sun. 10:30am-1:30am

FRENCH
Beacon Hill Bistro $$

The coziness of this bistro (which doubles as the lobby for the Beacon Hill Hotel) makes it a perfect place for a romantic date night as well as a prime spot to grab a paper and read with your omelet at the bar (and enjoy some great people-watching). The culinary team emphasizes local ingredients and produce, making the menu highly seasonal. Seafood usually takes top billing, but turf options like a bone-in pork chop with brown butter and apples from a local orchard are hard to pass up.

MAP 1: 25 Charles St., 617/723-7575, www.beaconhillhotel.com; Mon.-Tues. 11:30am-9pm, Wed.-Fri. 11:30am-10pm, Sat. 9am-10pm, Sun. 9am-9pm

COFFEE
Tatte Bakery & Café $

The Charles Street location of this popular local chain is worth your time, as it provides a great spot to relax and watch Beacon Hill natives and visitors go about their day. The bright interior and gorgeous, scrumptious pastries for sale make Tatte look equally inviting and intimidating, as it is reminiscent of a set from *The Barefoot Contessa*. Relax with a coffee and treat on the patio or in the usually crowded but cozy interior space.

MAP 1: 70 Charles St., 617/723-5555, www. tattebakery.com; Mon.-Fri. 7am-8pm, Sat. 8am-8pm, Sun. 8am-7pm

ICE CREAM
✪ J. P. Licks $

The original might be in Jamaica Plain, but the Beacon Hill J. P. Licks is most convenient for tourists needing a quick cone of creamy goodness. Boston's most popular local ice cream chain keeps locals coming back for ice cream sandwiches (called Lixwiches here), frozen yogurt, and gallons and gallons of its rotating flavors. They also take pride in their hot cocoa and coffee, the latter of which they roast themselves.

MAP 1: 150 Charles St., 857/233-2771, www.jplicks.com; daily 9am-11pm

FOOD MARKETS
❂ Savenor's Market $$$

Even if you don't have a kitchen in your hotel room, Savenor's is worth a trip just to gawk at its array of exotic meats, cheeses, and prepared foods. A favorite of Julia Child, Savenor's often features iguana and kangaroo meat as well as a variety of cheeses to make yours the most interesting charcuterie board in town. Accommodating staff and helpful butchers can help you work your way through the at-times-intimidating offerings to unleash your inner "French Chef."

Savenor's Market

MAP 1: 160 Charles St., 617/723-6328, www.savenorsmarket.com; Mon.-Fri. 11am-8pm, Sat.10am-8pm, Sun. noon-7pm

Government Center, North End, and Waterfront   Map 2

SEAFOOD
❂ Neptune Oyster $$$

Don't be deterred by the inevitable line outside this small seafood restaurant: It's worth it. Crowds arrive early for the raw bar and lobster rolls viewed as Boston's best, so it is recommended you arrive at least a half hour before it first opens for lunch to have a shot at finding a space in this legendary seafood hub.

MAP 2: 63 Salem St., 617/742-3474, www.neptuneoyster.com; Sun.-Thurs. 11:30am-9:30pm, Fri.-Sat. 11:30am-10:30pm

The Daily Catch $$

Not all North End restaurants are made the same, and this Sicilian pasta and seafood joint sets itself apart by featuring an open fire and cozy dining room that make the atmosphere more like Nona's kitchen than a traditional restaurant. Lines often run out the door, but lobster fra diavolo and black pasta are well worth the wait.

MAP 2: 323 Hanover St., 617/523-8567, www.thedailycatch.com; daily 11am-10pm

Il Molo $$

Despite its basement location, the bright, aquatic hues of Il Molo's dining room pair well with the delicious seafood and coastal Italian fare cranked out by the kitchen. Raw bars will be a faint memory after tasting the oysters Rockefeller, while seafood pastas and steamed lobsters are popular among the dinner crowd.

MAP 2: 326 Commercial St., 857/277-1895, www.ilmoloboston.com; Sun.-Wed. 4:15pm-10pm, Thurs.-Sat. 11am-11pm

James Hook & Co. $$

While this lobster shack might not be much—it's a portable trailer on the waterfront—the seafood served inside more than makes up for the lackluster architecture. Delicious lobster rolls with huge chunks of meat, as well as lobster mac-and-cheese, are hearty treats best enjoyed on the outdoor picnic tables. Tip: There is chatter about a more permanent facility getting built, so call ahead for availability.

MAP 2: 440 Atlantic Ave., 617/423-5501, www.jameshooklobster.com; Mon.-Thurs. and Sat. 10am-5pm, Fri. 10am-6pm, Sun. 10am-4pm

ITALIAN

Bricco $$$

One of the North End's more established establishments, Bricco's menu ranges from decadent *frittura mista* (lightly fried fish and veggies) to pasta mainstays (the gnocchi is particularly delightful) and steaks. Rich desserts and a late-night menu keep the dining room buzzing, and both should be washed down with the bar's delightful espresso martini.

MAP 2: 241 Hanover St., 617/248-6800, www.bricco.com; Sun.-Thurs. 4pm-11pm, Fri.-Sat. 4pm-2am

Mamma Maria $$$

Head to North Square for a refined Italian dinner. From expertly tended flower boxes outside to crisp white tablecloths inside, every detail is carefully executed at Mamma Maria. This precision translates to both the food and service: Fresh pastas along with meats and fish in decadent sauces are served underneath chandeliers, and an attentive sommelier ensures an excellent wine and meal pairing.

MAP 2: 3 North Square, 617/523-0077, www.mammamaria.com; Sun.-Thurs. 5pm-10pm, Fri.-Sat. 5pm-11pm

Giacomo's $$

Come for Italian staples in a cozy, exposed-brick dining room, but don't forget to bring cash! Lines are long, but the wait and service are usually quick. You'll be treated to some of the city's most affordable and delicious Italian classics (with ample servings to take home). The wine list has surprisingly reasonable prices. Save room for cannoli at Mike's Pastry across the street.

MAP 2: 355 Hanover St., 617/523-9026; Mon.-Thurs. 4:30pm-10pm, Fri.-Sat. 4:30pm-10:30pm, Sun. 4pm-9:30pm

Rigoletto Ristorante $$

It might not be as well known as other North End eateries, but Rigoletto lets the menu do the talking. Diners salivate over lobster ravioli, homemade pastas, and impossible-to-pick-just-one appetizers (but the ricotta *croccante* is a great launch to any meal). Friendly, knowledgeable staff and delicious cocktails make Rigoletto an Italian night filled with *la dolce vita*.

MAP 2: 115 Salem St., 857/350-3402, www.rigolettoristorante.com; Sun.-Thurs. noon-10pm, Fri.-Sat. noon-11pm

Tony & Elaine's $$

North Enders probably thought they were oversaturated with red sauce joints, but Tony & Elaine's has been a nice addition to Boston's Italian enclave since opening in 2018. Named after owner Nick Frattaroli's parents, the classic tile and red-checkered tablecloth joint offers sit-down service with favorite classics like lobster ravioli and chicken parmesan as well as take-out Italian subs.

It is relatively easy to find fresh produce and artisanal goods in Boston thanks to several farmers markets around the city. The city's Office of Food Access oversees nearly 30 farmers markets across Boston (a map of which can be found at www. boston.gov), including a year-round one at the Boston Public Market. Fresh food trucks change locations while popular markets pop up in Copley and Dewey Squares on Tuesdays from May until November.

MAP 2: 111 N. Washington St., 617/580-0321, www.tonyandelaines. com; Mon.-Thurs. 4:30pm-10pm, Fri. 4:30pm-11pm, Sat. 11:30am-11pm, Sun. 11:30am-10pm

PIZZA
The Original Regina Pizzeria $

You might be able to spot "Boston's Best Pizza" in several locations throughout the greater metro area, but there's only one original. Stray off the North End's main drag and head to Regina Pizzeria's neon sign to dine at the birthplace of the region's most popular pizza chain. Unpretentious pies, pitchers of beer, and a loyal following make this pizza a North End must-have.

MAP 2: 11 ½ Thacher St., 617/227-0765, www.reginapizzeria.com; Sun.-Thurs. 11am-11:30pm, Fri.-Sat. 11am-12:30am

JAPANESE
Kamakura $$

This multi-level, high-end Japanese restaurant in downtown Boston caters to business lunches and swanky nights on the town. Chef Youji Iwakura had many years under his belt at other Boston venues, like Uni, before opening Kamakura in 2018. Tasting menus at night have designated seating times, while lunch bento boxes are a more casual affair. Be sure to visit the third-floor lounge, boasting views of the Custom House Tower and a great spot for late-night Japanese wine and snacks.

MAP 2: 150 State St., 617/377-4588, www.kamakuraboston.com; Mon. 5:30pm-9:30pm, Tues.-Wed. 11:30am-2:30pm and 5:30pm-9:30pm, Thurs.-Fri. 11:30am-2:30pm and 5:30pm-midnight, Sat. 5:30pm-midnight

FOOD HALLS
Boston Public Market $$

The Boston Public Market above the Haymarket MBTA station has been a foodie find since it opened in 2015. More than 34 vendors are under one roof, offering everything from a chocolate bar to pastrami and fresh sandwiches to a wine and craft beer alley. Vendors do sometimes come and go, so check ahead to see the current lineup. Everything is locally produced, so you're helping the regional economy with every bite and sip! Local staples, such as Union Square Donuts, Bon Me, and George Howell Coffee, make this a true taste of Boston.

MAP 2: 100 Hanover St., 617/973-4909, www.bostonpublicmarket.org; Mon.-Sat. 8am-8pm, Sun. 10am-6pm

BAKERIES
Bricco Panetteria $

Head down the alley behind Bricco on Hanover and make a beeline to the sign advertising "Fresh Artisan Breads." Bakers downstairs in the white-tiled room might be making bread for other North End restaurants, but they also sell the loaves to visitors of the quaint shop. Be sure to ask for the meat bread: It's a perfect

CANNOLI WARS: MIKE'S VS. MODERN PASTRY

The streets of Boston may be known more for cute brunch spots and upscale shopping these days than they are for mob scenes out of *The Departed,* but one neighborhood rivalry still rages: Does Mike's Pastry or Modern Pastry have the rightful claim to the best cannoli in the North End? Cannoli is one of the city's best treats, and visitors flock to both establishments to taste the delightful desserts. Mike's might have the longer lines—and the pasty boxes typically seen around Boston—but Modern fills its customized pastries on the spot and even lets you have a drink in the bar downstairs. Join in the long-standing competition judging and try cannoli from both!

mid-Freedom Trail snack or great for later back at the hotel!

MAP 2: 241 Hanover St., 617/248-9859, www.briccopanetteria.com; Sun.-Thurs. 6am-8pm, Fri.-Sat. 6am-9pm

Mike's Pastry $

In the North End cannoli battle, Mike's Pastry garners the larger crowds (this is verified by all the Mike's boxes you'll see toted around well beyond the neighborhood). Lines run out the door, with guests looking to get their hands on the more than a dozen cannoli flavors as well as other Italian desserts and espresso.

MAP 2: 300 Hanover St., 617/742-3050, www.mikespastry.com; Sun.-Thurs. 8am-10pm, Fri.-Sat. 8am-11pm

Modern Pastry $

Locals often point their friends to Modern Pastry for cannoli. Flaky, ricotta-filled treats are customizable with such extras as chocolate chips and chocolate-dipped shells (filled on the spot!). Other desserts like chocolates, pastries, and cakes are also behind the case waiting to be taken home. Beat the line and enjoy the downstairs bar to pair your treat with an adult beverage.

MAP 2: 257 Hanover St., 617/523-3783, www.modernpastry.com; Sun.-Thurs. 7am-11pm, Fri.-Sat. 7am-midnight

FARMERS MARKETS
Haymarket $

If you stroll around the North End stretch of the Rose Kennedy Greenway on weekends, you might notice people swarming around a collection of fresh produce and seafood stands near Haymarket Station. Haymarket is one of the country's oldest open-air markets and has drawn people for its fresh food for nearly 300 years. Prices are low, vendors are friendly, and it's a great place to get picnic materials before heading to the nearby park.

MAP 2: 136 Blackstone St., www. haymarketboston.org; Fri.-Sat. 6am-7pm

Downtown, Chinatown, and the Theater District

Map 3

SEAFOOD

Ostra $$$

Boston's go-to Theater District seafood venue offers a night out just as entertaining as what is being performed on any of the nearby stages. Chef-owner Jamie Mammano offers daily shellfish, a raw bar, caviar, and a multicourse tour through the (extremely high-end) offerings of the sea in a modern yet simple dining room. **MAP 3:** 1 Charles St. S., 617/421-1200, www.ostraboston.com; Mon.-Thurs. 5:30pm-10pm, Fri.-Sat. 5:30pm-11pm, Sun. 5:30pm-9:30pm

AMERICAN

✪ Yvonne's $$

Part speakeasy, part supper club, Yvonne's is easy to locate (once you find the alley) because it has remained Boston's "it" restaurant well past its 2015 debut. While it's a top pick for the Instagram-your-food generation, local patrons of Locke-Ober, its venerable predecessor, will be equally pleased by classic cocktails churned out from the Library Bar and an eclectic American menu marked by Asian, Mediterranean, and British influences. **MAP 3:** 2 Winter Pl., 617/267-0047, www.yvonnesboston.com; kitchen daily 5pm-11pm, bar daily 4pm-2am

J. M. Curley $

American comfort food and an extensive beer and cocktail program rule the roost at this bar named for one of Boston's most colorful mayors (he served part of one term from

J. M. Curley

prison). The cast-iron mac-and-cheese and homemade Cracker Jacks can't be beat, but reserve ahead of time to get into Bogie's Place, the "secret" steak house in the rear.

MAP 3: 21 Temple Pl., 617/338-5333, www.jmcurleyboston.com; Mon.-Sat. 11:30am-2am (kitchen closes 1am), Sun. 11:30am-midnight

South Street Diner $

Boston is not known for its wild nightlife, but South Street Diner stays busy 24 hours a day. This retro diner in the shadow of South Station overlooks I-93 and casts a wide net for patrons looking for greasy staples like cheese fries, pancakes, eggs, and frappes (sometimes all in the same order).

MAP 3: 178 Kneeland St., 617/350-0038, www.southstreetdiner.com; daily 24 hours

MEDITERRANEAN
✪ No. 9 Park $$$

Whether you're looking to close a deal, pop the question, or gloat about whatever bill you just passed at the State House, Boston culinary queen Barbara Lynch's No. 9 Park is the peak of Boston "it" dining. Lynch's elegant French/Italian outpost features a casual-but-not-cheap front bar for cocktails and snacks. A front dining area offers views while the rear dining area is an intimate setting for savoring Lynch's decadent à la carte and chef's tasting menus.

MAP 3: 540 Atlantic Ave., 617/451-1234, www.no9park.com; Sun.-Mon. 5pm-9pm, Wed.-Sat. 5pm-10pm

Trade $$

The plates are small and the ceilings high in this Mediterranean hub perfect for happy hour snacks and cocktails or more romantic dinners when you find yourself in the mood to share nibbles and sips. Steps from Fort Point Channel, Trade features a raw bar, cold and hot small plates, and heartier options like flatbreads.

MAP 3: 9 Park St., 617/742-9991, www.trade-boston.com; Mon.-Thurs. 11:30am-11pm, Fri. 11:30am-midnight, Sat. 4pm-midnight

STEAK HOUSE
Mooo. . . . $$$

Try not to let the restaurant's name make you dwell on your dinner's past. Of Boston's steak houses, Mooo. . . . somehow manages to expertly cater to both the power deal crowd and those celebrating anniversaries under its high ceilings and modern decor. Überluxe cuts of meat, a well-researched wine menu, and a decadent dessert list make a meal at Mooo. . . . one you and your checking account won't soon forget.

MAP 3: 15 Beacon St., 617/670-2515, www.mooorestaurant.com; Mon.-Thurs. 7am-10pm, Fri. 7am-10:30pm, Sat. 8am-10:30pm, Sun. 10am-10pm

JAPANESE
O Ya $$$

Considered Boston's premier Japanese restaurant, O Ya has prices to match. This blink-and-you'll-miss-it venue in the city's Leather District feels like a speakeasy and is a far cry from the take-out sushi most are used to. Expertly prepared nigiri, sashimi, and wagyu beef rule the dimly lit dining room and contribute to a healthy tab—but it's worth it. James Beard Award-winning chef-owner Tim Cushman apprenticed with Nobu Matsuhisa, after all.

MAP 3: 9 East St., 617/654-9900, www.o-ya.restaurant; Tues.-Thurs. 5pm-9:30pm, Fri.-Sat. 5pm-10pm

South Street Diner

New York is the "City That Never Sleeps," and Boston is more than happy to cede that crown while it takes a slumber. But that doesn't mean night owls are left with just a chain pizza spot for a late-night bite. Most of the city's late-night spots are concentrated in Chinatown and the Leather District, with retro South Street Diner and its typical diner fare (think cheese fries and breakfast items) being the most popular. Dumpling Café stays open late, serving delicious dumplings and soups. Other spots along Beach Street in Chinatown are open well past last call as well.

CHINESE
China King $$
This red-awning-clad corner restaurant may not seem like much on the outside, but inside you'll find plenty of reasons to come back before your flight out. Homemade dumplings, Peking duck (order ahead!), and the house version of a scallion pancake are all delicious offerings that somehow skip the often oily trap of American takes on Chinese food. Leave your gluten aversions at the door and plan accordingly for an authentic neighborhood classic.
MAP 3: 60 Beach St., 617/542-1763, www. chinakingbostonma.com; Tues.-Sun. 11am-10pm

Dumpling Café $$
It might be a favorite of the late-night contingent, but the offerings at Chinatown's Dumpling Café are best enjoyed earlier in the day when liquid ambiguity isn't impacting the taste buds. Pan-fried dumplings, pork buns, soups, and soup dumplings are the top selections in this neon-lit dining room.
MAP 3: 695 Washington St., 617/338-8859, www.dumplingcafe.com; daily 11am-2am

Hei La Moon $$
The main dining hall might look like a ballroom from the 1980s, but crowds flock to this restaurant on the ground level of a downtown parking garage for some of the best dim sum in the city. Attentive staff roll out a wide array of scallion pancakes, dumplings, chicken feet, spare ribs, *bao* buns, and more. Amazing flavors washed down with Chinese beer give diners a taste

DIM SUM: THE BEST OF CHINATOWN

Though most visitors will think they know what to expect from Chinatown, it can be surprisingly intimidating thanks to its variety of options for dim sum, Peking duck, and delicious baked goods along Beach Street and several cross streets. Hei La Moon is a safe bet and usually packed with locals and tourists alike salivating over steamed dumplings, barbecue pork buns, and sweet custard tarts, served both downstairs and upstairs.

of Chinatown in the shadows of the neighborhood's *paifang* gate.
MAP 3: 88 Beach St., 617/338-8813, www. heilamoon.com; daily 8am-11pm

Five Spices House $

Brace your tongue—the Szechuan fare at Five Spices House will incinerate your taste buds, yet we can't get enough of it. Meats, veggies, and fish options are either "dry pot" (cooked with spices in a wok), stir-fried, or sautéed, all to the glee of diners in this smaller Chinatown restaurant. Lunch specials and generally affordable options across the entire menu make this a great stop along a Rose Kennedy Greenway stroll.
MAP 3: 58 Beach St., 617/574-8888, www.5spiceshouseboston.com; Mon.-Thurs. 11am-10:45pm, Fri.-Sun. 11am-midnight

GASTROPUBS
Bostonia Public House $$

Reminiscent of a well-appointed reading room or at-home library, Bostonia Public House offers New England classics with the occasional live musical act. Beer, wine, and a weekend Bloody Mary bar keep spirits lively, while hearty dishes like rosemary polenta fries, burgers, and a variety of seafood keep stomachs full.
MAP 3: 131 State St., 617/948-9800, www. bostoniapublichouse.com; Mon.-Tues. 11:30am-midnight, Wed.-Fri. 11:30am-2am, Sat. 10am-2am, Sun. 10am-midnight

FOOD HALLS
High Street Place $$

More than 20 food and cocktail vendors are on hand at this food hall tucked a few blocks in from the Rose Kennedy Greenway and South Station. *Top Chef* alum and Boston celeb chef Tiffani Faison has a Southern-New England fusion venue as well as a pizza and grinder sandwich concept at High Street. Other concepts include a burger joint, craft cocktails, and the organic food-focused Farmacy Café.
MAP 3: 100 High St., no phone, www. highstreetplace.com; hours vary

COFFEE
George Howell Coffee $

This coffeehouse's namesake founder was known locally for an earlier string of java joints that he eventually sold to Starbucks. He returned with his current coffee iteration with a focus on fair prices, direct sourcing, and regional offerings. The downtown branch in the Godfrey Hotel features pastries and cozy seating for visitors to unwind or cram for a looming final exam.
MAP 3: 505 Washington St., 857/957-0217, www.georgehowellcoffee.com; daily 6:30am-6:30pm

Gracenote $

This Leather District hole-in-the-wall has won over Boston's snobbiest coffee connoisseurs, who stop for a highbrow java to take to their office at one of the neighborhood's numerous startups.

Hip baristas stand by waiting to work their magic and showcase their skill at the espresso machine. The menu also features two daily espressos and a rotating mix of pastries.

MAP 3: 108 Lincoln St., no phone, www.gracenotecoffee.com; Mon.-Fri. 7am-4:30pm, Sat. 9am-4pm, Sun. 9am-3pm

Jaho Coffee and Wine Bar $

Jaho, the Greater Boston coffee chain, came downtown prepared for nightlife when it first opened in 2015, with a wine bar in addition to its standard fare. Daytime patrons will find Jaho's extensive menu of teas and coffees along with sandwiches and salads. Craft beer, wine, and espresso martinis beckon you to stay well past normal coffeehouse hours.

MAP 3: 665 Washington St., 857/233-4094, www.jaho.com; Mon.-Thurs. 6:30am-11pm, Fri. 6:30am-midnight, Sat. 7am-midnight, Sun. 11am-11pm

Sorelle Bakery & Café $

Don't let the bitter winters fool you: Iced coffee is Boston's morning drink of choice. Everyone can have a Dunkin' Donuts, but why not upgrade? Sorelle features made-to-order breakfast sandwiches, homemade pastries, and an extensive coffee lineup. Bright decor and picture windows add to this perfect start to a day.

MAP 3: 282 Congress St., 617-426-5475, www.sorellecafe.com; Mon.-Fri. 6:30am-6pm, Sat.-Sun. 8am-4pm

BAKERIES
Great Taste Bakery $

At 30 seats, the aptly named Great Taste Bakery and Restaurant is certainly not Chinatown's biggest restaurant, but it is among its tastiest. Head for reasonably priced dim sum off the menu in lieu of the usual pushcarts. Fried turnip cakes and congee are popular, but be sure to save room for the breads and cakes, which can also be taken home.

MAP 3: 63 Beach St., 617/426-6688, www. bostongreattastebakery.com; Sun.-Thurs. 8am-10pm, Fri.-Sat. 8am-11pm

Back Bay   Map 4

SEAFOOD
Atlantic Fish Company $$$

Just because Atlantic Fish Company is known for its patio as much as its seafood does not mean it is any less delicious than its fish-centric competitors. Best for the basics, Atlantic Fish is praised for its oysters, fresh fish, seafood platters, and an extensive wine and cocktail list. Located 1.5 blocks from the Boston Marathon finish line, it is especially worth a trip on Marathon Monday. Arrive early, as the patio gets crowded and rowdy for cocktails paired with the world's elite runners.

MAP 4: 761 Boylston St., 617/267-4000, http://atlanticfishco.com; Mon.-Thurs. 11:30am-11pm, Fri. 11:30am-11:30pm, Sat. 11am-11:30pm, Sun. 11am-11pm

Select Oyster Bar $$$

Boston might be known for its "chowdah," but that doesn't mean it shies away from refined seafood. Select Oyster Bar is a cozy retreat nestled just

Select Oyster Bar

From oysters and raw bars, steamers and lobster rolls, to just a great cup of clam chowder, Boston knows seafood—and it can sometimes be difficult to know where to begin or how much to spend. Places like Neptune Oyster ($20-40) and Select Oyster Bar ($30-50) take more refined approaches to tastes of the sea, and you can expect to pay a little extra for it, while James Hook & Co. ($15-30) and The Barking Crab ($14-30) have picnic table-style waterfront fried seafood dining options for bigger crowds (and lighter wallets). Expect to generally spend $20-40 for most fresh entrées, while clam chowder is usually always below $10. Many seafood spots are found along Boston Harbor in the Seaport, downtown, and the North End. Whichever dining experience you prefer, these spots are safe bets for visitors looking to taste the city's famously delicious seafood.

off Newbury Street and has emerged as a local favorite. Wine, oysters, and seafood towers at the industrial-style bar are decadently worth it, but unique takes like a Thai-style lobster salad as a main course will be what you brag about to friends.

MAP 4: 50 Gloucester St., 857/239-8064, http://selectboston.com; Mon.-Thurs. 11:30am-2:30pm and 4:30pm-9:30pm, Fri.-Sat. 11:30am-10:30pm, Sun. 11:30am-9:30pm

Saltie Girl $$

Don't be deterred: The tinned fish that made Saltie Girl famous is a far cry from the StarKist tuna your grandmother slapped on a sandwich. A no-reservations policy combined with it

being a local chefs' favorite has made this den of briny seafood the source of many foodie Instagram uploads. Mussels, mackerel, tuna (duh), and everything in between comes in a jar. Fried offerings and sandwiches are also available for visitors desiring an experience a little less Iberian!

MAP 4: 281 Dartmouth St., 617/267-0691, http://saltiegirl.com; Mon.-Wed. 11:30am-10pm, Thurs.-Sat. 11:30am-11pm, Sun. 11:30am-9pm

ITALIAN
Sorellina $$$

The red sauce establishments of the North End may as well be a continent away when staring down a bowl of squid ink spaghetti in

Eataly

the sophisticated dining room of Sorellina. Tucked behind the Boston Public Library, Sorellina allows diners to nibble on refined dishes like prosciutto-wrapped veal while catching a glimpse of the nearby Trinity Church. Be it a romantic night for two or a graduation celebration, dinner at Sorellina is perfect for a special occasion.

MAP 4: 1 Huntington Ave., 617/412-4600, http://sorellinaboston.com; Mon.-Thurs. 5:30pm-10pm, Fri.-Sat. 5:30pm-11pm, Sun. 5:30pm-9:30pm

Eataly $$

Why pick one Italian restaurant when you can have an Italian emporium? Eataly Boston is a Mediterranean temple featuring a variety of Italian restaurants in its 45,000 square foot nook within the Prudential Center. A popular piazza-inspired fast-casual court offers first-come, first-served seats for charcuterie, oysters, and plenty of wine. Dessert stands and cafés throughout Eataly offer grab and go treats to fuel you for your next attraction.

MAP 4: 800 Boylston St., 617/807-7300, http://eataly.com; daily 9am-11pm

MEDITERRANEAN
Porto $$$

Porto is the place where you want to cool off in the summer and be reminded of warmer times when Boston is in the pit of winter. And then there is the food: James Beard Award winner and *Top Chef Masters* contestant Jody Adams delivers Mediterranean-influenced dishes that change with the season. Oysters are always freshly shucked, grilled lamb chops pack a punch when paired with salsa verde, and Adams's meze and antipasti boards offer more comprehensive tastes of the Greek isles. An impressive beer and cocktail program pairs well with bar bites, which are available until close.

MAP 4: Ring Rd., 617/536-1234, http://porto-boston.com; Mon.-Thurs. 4pm-10pm, Fri.-Sat. 4pm-11pm, Sun. 4pm-9pm

spicy tuna and foie gras *tataki* at Uni

JAPANESE
Uni $$$

Ken Oringer has had a hand in guiding Boston's dining evolution for more than a decade. Born as a sushi lounge within a former Oringer fine-dining hub, Uni expanded and the city has heralded the growth. Chef Ken can be thanked for most of Back Bay now loving sea urchin (not to mention the cocktails served at the sexy, backlit bar). When in the mood for upscale sushi and Asian-inspired dishes amid chic decor, Uni has you covered.

MAP 4: 370A Commonwealth Ave., 617/536-7200, http://uni-boston.com; Sun.-Thurs. 5:30pm-10pm, Fri.-Sat. 5:30pm-10:30pm, with seasonal late-night hours

AMERICAN
Post 390 $$$

Whether you're settled into one of the high-tops around the downstairs tavern's fireplace for a burger or meat-and-cheese board, or upstairs with friends and family in the more exclusive dining room, Post 390 offers a rotating, seasonal lineup of American cuisine. "Farm to Post" prix-fixe menus change with the season but give visitors a taste of locally sourced dishes like oysters from the Cape or produce from Vermont farms.

MAP 4: 406 Stuart St., 617/399-0015, http://post390restaurant.com; Mon.-Fri. 11:30am-11pm, Sat. 5pm-11pm, Sun. 10am-10pm

✪ Stephanie's on Newbury $$

Brunch is a dish best served at Stephanie's on Newbury. Make a reservation for a patio table well before you even pack for your trip (the crowd is decidedly see-and-be-seen). Drinks are pricey, but their potency makes the bill sting less. Dishes like monkey bread (a gooey, necessary start to your meal) and a crab cake Benedict with jalapeno hollandaise are the perfect fuel for shopping later on Newbury Street.

FOOD TRUCKS

Looking for a taste of Boston without the hassle and cost of a sit-down restaurant? Boston's food truck scene has exploded over the last few years. From Dewey Square near South Station to Copley Square in Back Bay, these restaurants on wheels offer everything from Asian fusion to Middle Eastern bowls. Head to www.bostonfoodtruckblog.com to check out where the food trucks are on any particular day.

MAP 4: 190 Newbury St., 617/236-0990, http://stephaniesrestaurantgroup.com; Mon.-Wed. 7:30am-midnight, Thurs.-Fri. 7:30am-1am, Sat. 9am-1am, Sun. 9am-11pm

STEAK HOUSE
Grill 23 $$$

Ask any mover and shaker in Boston the first place they think of when closing a deal is suggested, and Grill 23 will be it. It's been renovated in recent years to update its bar (which features a menu of its own), but the two-story, mahogany-accented dining room is still *the* place in Boston to go for celebratory chops, seafood towers, and bottles of well-researched wine that fetch more than what a one-bedroom apartment goes for across the street.

MAP 4: 161 Berkeley St., 617/542-2255, http://grill23.com; Mon.-Thurs. 5:30pm-10:30pm, Fri. 5:30pm-11pm, Sat. 5pm-11pm, Sun. 5:30pm-10pm

GASTROPUBS
Parish Café $

When strolling the streets of Back Bay, it can be hard to settle on one restaurant—and at Parish Café, you don't have to. Several of the Boston area's top chefs passed along recipes for sandwiches, salads, appetizers, and more to make Parish Café a true taste of Boston. From a tuna burger from the team at luxe O Ya to a BLT from the city's favorite baker Joanne Chang, Parish Café has something for every palate.

MAP 4: 361 Boylston St., 617/247-4777, http://parishcafe.com; daily 11:30am-2am

FRENCH
Deuxave $$$

Part of the Dbar and Boston Chops family, Deuxave is the sophisticated sister who has spent the last few years in France and returned to tell Back Bay everything she learned. The plates are as visually appealing as they are delectable, and—trust me—they're pretty darn delicious. Seasonal offerings like duck breast and farm-fresh produce make it always a great idea to head to this dining room, which caters to romance and elegance (for the former, ask for the secluded "Alice in Wonderland" table).

MAP 4: 371 Commonwealth Ave., 617/517-5915, http://deuxave.com; Sun.-Thurs. 5pm-10pm, Fri.-Sat. 5pm-11pm

SOUTHERN
Buttermilk & Bourbon $$

Head down the stairs of this tucked-away, eclectically decorated Back Bay restaurant and you'll feel like you've stepped into the Big Easy. Chef Jason Santos's Southern-influenced cuisine tips its hat to Louisiana with oyster chowder, Cajun twice-fried duck, and beignets. The Hurricanes and "frozen voodoo" served at the bar might inspire you to start planning a trip to Mardi Gras.

MAP 4: 160 Commonwealth Ave., 617/266-1122, www.buttermilkbourbon.com; Mon.-Thurs. 5pm-10pm, Fri. 5pm-11pm, Sat. noon-11pm, Sun. 10:30am-3pm and 5pm-11pm

MEXICAN
Casa Romero $$

One of the city's favorite Mexican spots is tucked away down a Back Bay alley, so don't miss it! Bright decor, strong margaritas, and authentic Mexican fare keep locals coming back for repeat visits, but the friendly staff always has room for more visitors. Casa Romero's hidden treasure is its patio, perfect for a summer afternoon of south-of-the-border fun.

MAP 4: 30 Gloucester St., 617/536-4341, http://casaromero.com; Mon. 5pm-9pm, Tues.-Thurs. 5pm-10pm, Fri.-Sat. noon-11pm, Sun. 1pm-9pm

COFFEE
Pavement Coffeehouse $

Pavement is a Boston chain of cafés known for handmade, kettle-boiled bagels and friendly, knowledgeable baristas ready to brew you the perfect cup of java. The Newbury Street branch is usually packed with students, but it's well worth popping in for a bagel on the fly (take it to the nearby Commonwealth Avenue Mall for breakfast with a view).

MAP 4: 286 Newbury St., 617/859-9515, http://pavementcoffeehouse.com; daily 7am-7pm

FARMERS MARKETS
Copley Square Farmers Market $$

Everything from fresh lavender and rosemary to meats and smoked fish is offered by the more than two dozen vendors who line the Copley Square green each Tuesday and Friday afternoon. Dubbed the busiest farmers market in Massachusetts, this Copley Square staple is a favorite for workers nearby looking to grab lunch as well as visitors looking to get an authentic taste of Boston by local purveyors.

MAP 4: 139 St. James Ave., http://massfarmersmarkets.org; Tues. and Fri. 11am-6pm

South End   Map 5

SEAFOOD
✪ B&G Oysters $$$

Local celeb chef Barbara Lynch serves upscale seafood in an intimate, modern setting at this garden-level restaurant. The oysters and lobster rolls might be some of the priciest in town, but the perpetually packed dining room and back patio prove the cost is well worth it. Call ahead and reserve your spot for an afternoon oyster-shucking lesson!

MAP 5: 550 Tremont St., 617/423-0550, www.bandgoysters.com; Mon.-Wed. 11:30am-10pm, Thurs.-Fri. 11:30am-11pm, Sat. noon-11pm, Sun. noon-10pm

ITALIAN
✪ SRV $$

SRV has both a sleek bar that cozily beckons on a Boston winter night and a back patio that might confuse in the summer due to it feeling more West Hollywood chic than East Coast historic. Italian small plates and modern design have made SRV the trendy spot du jour in the South End, perfect for after-work cocktails or a special night out.

MAP 5: 569 Columbus Ave., 617/536-9500, www.srvboston.com; Sun.-Wed. 5pm-midnight, Thurs.-Sat. 5pm-1am

Bar Mezzana $$

What was once the old Boston Herald office has become Ink Block, a vibrant mixed-use development with some of the city's glitziest apartments and restaurants. Bar Mezzana beckons residents and visitors alike into a sleek, modern dining and bar area. Simple bar snacks like olives and fried mortadella are just as appealing as heartier pastas and Mediterranean entrées, most offered with optional wine pairings.

MAP 5: 360 Harrison Ave., 617/530-1770, www.barmezzana.com; Mon.-Wed. 4:30pm-midnight, Thurs.-Sat. 4:30pm-1am, Sun. 11am-midnight

Coppa $$

Cozy during the winter and breezy and cool during the summer, this Italian bistro by chefs Ken Oringer and Jamie Bissonnette offers house-made pastas, hearty pizzas, and a charcuterie lineup best enjoyed on the patio with a refreshing cocktail. Save room for weekend brunch—the Hangover pizza's Italian meats and peppers with runny eggs is the perfect way to forget that Monday approaches.

MAP 5: 253 Shawmut Ave., 617/391-0902, www.coppaboston.com; Mon.-Thurs. noon-10pm, Fri. noon-11pm, Sat. 11am-11pm, Sun. 11am-10pm

PIZZA
Picco $$

Come for the crispy pizzas, but save room for the decadent ice cream at this neighborhood favorite—just be prepared to wait, as reservations aren't accepted. The always-crowded Pizza and Ice Cream Company (Picco for short) keeps its menu simple: a couple of "snacks," well-executed pizzas and calzones, and a rotating list of ice cream that keeps the bar packed with people just looking for a cone to go.

MAP 5: 513 Tremont St., 617/927-0066, www.piccorestaurant.com; Sun.-Wed. 11am-10pm, Thurs.-Sat. 11am-11pm

BRUNCH
✪ The Beehive $$

This subterranean jazz club and restaurant offers the perfect balance of cool and comfort. Book reservations early in order to land a table closest to the dining room's stage, and enjoy delectable meze plates and eggs *shakshuka*—a popular Middle Eastern and North African dish comprised of poached eggs in a spicy tomato sauce—for a global brunch with a side of live music. Burlesque and dub nights keep a steady hip and sensual crowd years after The Beehive first arrived in the South End.

MAP 5: 541 Tremont St., 617/423-0069, www.beehiveboston.com; Mon.-Wed. 5pm-midnight, Thurs. 5pm-1am, Fri. 5pm-2am, Sat. 9:30am-2am, Sun. 9:30am-midnight

The Beehive

BRUNCH: THE OFFICIAL SPORT OF THE SOUTH END

What the South End lacks in museums and attractions it more than makes up in places to wine and dine. This eclectic neighborhood of weekend warriors is home to some of Boston's best restaurants, and weekend brunch is the best time to get a taste of the South End. Southern Proper is known for its cocktails and hearty Southern flair while The Beehive provides a subterranean, cool-cat jazz brunch to pair with a mimosa. Enjoy the weekend the way Bostonians do, with fine cuisine and boisterous dining companions. The brunch enthusiasm is contagious and extremely popular, so make reservations if you plan to participate in this South End sport.

Southern Proper $

Stepping into Southern Proper is a little like walking into an eccentric Southern relative's living room. Whimsical tchotchkes and overhead lighting provided by upside-down lamps are minor decor distractions from the main event: pimento cheese and popovers, fried okra, and, of course, fried chicken.

MAP 5: 600 Harrison Ave., 857/233-2421, www.southernproperboston.com; Mon.-Sat. 5pm-10pm, Sun. 11am-3pm

PAN-ASIAN
Banyan Bar + Refuge $$$

Small plates rule the wooded dining room of this upscale Asian gastropub. Mapo Frito Pie is a fun starter best shared over a Kirin Ichiban slushy or scorpion bowl at the bar. When ready to dive into something heartier, Banyan's ramen or rice bowls and shared plates like scallop Rangoon dip (because crab Rangoon is *so* last year) keep the cool crowds clamoring to get a seat in the outdoor patio or hip indoor space.

MAP 5: 553 Tremont St., 617/556-4211, www.banyanboston.com; Mon.-Thurs. 2pm-11pm, Fri. 2pm-1am, Sat. 11am-1am, Sun. 11am-11pm

Myers and Chang $$

Three words: cheap date night. Head to M&C on Monday or Tuesday for its $45 menu meant to be a full dinner of its popular Asian small plates for two (and add a bottle of wine for only $25). Nontraditional scallion pancakes and a Korean barbecue sloppy joe are just the tip of the innovative iceberg on chef-owner Joanne Chang's ever-changing menu.

MAP 5: 1145 Washington St., 617/542-5200, www.myersandchang.com; Sun.-Thurs. 11:30am-10pm, Fri.-Sat. 11:30am-11pm

GASTROPUBS
JJ Foley's Cafe $

One of Boston's oldest bars is also home to some of its best pub fare. JJ Foley's has been serving pints and burgers on Berkeley Street since 1909. Members of the Foley family still work the bar; be sure to save room for hearty classics and plenty of stories of Boston's yesteryear from the friendly crew.

MAP 5: 117 E. Berkeley St., 617/728-9101, www.jjfoleyscafe.com; Mon. 11am-10pm, Tues.-Thurs. 11am-11pm, Fri.-Sat. 11am-12:30am, Sun. 10:30am-10pm

FRENCH
Aquitaine $$
Aquitaine reigns supreme among the French bistros in the South End. An early pioneer in the neighborhood's restaurant revival, it has been offering a reliable menu of French classics for years. It underwent an extensive renovation in 2017 that spruced up the bar area and tweaked the menu to usher in a new era for the restaurant in the ever-changing neighborhood.

MAP 5: 569 Tremont St., 617/424-8577, www.aquitaineboston.com; Mon.-Wed. 11:30am-10pm, Thurs.-Fri. 11:30am-11pm, Sat. 9am-11pm, Sun. 9am-10pm

Bar Lyon $$
South Enders are flocking to this cozy corner spot to lap up Lyonnaise cuisine. Duck confit and escargot are rich, buttery starts to hearty entrées like an omelet with triple cream cheese or chicken paillard with whipped chickpeas. Copper pans hang along the open-concept kitchen, curtained windows block out the outside traffic (and drive home the feeling of actually being in Lyon), and a mural above the bar instructs patrons to *"Manger bien, riez souvent, aimez beaucoup"* (Eat well, laugh often, love a lot)—something most patrons in this dining room don't seem to have trouble executing.

MAP 5: 1750 Washington St., 617/904-4020, www.barlyon.com; Mon.-Thurs. 5:30pm-10pm, Fri.-Sat. 5pm-11pm, Sun. 5pm-9:30pm

Gaslight Brasserie du Coin $$
It's hard to get more French than baguette, brie, and escargot, and it's criminal if you leave Gaslight without trying all the above. This brasserie tucked away in the South End's gallery area is a cozy venue for brunch or date night. Simple classics like steak and *moules frites* (mussels and fries) are perfectly prepared, while special spins like Parisian gnocchi showcase the prowess of the kitchen.

MAP 5: 560 Harrison Ave., 617/422-0224, www.gaslight560.com; Mon.-Wed. 5pm-11pm, Thurs.-Fri. 5pm-midnight, Sat. 9am-midnight, Sun. 9am-11pm

MEXICAN
El Centro $$
Boston may not be known for its south-of-the-border fare, but Shawmut Avenue's El Centro is viewed as the city's best. The intimate dining room fills up quickly, and service may run on the slow side, but novel takes on Mexican cuisine—like shrimp wrapped in bacon and stuffed with cheese—make it worth the wait.

MAP 5: 472 Shawmut Ave., 617/262-5708, www.elcentroinboston.com; Mon.-Thurs. 11am-3pm and 5pm-10pm, Fri.-Sun. 11am-10pm

TAPAS
Toro $$
Open since 2005, Toro is still a source of ire for diners facing two-hour waits even on a Tuesday night. The überpopular tapas restaurant has garnered international acclaim for its killer cocktails and bevy of small plates. Eat the richly butter-coated corn (easily the most popular dish) in relative seclusion in the cozy, dimly lit dining room—perfect for first dates and anniversaries alike.

MAP 5: 704 Washington St., 617/536-4300, www.toro-restaurant.com; Mon.-Thurs. noon-3pm and 5pm-10pm, Fri. noon-3pm and 5pm-11pm, Sat. 4pm-11pm, Sun. 10:30am-2:30pm and 5pm-10pm

AMERICAN
Black Lamb $$

Business partners (and husband and wife) Colin and Heather Lynch have built a South End restaurant empire since opening Bar Mezzana. Black Lamb, a self-described American brasserie, is a neighborhood staple, and dishes like 17-layer chocolate cake, oysters, the Black Lamb burger, and duck breast *frites* give locals ample reason to return again and again.

MAP 5: 571 Tremont St., 617/982-6330, www.blacklambsouthend.com; Mon.-Wed. 11am-midnight, Thurs.-Fri. 11am-1am, Sat. 10am-1am, Sun. 10am-midnight; kitchen closes 10pm Sun.-Wed., 11pm Thurs.-Sat.

The Gallows $$

Parts of the menu may change on a whim (actually every week), but the burgers and poutine at the Gallows are anchors that keep tables busy and stomachs full. The raucous but no less inviting hangout offers fun takes on American staples. Sassy cocktails like the Gretchen Wieners for *Mean Girls* aficionados and the jalapeno-infused vodka Brazen Bull are perfect for after-work libations.

MAP 5: 1395 Washington St., 617/425-0200, www.thegallowsboston.com; Mon.-Thurs. noon-11pm, Fri. noon-1am, Sat. 10am-1am, Sun. 10am-11pm

STEAK HOUSE
The Butcher Shop $$$

It might be intimidating entering a place that advertises $16 roast beef sandwiches on the chalkboard outside, but trust us—it's worth every penny. Chef Barbara Lynch's red-meat outpost in her greater restaurant empire contrasts well with the fishy offerings across Waltham Street at her delightful B&G Oysters. Perfect cuts of meat and sides served à la carte connect well with the extensive wine list.

MAP 5: 552 Tremont St., 617/423-4800, www.thebutchershopboston.com; Mon.-Wed. 4pm-10pm, Thurs. 4pm-11pm, Fri.-Sat. 11:30am-11pm, Sun. 11:30am-10pm

Boston Chops $$

Part steak house, part campy after-hours den, Boston Chops is a steak joint for all budgets. Cheaper cuts of meat come with limitless french fries (most under $30), while dishes usually saved for anniversaries or the close of a big acquisition are just one column over on the menu. The variety keeps the dining room hopping with a blended crowd of LGBTQ youth, businesspeople, and couples looking for a casual night out.

MAP 5: 1375 Washington St., 617/227-5011, www.bostonchops.com; Mon.-Thurs. 5pm-midnight, Fri.-Sat. 5pm-1am, Sun. 10am-midnight

JAPANESE
Douzo Sushi $$

Douzo is always buzzing—perhaps because it's adjacent to Back Bay Station and has a perpetually busy to-go order kiosk, or maybe because the sushi here is just that good. The lounge setting of the dining room keeps a stream of couples and guests from nearby hotels flowing in, and it's easy to see why: classic sushi done well along with a few local takes (lobster maki rolls are a must).

MAP 5: 131 Dartmouth St., 617/859-8886, http://douzosushi.com; daily 11:30am-11:30pm

COFFEE
Blackbird Doughnuts $

Halfway through her Boston stop on her 2016 world tour, Adele took time to give Blackbird Doughnuts a shout

Flour Bakery

(she was a fan of the Boston Cream) because it was so delicious. Step in and you'll immediately feel miles away from the offerings of a Dunkin' Donuts. Boston Cream Bismarcks and Coconut Nests are just a sampling of the rotating menu, which also includes soft-serve ice cream.

MAP 5: 492 Tremont St., 617/482-9000, www.blackbirddoughnuts.com; Mon.-Fri. 7am-6pm, Sat.-Sun. 8am-6pm

Café Madeleine $

Step into this corner café for the ultimate taste of France. James Beard Award-winning pastry chef Frederic Robert gained fame in Monaco, London, and, yes, Paris for his croissants and macarons—and luckily for South Enders, he decided to bring them to Boston. Light lemon tarts and éclairs can also be found behind the glass display, while salads and sandwiches keep the guests coming past breakfast.

MAP 5: 517 Columbus Ave., 857/239-8052, www.cafemadeleineboston.com; daily 6:30am-6:30pm

Charlie's Sandwich Shoppe $

Even former president Barack Obama couldn't resist sidling up to the counter at Charlie's for a sandwich. Extensively renovated under new ownership in 2016, Charlie's offers breakfast and lunch staples from a simple BLT to Cape Cod french toast (deliciously buried in cranberry compote!). Affordable prices for large portions keep the clientele varied and steady.

MAP 5: 429 Columbus Ave., 617/536-7669, www.charliesboston.com; daily 7am-3pm

Flour Bakery $

James Beard Award-winning chef Joanne Chang's local chain of bakeries got its start in the South End. The line routinely coils around the small dining area for treats like parmesan chive scones and house-made toaster pastries as well as scrumptious sandwiches and soups. Order ahead for

105

bigger features like cakes, and save room for a slice of raspberry cheesecake—it's a *Today Show* favorite.

MAP 5: 1595 Washington St., 617/267-4300, www.flourbakery.com; Mon.-Fri. 6:30am-8pm, Sat. 8am-6pm, Sun. 8am-5pm

South End Buttery $

A Saturday-morning stroll in the South End isn't complete without popping into the Buttery for a cup of coffee and a pre-breakfast pastry (calories don't count until 10am, right?). Equator coffees, cupcakes of the month, and other grab-and-go treats are served in the café, while sit-down service is offered in a restaurant below.

MAP 5: 314 Shawmut Ave., 617/482-1015, www.southendbuttery.com; daily 6am-10pm

Fenway and Kenmore Square   Map 6

SEAFOOD

Island Creek Oyster Bar $$$

Seafood comes in a sleek environment at this Kenmore Square staple. With its own oyster farm on the South Shore, Island Creek is a sea-to-table experience right down to the oyster shell wall in the dining room. Guests gush for items from the raw bar, and the lobster roll and chowder routinely take awards for being the best in the city.

MAP 6: 500 Commonwealth Ave., 617/532-5300, www.islandcreekoysterbar. com; Mon.-Thurs. 4pm-11pm, Fri. 4pm-11:30pm, Sat. 11:30am-11:30pm, Sun. 10:30am-11pm

Eventide Fenway $$

Raw bars might seem as common in Boston as the city's beloved Dunkin' Donuts, but Portland, Maine-based Eventide Oyster Co. gets particularly high marks from even the most discerning of New England seafood fans. The counter-service eatery features many of the delectable options found at its full-service cousin to the north.

The menu can shift, but oysters (duh) and the cold lobster roll are classics you can't pass up.

MAP 6: 1321 Boylston St., 617/545-1060, www.eventideoysterco.com; daily 11am-10pm

PAN-ASIAN

Tiger Mama $$

Top Chef alum Tiffani Faison's Southeast Asian-inspired outpost proves she has the Midas touch for Fenway dining. Occupying the same building as her wildly popular Sweet Cheeks Q, Tiger Mama serves potent tiki cocktails and delicious small plates—lucky for you, tables come equipped with lazy Susans to make sharing all the easier. The menu changes frequently, but the spicy okra is usually available and is easily the crowd favorite.

MAP 6: 1363 Boylston St., 617/425-6262, www.tigermamaboston.com; Mon.-Thurs. 5pm-11pm, Fri.-Sat. 5pm-midnight, Sun. 11am-2:30pm and 5pm-11pm

JAPANESE
Hojoko $$

The Verb Hotel's *izakaya* (a Japanese gastropub) serves small plates with a side of rock and roll. Sushi, spicy "funky" chicken ramen, and tuna nori—served in what's best described as a white exoskeleton platter—are filling dishes to complement a perfect cocktail list. Bathrooms wallpapered in Japanese fashion magazines, Hello Kitty decor on the slushie machine, and anime on the TVs round out the hipster conducive ambience.

MAP 6: 1271 Boylston St., 617/670-0507, www.hojokoboston.com; daily 5pm-2am

GASTROPUBS
Citizen Public House & Oyster Bar $$

Plenty of dimly lit watering holes populate Fenway, but if you're more in the mood for Manhattans, oysters, and refined bar bites in lieu of PBR and nachos, this is the place for you. This neighborhood tavern arrived when gourmet was not a word normally associated with the neighborhood, and it ushered in a new and delectable era. Evolved pub grub like meatball parm sliders is washed down with a "bartender's choice" shot and a beer.

MAP 6: 1310 Boylston St., 617/450-9000, www.citizenpub.com; Mon.-Sat. 5pm-2am, Sun. 11am-2am

FOOD HALLS
Time Out Market $$

If you're looking for proof Boston's Fenway neighborhood is trying to shed its hot dog and beer reputation when it comes to dining, look no further than Time Out Market. The Fenway outpost includes 15 food stalls and two bars under the same roof. Local restaurateurs like Tony Maws of Craigie on Main and the team behind O Ya and Hojoko work side-by-side to offer

Citizen Public House & Oyster Bar

some of the best bites in Boston in an easy-to-access format.

MAP 6: 401 Park Dr., 978/393-8088, www.timeoutmarket.com/boston; Mon.-Thurs. 7:30am-11pm, Fri. 7:30am-midnight, Sat. 9am-midnight, Sun. 9am-11pm

FRENCH
Eastern Standard $$

Eastern Standard is the gold standard for Fenway dining. Whether it's a Vermont cheddar omelet at sunrise, an alfresco dinner date, or late-night oysters, champagne, and escargot with the most fabulous of friends, the time is always right for this brasserie that's close but not *too* close to Fenway Park. Dark decor gives a nod to the romantic while the popular patio keeps a lively crowd even as the temperatures drop and heat lamps emerge.

MAP 6: 528 Commonwealth Ave., 617/532-9100, www.easternstandardboston.com; daily 7am-2am

BURGERS
Tasty Burger $

Boston's answer to In-N-Out was born in Fenway. It may have retro style, but don't call it fast food. It has classic options like the Big Tasty and more adventurous choices like the Gorgonzola. Split a 50/50 side, as this box of fries and onion rings is more than a hungry group of four can share. Tasty knows Boston: College students get the

Tasty Burger

"Starvin' Student" with burger, fries, and a beer for $10.

MAP 6: 1301 Boylston St., 617/425-4444, www.tastyburger.com; daily 11am-2am

SOUTHERN
Sweet Cheeks Q $$

Boston doesn't usually conjure images of bourbon and biscuits, but thanks to *Top Chef* alum Tiffani Faison, it should. Arrive starving to her family-style Southern outpost, as an order of barbecue pulled pork means a mile-high pile. Fret not, vegetarians: The sides are as much of a delectable draw as the meatier options. Fried green tomatoes, mac-and-cheese with a Ritz cracker crust, and buttermilk biscuits keep veggie lovers just as stuffed as their carnivorous counterparts.

MAP 6: 1381 Boylston St., 617/266-1300, www.sweetcheeksq.com; Sun.-Thurs. 11:30am-10pm, Fri.-Sat. 11:30am-11pm

SEAFOOD

Row 34 $$$

Row 34 simply gets everything right, and it's recommended you reserve a table in advance for this popular seafood-heavy venue. Oysters are a must, as there isn't a bad choice from the extensive raw bar. Contemporary entrées like seared bluefish wow, while an array of dipping sauces innovate fried staples like calamari and beer-battered fish. An impressive craft beer and wine list will appeal to all palates and hit the right spots in this sleek Fort Point establishment.

MAP 7: 383 Congress St., 617/553-5900, www.row34.com; Mon.-Thurs. 11:30am-10pm, Fri.-Sat. 11:30am-11pm, Sun. 10:30am-10pm

✪ The Barking Crab $$

Amid the steel and glass boxes rising in the Seaport, the carnival tent of The Barking Crab remains a throwback landmark to the ever-changing neighborhood. Originally an outdoor summer seafood hangout, the restaurant is open year-round and features shellfish galore served at communal tables with views of Fort Point Channel and the downtown skyline. Popular for oyster shooters at the bar and seafood platters (fried, grilled, and shelled) best shared with larger groups, this hot spot is a go-to for picture-perfect meals.

MAP 7: 88 Sleeper St., 617/426-2722, www.barkingcrab.com; Sun.-Thurs. 11:30am-9pm, Fri.-Sat. 11:30am-10pm

The Barking Crab

✪ Legal Harborside $$

This flagship in the Legal Sea Foods empire is a waterfront temple celebrating the bounty of the sea. The casual first floor provides a traditional seafood menu and raw bar while the second floor has a more refined setting with dark wood accents and a surf-and-turf lineup priced more for special occasions than a typical night out. The top level is a singles haven with its rooftop lounge, alcoholic punches, and Boston Harbor views.

MAP 7: 270 Northern Ave., 617/477-2900, www.legalseafoods.com; Sun.-Thurs. 11am-11pm, Fri. -Sat. 11am-midnight

ITALIAN
Capo $$

Southie's dining scene has come a long way from the corned beef and cabbage many kitchens in this historically Irish enclave are known to produce. Capo's Italian fare keeps lines out the door and the dining room abuzz as excited diners wait for classics like chicken parmigiana and homemade pastas. A crackling fireplace makes this a perfect spot for a winter night out.

MAP 7: 443 W. Broadway, 617/993-8080, www.caposouthboston.com; Mon.-Fri. 5pm-1am, Sat.-Sun. 10am-1am

Fox & the Knife $$

One of West Broadway's newest restaurants is garnering rave reviews from neighbors and local press for bar bites and main courses. Salivate over handmade pastas, focaccia stuffed with gooey Tallegio cheese, and a grilled broccoli Caesar salad. Chef Karen Akunowicz's restaurant was named a Best New Restaurant by *Food & Wine* in 2019—not bad for a spot that was formerly Triple O's, notorious mobster Whitey Bulger's go-to watering hole.

MAP 7: 28 W. Broadway, 617/766-8630, www.foxandtheknife.com; Sun.-Thurs. 4pm-10pm, Fri.-Sat. 4pm-11pm

Sportello $$

This isn't your grandparents' diner. Barbara Lynch's upscale Italian luncheonette and dinner spot in Fort Point is dominated by a communal counter where pasta dishes and entrées are served to devoted fans of Boston's star chef. Crostini, charcuterie, and cheeses are smart starters to decadent carb-heavy offerings later in the meal; the *strozzapreti* pasta with braised rabbit is reason enough to come back multiple times over a visit to Boston.

MAP 7: 348 Congress St., 617/737-1234, www.sportelloboston.com; Sun.-Wed. 11:30am-10pm, Thurs.-Sat. 11:30am-11pm

MEDITERRANEAN
Chickadee $$

The industrial eastern edge of the Seaport has upped its gourmet game thanks to the arrival of Chickadee. Bright, warm decor in this space inside the Industrial & Design Building pairs well with New England-Mediterranean fusion meals. Smoked trout dip and Scotch olives are great kickoffs to any meal. Staff regularly recommend the rib eye for two. Save room for popcorn *crémeux*, Chickadee's decadent version of caramel corn.

MAP 7: 21 Drydock Ave., 617/531-5591, www.chickadeerestaurant.com; Mon.-Fri. 11am-10pm, Sat. 11am-2pm and 5pm-10pm, Sun. 11am-2:30pm

Committee $$

Locals often chide the Seaport's massive restaurants for lacking the intimate character of venues seen elsewhere, but the Mediterranean dishes served at Fan Pier's Committee please even the staunchest critics. Meze plates feature classics like artichoke moussaka and a delicious tzatziki trio. A gargantuan platter of grilled meats called Poikilia Kreaton is a great way to sample a lot with friends and is best accompanied by the alcoholic punches popular among the restaurant's patio crowd.

MAP 7: 50 Northern Ave., 617/737-5051, www.committeeboston.com; Mon.-Wed. 11:30am-midnight, Thurs.-Fri. 11:30am-2am, Sat. 11am-2am, Sun. 11am-11pm

PAN-ASIAN
Blue Dragon $$
Chef Ming Tsai is known for his East-West fusion (and his popular *East Meets West* on Food Network). While his longtime Wellesley flagship Blue Ginger closed in 2017, younger sister restaurant Blue Dragon serves Tsai's signature style in gastropub form. Teriyaki bison sliders, panko cod-and-chips (with Chinese black vinegar aioli), and "the cookie" are reason enough to stray from Chinatown and head to Fort Point when craving Asian fare that has a taste of Boston.

MAP 7: 324 A St., 617/338-8585, www. ming.com; Mon.-Wed. 11:30am-11pm, Thurs.-Fri. 11:30am-midnight, Sat. 5pm-10:30pm

Empire $$
If you're looking for your sushi to be accompanied by a wow factor, the Hong Kong-inspired Empire on Fan Pier is your go-to hangout. Takeout mainstays like scallion pancakes and crab Rangoon top the menu, which is dominated by sushi rolls crafted in an open-concept kitchen in the middle of this 14,000-square-foot restaurant. A mammoth bar and lounge area at the entrance is popular both with

twentysomething singles and businesspeople in town looking to impress.

MAP 7: 1 Marina Park Dr., 617/295-0001, www.empireboston.com; Mon.-Thurs. 4:30pm-1am, Fri.-Sat. 4:30pm-2am, Sun. 4:30pm-11pm

GASTROPUBS
Lincoln Tavern $$
Maybe it's the fried zucchini fritters and a pulled pork sandwich, or maybe a cold pint of a local IPA and a crispy artichoke and soppressata pizza—no matter your comfort zone with your comfort food, the hearty dishes and the affable staff make Lincoln the clear catalyst in shifting Southie's dining scene from pub grub to gourmet. Popular for both its dining and bar, Lincoln will keep you preoccupied for an entire night in Boston's Irish enclave.

MAP 7: 425 W. Broadway, 617/756-8636, www.lincolnsouthboston.com; Mon.-Fri. 10am-2am, Sat.-Sun. 9am-2am

Local 149 $$
Often referred to by Southie natives by its old moniker, the Farragut House, Local 149 (named for the union that used to reside in the building) shows the Irish bastion isn't afraid of American cuisine. Delicious comfort food like chicken and waffles, fried pickles, and a daily "Really Fresh Fish" from local fishers give visitors reason to go to the eastern stretch of South Boston.

MAP 7: 149 P St., 617/269-0900, www. local149.com; Mon.-Thurs. 4pm-midnight, Fri.-Sat. 11am-1am, Sun. 10am-midnight

FRENCH
Bastille Kitchen $$$
Despite its French penitentiary namesake, Bastille Kitchen is a cozy Fort Point bistro perfect for hearty dishes

and relaxing during a cold Boston winter. Burgundy escargot, black truffle and beef short rib flatbreads, and entrées like bacon-wrapped rabbit can't be missed, while the impressive dessert lineup will leave diners squealing *"sacré bleu!"*

MAP 7: 49 Melcher St., 617/556-8000, www.bastillekitchen.net; Mon.-Wed. 4:30pm-10pm, Thurs.-Sat. 4:30pm-11pm

Menton $$$

Part of the Barbara Lynch empire, Menton offered über-fine dining tasting menus when it first opened at the peak of the Great Recession. Lynch has since toggled the space to where it is open for "modern fine dining," à la carte or a $165 "chef's whim" tasting menu with an optional $130 wine pairing. Craft cocktails and small bites are featured in the Bar at Menton, all in a celebratory environment that's no longer so stuffy.

MAP 7: 354 Congress St., 617/737-0099, www.mentonboston.com; Sun.-Mon. 5:30pm-9pm, Tues.-Sat. 5:30pm-10pm

MEXICAN

Loco Taqueria & Oyster Bar $$

Every day is Cinco de Mayo at this popular Southie Mexican restaurant on bustling Broadway. The rustic cantina is popular with the neighborhood's increasing young professional population, who come for the tequila and stay for dishes like cola pork carnitas tacos, oyster ceviche, and a variety of guacamole (bacon and smoked fish are popular options). South-of-the-border weekend offerings make Loco a perfect spot for Sunday brunch, too.

MAP 7: 412 W. Broadway, 617/917-5626, www.locosouthboston.com; Mon.-Fri. 5pm-1am, Sat.-Sun. 10am-1am

Local 149

Temazcal Tequila Cantina $$

It's rare for Bostonians to find an instance where lobster can't be applied, and Tex-Mex cuisine is no exception. The lobster guacamole at Temazcal is probably the only thing more incredible than the restaurant's harborside views. Watch planes take off and land from Logan Airport while sipping one of the 250-plus tequilas and perusing a menu of upscale Mexican staples, including a lobster mac poblano.

MAP 7: 250 Northern Ave. #2, 617/439-3502, www.temazcalcantina.com; daily 11am-2am

COFFEE
Caffè Nero $

The London-based Caffè Nero arrived stateside in Boston in 2014, and it has been on an aggressive expansion ever since. Known for Italian espresso, drip coffees, and pastries served in a cozy setting, Nero's Fort Point location is down the street from its American corporate headquarters and features reclaimed furniture and baked goods more in line with a one-off shop instead of something from a 650-plus-store chain.

MAP 7: 368 Congress St., 857/233-5385, http://us.caffenero.com; Mon.-Fri. 6am-9pm, Sat.-Sun. 7am-9pm

Cambridge   Map 8

ITALIAN
Giulia $$$

Giulia has the exposed red brick and the red sauce to make you feel like you're at grandma's, while the menu's deeper cuts give a new gourmet approach to everyone's favorite Mediterranean boot. Good luck getting a reservation. If you say a prayer, friendly hosts *might* be able to give you a seat at the bar. It's worth it: fresh pastas, meats, and fishes in a cozy setting north of Harvard Square keep the dining room and stomachs full.

MAP 8: 1682 Massachusetts Ave., Cambridge, 617/441-2800, www. giuliarestaurant.com; Mon.-Thurs. 5:30pm-10pm, Fri.-Sat. 5:30pm-11pm

Pammy's $$

A white tile-encased fireplace and simple, bright decor allow Pammy's to exude cozy and chic. It serves up delectable Italian-American plates like marinated artichokes, a Bolognese, and a 45-day dry-aged rib eye. A restaurant as beautiful and simply elegant as this one is meant to be enjoyed with a drink, so take time to peruse the cocktail and wine list—a Reposado tequila with hazelnut, lime, rose water, and nutmeg is the spiced south of the border libation you never knew you needed.

MAP 8: 928 Massachusetts Ave., Cambridge, 617/945-1761, www. pammyscambridge.com; Mon.-Thurs. 4:30pm-midnight, Fri.-Sat. 4:30pm-1am

PIZZA
Area Four $$

Farm-to-table doesn't have to be pretentious—especially if it primarily comes in the form of pizza! This Kendall Square restaurant-café is known for its pizzas made from dough fermented more than 30 hours. Ever-changing pies, seasonal vegetables, and a bevy of meat and hearty vegetarian offerings keep this venue abuzz with the neighborhood's tech and life science workers.

MAP 8: 500 Technology Square, Cambridge, 617/758-4444, www.areafour. com; Mon.-Fri. 11:30am-10pm, Sat.-Sun. 10:30am-10pm

AMERICAN
Harvest $$$

Some of the top chefs in the world have passed through Harvest's kitchen during its more than 40-year reign as the peak of Harvard Square dining. The owners used to keep goldfish crackers behind the bar for frequent guest Julia Child, who was a fan of the burger (to the dismay of chefs looking to flex their gourmet muscle!). Today, it's still the scene of power lunches and dinners by Harvard professors and visiting speakers in the mood for seasonal New England fare with an upscale twist. Don't miss the back patio for the neighborhood's best alfresco dining.

MAP 8: 44 Brattle St., Cambridge, 617/868-2255, www.harvestcambridge. com; Mon.-Thurs. 11:30am-10pm, Fri. 11:30am-11pm, Sat. 11am-11pm, Sun. 11am-10pm

Oleana $$$

Greater Boston's best backyard happens to come with impeccable Mediterranean fare. Chef Ana Sortun is a favorite of diners and local chefs alike. Bite into the menu's extensive supply of fish, meats, and hot and cold meze offerings, and it will be easy to see why.

MAP 8: 134 Hampshire St., Cambridge, 617/661-0505, www.oleanarestaurant. com; Sun.-Thurs. 5:30pm-10pm, Fri.-Sat. 5:30pm-11pm

Alden & Harlow $$

Do yourself a favor and make a point of popping by Alden & Harlow for the French onion dip and corn pancakes. It might sound like 7-Eleven fare, but, rest assured, it tastes more like the Four Seasons. The American small plates are addictive and range from grilled fishes and braised meats to a select few burgers that largely sell out by 8pm.

MAP 8: 40 Brattle St., Cambridge, 617/864-2100, www.aldenharlow.com; Mon.-Wed. 5pm-1am, Thurs.-Fri. 5pm-2am, Sat. 10:30am-2pm and 5pm-2am, Sun. 10:30am-2:30pm and 5pm-1am

Alden & Harlow

Beat Brew Hall $$

The funky art on the walls matches the eclectic menu at Beat Brew Hall, which lures Harvard professors and first-daters alike for its innovative cuisine and potent libations. This subterranean lair features an array of dishes, ranging from earth bowls and buffalo cauliflower to charred octopus and steak. Its massive bar area is the perfect spot to grab a drink and listen to live music acts that arrive later on weekend nights.

MAP 8: 13 Brattle St., Cambridge, 617/499-0001, www.beatbrasserie. com; Mon.-Wed. 4pm-midnight, Thurs. 4pm-1am, Fri. 4pm-2am, Sat. 2pm-2am, Sun. 2pm-midnight

JULIA CHILD IN BOSTON

She may have been known as *The French Chef,* but Julia Child spent 40 years living in Cambridge at 101 Irving Street. While her kitchen has been donated to the Smithsonian, her spirit lives on in Greater Boston dining rooms. The bartender at Harvest kept a bowl of goldfish crackers (Julia's favorite) behind the bar just for her when she stopped in for dinner. Savenor's Market was her go-to for ingredients like top cuts of meat. Julia's admirers and local chefs Barbara Lynch and Lydia Shire went on to open some of the city's most treasured spaces, such as No. 9 Park and Scampo, respectively.

Catalyst $$

Just because you are in America's hub of life science research doesn't mean you should skimp on gourmet eats. Catalyst serves local fare under a scientific moniker in the heart of Kendall Square. Be it the venture capital scene at the sleek bar or the hungry nibbling on chef William Kovel's delicacies in the airy, modern dining room, this restaurant is a catalyst for stomach satisfaction.

MAP 8: 300 Technology Square, Cambridge, 617/576-3000, www. catalystrestaurant.com; Mon. Thurs. 11am-10pm, Fri. 11am-11pm, Sat. 5pm-11pm

SEAFOOD
Waypoint $$$

This trendy seafood restaurant and raw bar just outside Harvard Square

whole branzino at Waypoint

offers a taste of the sea with upscale presentation. A bar with power outlets at every seat keeps the cocktail crowd pleased while oysters, seafood pizzas, and an array of meat and seafood plates keep the dining room abuzz with guests vying for a bite of what their tablemate ordered.

MAP 8: 1030 Massachusetts Ave., Cambridge, 617/864-2300, www. waypointharvard.com; Mon.-Wed. 11:30am-3pm and 5pm-11pm, Thurs.-Fri. 11:30am-3pm and 5pm-midnight, Sat. 5pm-midnight, Sun. 10am-2:30pm and 5pm 11pm

GASTROPUBS
Little Donkey $$$

Chef duo Ken Oringer and Jamie Bissonnette have made names for themselves serving as the gourmet canonization that a Boston neighborhood is officially hip. Small plates here nod to the Middle East, Africa, Europe, and Asia. Kimchi fried rice, lobster Rangoon, and snapper nachos are but a few bites waiting for you at the other side of a healthy wait for a table.

MAP 8: 505 Massachusetts Ave., Cambridge, 617/945-1008, www. littledonkeybos.com; Mon.-Thurs. noon-1am, Fri. noon-2am, Sat. 10am-3pm and 5pm 2am, Sun. 10am-3pm and 5pm-midnight

FRENCH

Bondir $$$

The French countryside is ideal, but airfare could cost you gobs of cash. Don't fret: Bondir, between Harvard and Central Squares, aptly handles your rustic cravings. Its 28 seats cloister around a fireplace, and waiters deliver the best vintages to pair with a carefully curated menu of fresh fish and farm-to-table fare that'll have you thinking you're in a cabin in Chamonix instead of a stone's throw from big pharma labs.

MAP 8: 279 Broadway, Cambridge, 617/661-0009, www.bondircambridge.com; Sun. and Wed.-Thurs. 5pm-9pm, Fri.-Sat. 5pm-10pm

Café ArtScience $$$

Don't call it a kitchen! The "culture lab" at Café ArtScience churns out food and drinks up to snuff for those working in innovation labs nearby. The vast bar space is light enough for summer and the perfect spot to forget how dreadful winter can be. Cool, modern design is complemented by ever-changing food that is described as art on a plate.

MAP 8: 650 E. Kendall St., Cambridge, 857/999-2193, www.cafeartscience. com; Mon.-Fri. 11:30am-midnight, Sat. 5pm-midnight

Craigie on Main $$

The upscale French fare at Craigie on Main keeps it on many a "Best of Boston" list, and the unpretentious staff make it more enjoyable than most high-end brasseries in town. But locals don't go here just for the ever-changing prix fixe menu; they come for the burger. Pop in right at 5:30pm to get one of the original burgers or the 10 specialty burgers made available each night at the Craigie on Main Bar (COMB), which stays open after the restaurant closes, until midnight.

MAP 8: 853 Main St., Cambridge, 617/497-5511, www.craigieonmain.com; Tues.-Sun. 5:30pm-10pm

SOUTHERN

Smoke Shop $$

Barbecue in . . . Boston? Believe it or not, Beantown knows how to smoke some meat, and you'd be missing out if you didn't pop into this temple to 'cue and whiskey. Chef Andy Husbands offers a gourmet spin on the deviled egg, pimento mac-and-cheese, ribs, burnt ends, pulled pork—yeah, you get the idea. Wash it down with one of the more than 100 whiskeys on the menu, and you'll begin to think you're really in Tennessee.

MAP 8: 25 Hampshire St., Cambridge, 617/577-7427, www.thesmokeshopbbq. com; Sun.-Wed. 11am-midnight, Thurs.-Sat. 11am-1am

MEXICAN

Felipe's Taqueria $

Not all good meals in town require white tablecloth service. Felipe's offers fast-casual Mexican dishes, margaritas, and one of the more popular roof decks in Harvard Square. The line to get a burrito or any of the other items made right before your eyes may seem long, but service is quick and ingredients are fresh—which is likely why the line never seems to get any shorter.

MAP 8: 21 Brattle St., Cambridge, 617/354-9944, www.felipestaqueria.com; Sun.-Wed. 11am-midnight, Thurs.-Sat. 11am-2am

Veggie Galaxy

VEGETARIAN
✪ Veggie Galaxy $

The interior might scream *Happy Days*, but don't expect a burger or hot dog from this vegetarian diner. Breakfast is served all day, everything can be made vegan, and just about everything can come gluten-free. It's a sin to be on this side of the river and *not* taste the potato salad. Beyond, expect everything you would find on a normal diner menu—albeit made with seitan or chickpea bases.

MAP 8: 450 Massachusetts Ave., Cambridge, 617/497-1513, www.veggiegalaxy.com; Sun.-Thurs. 9am-10pm, Fri.-Sat. 9am-11pm

COFFEE
Darwin's $

When you're tired from exploring Harvard and its surrounding neighborhood, there's no better spot to unwind and recharge than Darwin's. Affordable breakfast sandwiches and baristas with extensive java knowledge make this a go-to spot for students and professors to cram before an exam or just relax with the morning paper.

MAP 8: 148 Mt. Auburn St., Cambridge, 617/354-5233, www.darwinsltd.com; Mon.-Sat. 6:30am-8pm, Sun. 7am-8pm

ICE CREAM
Toscanini's $

Cool off with a refreshing treat long prized by MIT students. The *New York Times* once labeled Toscanini's in Central Square as the best ice cream in the world, and the steady crowd would agree! Burnt caramel, B3 (brown sugar, brown butter, and brownies), and peanut butter cheesecake are but a few of the 32 rotating flavors on hand—don't worry, they let you sample before making a final pick.

MAP 8: 159 1st St., Cambridge, 617/491-5877, www.tosci.com; daily 10am-11pm

ITALIAN

Legal Oysteria $$

Legal Oysteria is the swank, one-off Italian cousin to the Legal Sea Foods empire. Oysteria is perfect for a cocktail, expertly crafted northern Italian classics, and, yes, even chowder (it is in the Legal family, after all). Dine at the bar, as the bartenders are great sources of local knowledge while you wait for a meal to emerge from the brick oven.

MAP 9: 10 City Square, Charlestown, 617/712-1988, http://legalseafoods.com; Mon.-Wed. 11:30am-11pm, Thurs.-Sat. 11:30am-1am, Sun. 10am-11pm

Rino's Place $$

Rino's in Eastie routinely tops lists for Boston Italian fare, but its tiny dining room and no-reservations policy mean you'll wait hours at a pub down the street before your first bite. It's worth the wait. Affordable, mouthwatering classics like chicken parmigiana and lobster ravioli make the trek to this cash-only spot worth your time investment.

MAP 9: 258 Saratoga St., Boston, 617/567-7412, http://rinosplace.com; Mon. 4pm-9pm, Tues.-Thurs. 11am-9pm, Fri. 11am-10pm, Sat. 3pm-10pm

Santarpio's Pizza $

Santarpio's is often the first or final stop for visitors to Boston, as it's located at the mouth of the Callahan Tunnel near the airport. The pizzas and barbecue are delicious enough to overcome the slow service and reward your patience. The New York-style pies usually get awards for best in town, and you should add a sausage, beef, or lamb skewer on the side.

MAP 9: 111 Chelsea St., Boston, 617/567-9871, http://santarpiospizza.com; Mon.-Thurs. 11:30am-11pm, Fri.-Sat. 11:30am-11:30pm, Sun. noon-11pm

GASTROPUBS

Brewer's Fork $$

Don't let the cinder block and brick fool you: Charlestown upped its brunch game with this trendy wood-fired eatery. Thirty beers rotate on the draft menu while small plates like burrata and the cornmeal hoecake are excellent for pairing with a cold craft brew. Sunday brunch is perfect for a post-Freedom Trail refuel, with the duck fat home fries and brunch pizzas the scrumptious highlights.

MAP 9: 7 Moulton St., Charlestown, 617/337-5703, http://brewersfork.com; Mon.-Fri. 11:30am-11:30pm, Sat.-Sun. 10:30am-11:30pm

Dbar $$

Part gastropub, part LGBTQ hot spot, Dbar is a Dorchester draw both for chef Chris Coombs's cuisine and for campy events like Showtunes Tuesday and Magnum Saturdays (infer what you will). Arrive early for Dbar's take on mac-and-cheese and other comfort staples, and then dance them off when the lights go down and the bar crowd builds for the mixologists' latest creations.

MAP 9: 1236 Dorchester Ave., Dorchester, 617/265-4490, http://dbarboston.com; Mon.-Sat. 5:30pm-10pm, Sun. 11am-3pm and 5:30-9pm

Monument Restaurant & Tavern $$

Monument's open-concept kitchen gets you as close to the cooking action as possible without you being asked to don an apron and plate an entrée for table 16. Appetizers like baked goat cheese dip are hearty accompaniments to the extensive beer, wine, and cocktail offerings. Seasonal pizzas and upscale pub grub keep this high-ceilinged hangout steadily full.

MAP 9: 251 Main St., Charlestown, 617/337-5191, http://monumentcharlestown.com; Mon.-Fri. 11:30am-1am, Sat.-Sun. 9am-1am

COFFEE
Sorelle Bakery & Café $

After walking the Freedom Trail, you're going to need a java jolt. One of Boston's popular coffee chains was born in Charlestown. Sorelle offers homemade baked goods at breakfast while pressed sandwiches keep visitors streaming in for lunch. Modern decor and free Wi-Fi give you the perfect spot to relax and upload a few pictures from your trip to social media.

MAP 9: 100 City Square, Charlestown, 617/242-5980, http://sorellecafe.com; Mon.-Fri. 7am-6pm, Sat. 8am-6pm, Sun. 8am-5pm

Brewer's Fork

NIGHTLIFE

It's often said that Boston is a city that sleeps—most evident in its firm 2am closing time for nightlife (with many spots closing even earlier). However, Boston

knows how to have fun within its time constraints. Local music venues churn out hot acts while dance clubs bring in celebrity DJs from around the world. From local Irish pubs to waterfront whiskey bars, it's not hard to find a stiff drink within city limits. South Boston has gone from the den of cheap beer and gruff watering holes along Broadway to trendy nightclubs and speakeasies while the Theater District is home not only to dazzling marquees, but also the city's rowdiest dance clubs.

Franklin Café

HIGHLIGHTS

✪ **BEST COMEDY:** Stomachs don't always leave the North End hurting from eating too much pasta: They also ache from laughter at the performances at the Improv Asylum (page 125).

✪ **BEST IRISH PUB:** You may be thousands of miles from Temple Bar in Dublin, but the warm bartenders, flowing pints of Guinness, and fiddles at Mr. Dooley's Boston bring you the luck of the Irish without the airfare (page 127).

✪ **BEST NIGHT OF UNKNOWNS:** Promoters at Royale make sure there's a little something for everyone, whether hosting the cast of *RuPaul's Drag Race* or DJs that make for a fist-bumping bro's paradise (page 127).

✪ **BEST SPEAKEASY:** It's not *impossible* to find Wink & Nod, so what it lacks in true speakeasy covertness it makes up in Prohibition-inspired libations (page 130).

✪ **BEST JAZZ CLUB:** The South End may be known for brunch over jazz these days, but Wally's Café takes guests back to the 1940s, when there was a jazz or juke joint on every corner (page 133).

✪ **BEST SPORTS BAR:** There are sports bars and then there's the Bleacher Bar, built into the outfield wall at Fenway Park (page 133).

✪ **BEST COZY LOUNGE:** Crowd-controlled and impeccably decorated, The Hawthorne is *the* place to take that friend who would always rather make drinks at home (page 134).

✪ **BEST COCKTAILS:** Sometimes it's hard to settle on one cocktail, so let the team at Drink craft a beverage to your liking (page 134).

✪ **BEST DRINK WITH A VIEW:** Lookout Rooftop and Bar at the Envoy Hotel has quickly become the place to see and be seen while sipping cocktails amid an Instagram-able backdrop of the downtown skyline (page 134).

✪ **BEST CRAFT BEER TASTING:** Boston Lager may be the city's best-known brew, but Harpoon Brewery and Beer Hall in the Seaport offers 20 taps of the local favorite brand as well as an outdoor keg yard with lawn games and pretzels (page 135).

✪ **BEST LIVE MUSIC:** Whether you're looking for Top 40 and vodka sodas or "Emo Night" to go with the tears in your beer, The Sinclair keeps a busy set list for all music (and cocktail) tastes (page 138).

Beacon Hill and the West End

Map 1

BEER & COCKTAILS

Alibi

Be your baddest self behind bars at this bustling watering hole inside the Liberty Hotel. Incorporated into what used to be the Charles Street Jail's drunk tank, Alibi is dimly lit and serves potent cocktails. The bar features a patio prime for warm-weather rowdiness, while celebrity mug shots and their crimes line the walls inside.

MAP 1: 215 Charles St., 857/241-1144, www.alibiboston.com; Mon.-Fri. 5pm-2am, Sat.-Sun. 3pm-2am

Cheers

It's where everybody knows your name, and even though its namesake television show went off the air more than 25 years ago, tourists still come here in droves for a pint and a selfie. This Cheers may lack Sam and Diane, but it is still worth a quick stop to take in the television nostalgia. While it might not look like the set (that can be found in the sister location in Faneuil Hall Marketplace), it's a good spot to get a relatively overpriced beer and a Cheers T-shirt or other branded merchandise to take back home.

MAP 1: 84 Beacon St., 617/227-9605, www.cheersboston.com; Sun.-Wed. 11am-10:30pm, Thurs. 11am-11:30pm, Fri.-Sat.11am-midnight

Night Shift Brewing

TOP EXPERIENCE

GRAB A PINT

Any visit to Boston is worth darkening the door of a few of the city's bars and pubs. Cheers boosted the global profile of the Boston barroom. You could say Sam Adams kicked off the ongoing trend of craft beer snobbery, and now beer gardens and breweries are found in neighborhoods across the city. Sure, everyone may not know your name at each one, but all that matters is that the bartender remembers the name of your new favorite New England IPA.

Sam Adams Brewery

- **Visit Boston's most iconic brewery:** Learn the back story of the country's biggest craft beer at Sam Adams Brewery (page 81).

- **Go where everyone knows your name:** Norm! Relive a pop culture phenomenon with a pint at Cheers (page 122).

- **Hunker down at an Irish pub:** Every day is reason to wear your Irish pride at Mr. Dooley's Boston (page 127).

- **Cheer on your favorite team:** Don't even think about wearing a Yankees jersey at Bleacher Bar at Fenway Park (page 133)!

- **Try the locals' favorite craft beer:** Bostonians call the offerings from Harpoon Brewery and Beer Hall the city's "real" craft beer (page 135).

Night Shift Brewing

Everett-based Night Shift Brewing is one of Greater Boston's more popular and fast-growing craft brewers. This downtown taproom, kitchen, coffee bar, and store offers experimental small-batch beers, comfort food, coffee, and beers to go—making this a perfect spot before or after a concert or game at the nearby TD Garden.

MAP 1: 1 Lovejoy Wharf, Suite 101, 617/456-7687, www.nightshiftfamily.com; Mon.-Tues. 6am-midnight, Wed.-Fri. 6am-1am, Sat.-Sun. 8am-midnight

Ward 8

Located in a bit of a purgatory between the North End and North Station, Ward 8 was named for a cocktail first crafted in the late 1800s at Boston's iconic Locke-Ober. While the 19th-century creation honored a Democratic politician's election, the 21st-century venue is a great industrial spot to grab classic cocktails and comfort food before dinner or a show at TD Garden.

MAP 1: 90 N. Washington St., 617/823-4478, www.ward8.com; Mon.-Wed. 11:30am-1am, Thurs.-Fri. 11:30am-2am, Sat. 10am-2am, Sun. 10am-1am

DIVE BARS
Beacon Hill Pub

Just because Beacon Hill is an exclusive enclave doesn't mean it is too snooty to have a good old-fashioned dive bar. It might smell a little like urine, and you may have to wait in line to play Big Buck Hunter, but the Beacon Hill Pub's drinks are cheap and stiff, the crowd is friendly, and this place is a great alternative if the bars at the nearby Liberty Hotel are at max capacity.

MAP 1: 149 Charles St., 617/523-1895, www.thebeaconhillpub.com; Sun.-Wed. 4pm-1am, Thurs.-Sat. 4pm-2am

Government Center, North End, and Waterfront   Map 2

BEER & COCKTAILS

The Landing

Because not even a day of whale-watching should come without a cocktail, the Landing is perfectly positioned to offer libations from its outdoor bar at Boston's Long Wharf. Whether you're needing a summer beer after visiting the New England Aquarium or killing time before you hop on the Provincetown fast ferry, the Landing is a great place to enjoy fruity, frozen cocktails alfresco.

MAP 2: 1 Long Wharf, 617/227-4231, www.bostonharborcruises.com/the-landing; Sun.-Tues. 10am-9pm, Wed.-Sat. 10am-11pm (open seasonally, hours dependent on weather)

Parla

The sauce served at this North End cocktail bar is certainly not red! Parla's speakeasy decor (including wood from an old barn in Kentucky) is a nod to the years when most of Boston's sipping fun had to be hush-hush. Mixed drinks from the menu are always refreshing, but if you're daring, roll the dice and enjoy a mystery beverage crafted by one of Parla's friendly bartenders.

MAP 2: 230 Hanover St., 617/367-2824, www.parlaboston.com; Mon. noon-11:30pm, Tues. 4:30pm-midnight, Wed.-Thurs. 11:30am-midnight, Fri. 11:30pm-12:30am, Sat. 11am-12:30am, Sun. 11am-11:30pm

Sam Adams Downtown Boston Taproom

The original Sam Adams is miles away in the Jamaica Plain neighborhood, but a beer named after a founding father surely needs an outpost on the Freedom Trail; hence, Sam Adams's downtown taproom offers all the massive craft brewer's classics, including the Boston Lager and seasonal Sam Summer, while also pouring a few test brews for the curious traveler.

MAP 2: 60 State St., www.samueladams.com; hours vary

DIVE BARS
Durty Nelly's
Billed as Boston's friendliest dive bar, Durty Nelly's is a two-story Irish pub named for the perpetually unwashed shawl of a woman named Nelly, whom the bar's original owner used to see back in Ireland. The pub might not have complicated cocktails, but the beer is cold and cheap. Locals and tourists pour in for the lively atmosphere and secluded patio to chat away problems and enjoy a stiff drink in the heart of old Boston.

MAP 2: 108 Blackstone St., 617/742-2090, www.durtynellysboston.com; Mon.-Thurs. 9am-2am, Fri.-Sat. 8am-2am, Sun. 11am-2am

IRISH PUBS
Bell In Hand
With its first pour tipping into the pint glass in 1795, Bell in Hand claims it is America's oldest tavern. The crowd it attracts skews younger, as a collegiate mob tends to swarm the place most nights. Pop in for a sip of history as well as live music and a cozy place to recharge when walking through Faneuil Hall on the Freedom Trail.

MAP 2: 45 Union St., 617/227-2098, www.bellinhand.com; daily 11am-2am

LIVE MUSIC
The Black Rose
The Black Rose takes its Irish pub status seriously: Irish county flags adorn the walls, and a local paper deemed it the Fenway Park of Irish bars. Grab a Guinness and corned beef and try to secure a seat for the Black Rose's nightly live Irish band. Be sure to make your drink a double, as sing-alongs are a guarantee.

MAP 2: 160 State St., 617/742-2286, www.blackroseboston.com; daily 9am-2am; no cover

Ned Devine's Pub
The cute dining room with Irish pub grub during the week becomes one of Faneuil Hall's busiest nightclubs and live music venues on the weekends. Ned Devine's somehow manages to serve standard bar fare while also being a hotbed for live music and DJ-hosted events for tourists and younger crowds looking for a clubby end to their night.

MAP 2: 1 Faneuil Hall Marketplace, 617/248-8800, www.neddevinesboston.com; daily 11am-2am, $10 cover Fri.-Sat.

COMEDY
✪ Improv Asylum
This nondescript subterranean space is home to some of Boston's best comedy. Improv Asylum is an improv comedy theater in the heart of the North End, where it performs several shows throughout the week and holds group events and improv classes. The troupe has been featured on HBO and bills itself as part *Whose Line Is It Anyway?*, part *Saturday Night Live*.

MAP 2: 216 Hanover St., 617/263-6887, www.improvasylum.com; $15-30

POP-UP SUMMER BEER GARDEN

If you're visiting Boston in the warmer months, head to the Wachusett Brew Yard (daily May-early fall), to the right of the stairway landing on City Hall Plaza. This annual pop-up beer garden by the Westminster-based brewing company features brews, spiked seltzers, and wine served up from an Airstream trailer. It's part of an ongoing city plan to revitalize the plaza and turn it into a destination. The presence of the pop-up has certainly added a spring to many a locals' step when summoned to City Hall. A stop here is a great way to start a summer night out or enjoy a crisp evening in the fall with a beer and views of Faneuil Hall below. Hours vary by season, with last call no later than 10pm, and the season's beginning and end are weather dependent.

Downtown, Chinatown, and the Theater District   Map 3

COCKTAILS
Carrie Nation Cocktail Club

It gets its moniker from the woman who famously attacked alcohol-serving establishments with a hatchet in her support of Prohibition, but Carrie Nation Cocktail Club lets the hooch flow freely! Designed with a nod to the 1920s, Carrie Nation is bright and lively up front and offers a more intimate speakeasy in the back with pool tables and jazz to pair with its libidinous offerings.

MAP 3: 11 Beacon St., 617/227-3100, www.carrienationcocktailclub.com; Sun.-Thurs. 11am-midnight, Fri.-Sat. 11am-2am

Explorateur

Part-café, part-cocktail bar, Explorateur is "French in spirit" and where Bostonians can spend all day working at one of several cozy tables with reading lamps then segue into happy hour. Leather banquettes are where many pre- or post-theater attendees cozy up with an espresso martini.

MAP 3: 186 Tremont St., 617/466-6600, www.explorateur.com; Sun.-Wed. 7:30am-5:30pm, Thurs.-Sat. 7:30am-11pm

Rooftop at the Revere Hotel

The pool shouldn't be the only thing splashing in warm months. The Revere Hotel's rooftop lounge overlooks Back Bay and features a heated indoor pool as well as outdoor cabanas to take in the sights and sip a cool cocktail while enjoying seasonal snacks. High-rise fabulousness doesn't come cheap. Arrive early, as longer visits can make the steep cover charge a little bit more justifiable.

MAP 3: 200 Stuart St., 617/482-1800, www.reverehotel.com; daily 11am-midnight; $30 cover

DIVE BARS
Biddy Early's

The food is incredibly Irish and the drinks are incredibly strong at this downtown dive favored by workers coming off the night shift as well as financiers looking for a quick liquid break from the office at one of the many neighboring skyscrapers. The lighting is low and the drinks are simple, and that's what makes Biddy Early's a favorite spot year after year.

MAP 3: 141 Pearl St., 617/654-9944; Mon.-Sat. 10am-2am, Sun. noon-2am

IRISH PUBS
✪ Mr. Dooley's Boston

The Financial District crowd shouldn't fool you: Mr. Dooley's is arguably Boston's best Irish pub. It's not uncommon to hear an impromptu fiddle session break out while you're ordering your second (or fourth) Jameson of the night. Service is fast, food is authentic, and some say the Guinness here tastes as close to how it does back in the homeland!

MAP 3: 77 Broad St., 617/338-5656, www. mrdooleys.com; Mon.-Fri. 11:30am-2am, Sat.-Sun. 9am-2am

Emmets Irish Pub & Restaurant

Some of the best taste and luck of the Irish in Boston is also along the early steps of the Freedom Trail. Emmets Irish Pub serves Irish classics like shepherd's pie to give guests a slice of the Emerald Isle at affordable prices. Attentive staff and bartenders (several with Irish accents) are more than helpful with beer and whiskey selections.

MAP 3: 6 Beacon St., 617/742-8565, www. emmetsirishpubandrestaurant.com; daily 11am-2am

DANCE CLUBS
✪ Royale

This expansive nightclub attracts a see-and-be-seen crowd for live music, DJs, and dancing on sporadic nights of the week. Acts ranging from Emile Sandé to the cast of *RuPaul's Drag Race* perform on the main stage before the venue turns into a popular nightclub on weekends. Drinks can be

Rooftop at the Revere Hotel

Royale

pricey ($10-15), but one goes to Royale for the people more than the cocktails.
MAP 3: 279 Tremont St., 617/338-7699, www.royaleboston.com; hours vary; cover varies

KARAOKE
Limelight Stage and Studios

Order from the bar and then channel your inner Material Girl, T-Swift, or Justin Bieber on the stage at Boston's leading karaoke bar. Whether it's in private party booths ($60-250 per hour, depending on the studio size) or on the main stage, Limelight is sure to offer singing entertainment at a wide array of embarrassment levels. (Except you, of course. Your voice is marvelous!). A $5 cover charge is waived if you reserved a private booth ahead of time.
MAP 3: 204 Tremont St., 617/423-0785, www.limelightboston.com; Sun.-Thurs. 5pm-2am, Fri.-Sat. 2pm-2am

LGBTQ
Jacques Cabaret

Life can be a drag, so let the drag performers at Jacques Cabaret boost your spirits! Jacques features drag queen and cabaret performances every night of the week, and it has become a spot for bachelor and bachelorette parties, so reserve a table well in advance. The bar itself is not that glitzy; the razzle-dazzle is reserved for each of the ladies who courageously take the stage and lip-sync for their life.
MAP 3: 79 Broadway, 617/426-8902, http://jacques-cabaret.com; Mon.-Sat. 11am-midnight, Sun. noon-midnight; $7-15 cover

COMEDY
Wilbur Theatre

While musical and theater acts do appear on the Wilbur Theatre's stage, the orchestra pit's table seating and bar service make this a must-stop for comedians and have made the Wilbur Boston's biggest comedy stage. Everyone from Kathy Griffin to Dana

Carvey has filmed specials from the theater. Be advised: Later shows tend to get rowdy.

MAP 3: 246 Tremont St., 617/248-9700, www.thewilbur.com

Back Bay

Map 4

COCKTAILS

Lolita Cocina and Tequila Bar

The room is dark and cool, so that can only mean one thing: time for a margarita! Lolita serves up more than 200 varieties of tequila in its Gothic-inspired dining room and bar. The bar and lounge area is a haven for young professionals looking for after-work libations with a south-of-the-border kick. Spicy margaritas are a house (and author) favorite. Arrive early on weekends to avoid waiting too long for a seat.

MAP 4: 271 Dartmouth St., 617/369-5609, http://lolitatequilabars.com; daily 4pm-2am

Oak Long Bar + Kitchen

Oak Long Bar + Kitchen

The Oak Room in the Fairmont Copley Plaza was one of the first of old Boston's dining bastions to get an overhaul when multicourse fine dining in the city went the way of the dodo. Its rebrand as a cocktail bar has been a resounding success. Mixed crowds of twentysomethings and con-ventioneers flock to the aptly named long bar for martinis, Manhattans, and bar bites. Enjoy the drinks while seated in fine leather upholstery.

MAP 4: 138 St. James Ave., 617/585-7222, http://oaklongbarkitchen.com; daily 7am-1am

DIVE BARS

Bukowski Tavern

Time once called writer Charles Bukowski "a laureate of American low-life," and this Back Bay beer bar would like visitors to believe it is catering to said types. Bragging about its "surly service" (which this author never experienced), Bukowski's *is* rather grungy. Featuring a global beer selection and not much else, Bukowski's is the perfect dark room in which to hide and have a few pints before having to face the outside world.

MAP 4: 50 Dalton St., 617/437-9999, http://bukowskitavern.net; Mon.-Sat. 11:30am-2am, Sun. noon-2am

IRISH PUBS

McGreevy's

Named for the owner of the 3rd Base Saloon, a Boston bar viewed as the first sports bar in the United States (it was shut down by Prohibition), McGreevy's is a perennial favorite for St. Patrick's Day, Marathon Monday, and the annual Santa Speed Run. Owned by Dropkick Murphys lead

LGBTQ BOSTON

Massachusetts led the country in legalizing gay marriage in 2004, 11 years before it was legal coast-to-coast. Despite the progressive spirit and embrace of gay culture (Boston's Pride Festival each June is among the country's largest), the city lacks a distinct "gayborhood," though areas like the South End and pockets of Dorchester are particularly gay friendly, with several gay bars and nightclubs. Club Café is the city's most popular gay bar, while places like The Eagle in the South End are rougher around the edges but still fun nights out with friends. Provincetown on the Outer Cape is the hub of New England gay culture and is easily accessible via fast ferry from Long Wharf and the World Trade Center at the Seaport Hotel.

singer Ken Casey, the bar features plenty of Red Sox memorabilia and opportunities to listen to Casey's Irish punk rock.

MAP 4: 911 Boylston St., 617/262-0911, http://mcgreevysboston.com; Mon.-Fri. 11am-2am, Sat.-Sun. 10am-2am

LGBTQ
Club Café

The drinks are strong, the music is loud and remixed, and the dance floor is always packed at Boston's biggest LGBTQ dance club. Club Café has been a staple of Boston nightlife for decades, and it has evolved with the times. Drag brunches, Sunday teas, charity benefits, and, yes, weekend DJs make Club Café a community center just as much as it is a nightlife hub.

MAP 4: 209 Columbus Ave., 617/536-0966, http://clubcafe.com; daily 11am-2am; $10 cover

South End

Map 5

COCKTAILS
✪ Wink & Nod

While the kitchen changes every six months thanks to Wink & Nod's pop-up culinary program, the cocktails and ambience always nod toward Prohibition-era Boston. The mixologists behind the bar have a way with seasonal cocktails, beer and wine suggestions, and higher-end Black Card cocktails (think $50/glass), which, along with the Tuesday night Scotch Club, keep this bar decidedly highbrow.

MAP 5: 3 Appleton St., 617/482-0117, www.winkandnod.com; Mon.-Sat. 5pm-2am

Franklin Café

This dark hole-in-the-wall is ideal for a clandestine rendezvous. The Franklin draws an industry crowd that skews young and hip thanks to a kitchen that stays open late. Friendly bartenders deliver heavy pours of wine

Franklin Café

and cocktails that seduce you into ordering from the menu's hearty lineup of delicious comfort food.

MAP 5: 278 Shawmut Ave., 617/350-0010, www.franklincafe.com; daily 5pm-2am

Lion's Tail

Lion's Tail may be part of a new mixed-use development, but it's easy to forget that when you're inside its sleek, dark interior, which looks like it's been part of the South End establishment for decades. The bar focuses on local ingredients and spirits with rotating pop culture names (the gin-based Lady Sansa almost makes one forget about that last season of *Game of Thrones*).

MAP 5: 354 Harrison Ave., 857/239-9276, www.lionstailboston.com; Mon.-Wed. 5pm-midnight, Thurs.-Fri. 5pm-2am, Sat. 4pm-2am, Sun. 11am-11pm

Stella

In Puritan Boston, it's sometimes difficult to find a bar and kitchen open late, but Stella manages to keep things humming until last call. The restaurant has evolved from chic hot spot to neighborhood staple in recent years, but the ever-changing cocktails are strong and the bar snacks remain tasty. It's the place these days where (almost) everybody knows your name.

MAP 5: 1525 Washington St., 617/247-7747, www.bostonstella.com; Mon.-Thurs. 4pm-11pm, Fri.-Sat. 4pm-midnight, Sun. 10am-3pm and 4pm-midnight

Trophy Room

Rumor was that owners tried to make this space—formerly occupied by a rowdy LGBTQ sports bar—a bit more family friendly, but Trophy Room continues to draw the same delightfully raucous crowd most nights. The bartenders concoct potent cocktails, and

the food isn't half bad either. While most of the room imbibes vodka sodas, the cocktail list is certainly worth your try—after all, they are trying to please the entire spectrum these days.

MAP 5: 26 Chandler St., 617/482-4428, www.trophyroomboston.com; Mon.-Fri. 4pm-2am, Sat.-Sun. 11am-2am

CRAFT BEER
Five Horses

Come for tater tots and blink-and-you'll-miss-it rotating pizzas (the Foghorn Leghorn's fried chicken on a pie was the best sampled over several visits), but stick around for the expansive bar and over 40 beers on tap. Perfect for any craft beer snob, Five Horses and its pint masters will dissect the menu with you and serve up just what you wanted—or have been too scared to try.

MAP 5: 535 Columbus Ave., 617/936-3930, www.fivehorsestavern. com, Mon.-Fri. 11:30am-midnight, Sat.-Sun. 10am-midnight

Five Horses

DIVE BARS
Delux Café

The food is limited (a one-man kitchen can only handle so much!), but the cocktails pack a punch at this popular dive, which in this neighborhood

SUNDAY FUNDAY

Boston embraces the waning hours of the weekend with Sunday Funday, which typically means brunch that turns boozy that in turn causes you to wake up 20 minutes before work starts on Monday. Neighborhoods like the South End, South Boston, and the Seaport are all home to brunch hot spots with nearby pubs and cocktail bars to keep the fun going. Lawn on D in the Seaport is a particularly popular weekend haunt in nicer weather.

means the drinks are under $10. Records from the Mamas and the Papas and Dolly Parton line the wall, along with red Solo cup Christmas lights. You'll share the bar with an Elvis lamp, and the bartender might try to get you to buy a $5 mystery shot. MAP 5: 100 Chandler St., 617/338-5258; daily 5pm-1am

SPORTS BARS
Clery's

Pints, pub grub, and the Patriots (plus the other three major Boston teams) dominate this sports bar where Back Bay meets the South End. Plenty of big screens and cheap drinks keep the crowd alive upstairs on game day, and a popular dance floor downstairs causes a hefty line to form up Dartmouth Street on Friday nights. MAP 5: 113 Dartmouth St., 617/262-9874, http://clerysboston.com; daily 11am-2am

LGBTQ
The Eagle

The drinks arrive cheap with a side of sass at Boston's most notorious gay dive bar. The bathroom may reek, and a gin and tonic may come in separate glasses (usually because the bartender was too busy recounting a run-in with

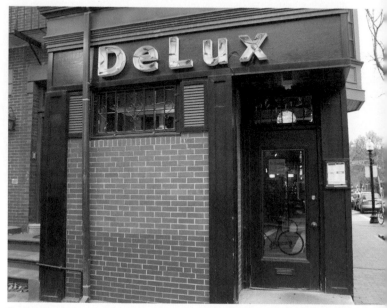

Delux Café

Cher back in '83 to remember to stop pouring the Tanqueray), but there's something endearing about this unpretentious standout amid the increasingly gentrifying neighborhood.

MAP 5: 520 Tremont St., 617/542-4494; Mon.-Sat. 4pm-2am, Sun. noon-2am

LIVE MUSIC
✪ Wally's Café

Founded in 1947 and featuring live music every day of the year, Wally's is one of the oldest jazz clubs in town. Nights start out behind its red door with a 6pm-9pm jam session before the evening's theme (usually jazz, funk, blues, or similar) gets going by professionals at around 9:30. Combined with the music a few blocks over at the Beehive, Wally's maintains the South End's roots as a jazz mecca.

MAP 5: 427 Massachusetts Ave., 617/424-1408, www.wallyscafe.com; daily 5pm-1:30am; no cover

Fenway and Kenmore Square

Map 6

COCKTAILS
Fool's Errand

Chef Tiffani Faison's Midas touch with Fenway dining now extends to hole-in-the-wall barrooms—admittedly, very nice hole-in-the-wall barrooms. Fool's Errand, an "adult snack bar" between Faison flagships Sweet Cheeks and Tiger Mama, has no chairs but plenty of bar bites (think pigs in a blanket and caviar) and hand-crafted cocktails, proving you don't have to go see the Red Sox to have a night in Fenway.

MAP 6: 1377 Boylston St., no phone, www.foolserrandboston.com; Mon.-Wed. 5pm-11pm, Thurs.-Sat. 5pm-1am, Sun. 3pm-11pm

SPORTS BARS
✪ Bleacher Bar

Don't have tickets to the game? Head to Bleacher Bar and drink in the outfield! Located in the center field wall of Fenway Park, this sports bar makes guests feel like one of the Red Sox players minus all the stress of having to catch the ball. Arrive early on game day to get a seat with a view of the playing field—the wings and beer aren't half bad, either!

MAP 6: 82A Lansdowne St., 617/262-2424, www.bleacherbarboston.com; Sun.-Wed. 11am-1am, Thurs.-Sat. 11am-2am

Cask 'N Flagon

One of the most popular sports bars in Boston, Cask 'N Flagon has been called a "Top Baseball Bar in America" by ESPN. Judging from the long lines to get in on game day, they may be onto something. Hearty potato wedge nachos, burgers, and a slew of beers on tap make for an eventful pregame spot, but be warned—service can get slow.

MAP 6: 62 Brookline Ave., 617/536-4840, www.casknflagon.com; Sun.-Wed. 11am-1am, Thurs.-Sat. 11am-2am

Game On Fenway

Over 30 TVs dot Game On Fenway's mammoth dining rooms, making it impossible to miss any sporting event while you sip and nosh. The batting cage inside is the perfect way to kill time while you wait for a beer or appetizer (or if you're looking to take out your frustration in the event the Sox somehow lose). Fried pickles and cold beer on the patio are a good summer combo while you wait for the gates across the street to open on game day.

MAP 6: 82 Lansdowne St., 617/351-7001, www.gameonboston.com; Sun.-Wed. 11:30am-1am, Thurs.-Sat. 11:30am-2am

LOUNGES
✪ The Hawthorne
Fenway is home to countless sports bars, but one of the city's trendiest lounges is also by the park. The Hawthorne serves cocktails from a perch that seems more like a chic town house than a bustling bar. The El Diablo is a tequila concoction that packs just the right level of spice, while bar snacks like the potato gaufrettes are perfect holdovers while waiting for a table at Island Creek Oyster Bar next door.

MAP 6: 500A Commonwealth Ave., 617/532-9150, www.thehawthornebar.com; daily 4pm-1am

South Boston   Map 7

COCKTAILS
✪ Drink
Even if you are a rigid "I only drink whiskey neat" kind of person, let your inhibitions fly and allow the gifted bartenders at Drink to ask a few questions and make a cocktail based off your responses. This subterranean cocktail bar has been nationally recognized for its libations, which are worth the usual wait to get in. For the hungry, a limited number of burgers are available each night, but order fast—they go quickly.

MAP 7: 348 Congress St., 617/695-1806, www.drinkfortpoint.com; daily 4pm-1am

✪ Lookout Rooftop and Bar
Rooftop bars are rare in Boston, but Lookout offers elevated cocktails overlooking downtown and Boston Harbor. Crowds flock early, so arrive at the lobby by 5pm to avoid the two-plus-hour wait that usually greets guests upon entry. The design skews modern, but it goes largely unnoticed by the swarm of twentysomethings angling to get a drink at the understaffed bar—despite the wait(s), the view and people-watching are worth your happy hour.

MAP 7: 70 Sleeper St., 617/338-3030, https://outlookkitchenandbar.com; Mon.-Wed. 4pm-11pm, Thurs.-Sat. 4pm-midnight, Sun. noon-11pm

Lucky's Lounge
While the Seaport and Fort Point are known for open-concept, glassed-in bars, Lucky's Lounge is a dark, subterranean watering hole with a Sinatra-esque hue. More neighborhood hangout than tourist haven, Lucky's serves relatively cheap cocktails amid Rat Pack-era decor. Keep an eye out, though: The front door is easy to miss!

MAP 7: 355 Congress St., 617/357-5825, www.luckyslounge.com; Mon.-Fri. 11:30am-2am, Sat.-Sun.10am-2am

Scorpion Bar

The Seaport branch of Scorpion Bar, a Mexican-inspired restaurant, often feels more nightclub than cocina. While most clubgoers in this part of town will head to The Grand nearby, Scorpion is a fun spot for a margarita to get the night going.

MAP 7: 58 Seaport Blvd., Ste. 200, 617/322-0200, www.scorpionboston.com; Mon.-Wed. 2pm-midnight, Thurs.-Sat. 2pm-2am, Sun. 2pm-11pm

CRAFT BEER
✪ Harpoon Brewery and Beer Hall

The team at Harpoon Brewery likes to say their brew is Boston's real craft beer. The company has churned out beer from its Seaport warehouse since the late 1980s and has become a major community player thanks to its annual fund-raisers. The European-style beer hall has 20 Harpoon brews on tap, accompanied by beer pretzels. The Keg Yard is open in the summer and features lawn games and movie nights.

MAP 7: 306 Northern Ave., 617/456-2322, www.harpoonbrewery.com; Sun.-Thurs. 11am-8pm, Fri.-Sat. 11am-11pm

Trillium Brewing Company

Trillium finally has elbow room. The brewery expanded from its original, small Fort Point space to around the corner to an expansive, three-story venue complete with a taproom, restaurant, and rooftop terrace. While the restaurant is popular, Trillium's beers—including citrusy New England IPAs and their hoppier cousins—are the main draw.

MAP 7: 50 Thomson Pl., 857/449-0083, www.trilliumbrewing.com; daily 11am-11pm

SPORTS BARS
Stats Bar & Grille

Based on the omnipresent line, it's quite possible the entirety of South Boston heads to Stats for any given game day. No matter if you're in sweatpants or a three-piece suit, there is a spot for you at this bar near the junction of Broadway and Dorchester Street. Despite the insanity of the crowds, the bartenders are quick in pouring pints and getting pub grub to enthusiastic weekend fans glued to the lineup of televisions.

MAP 7: 77 Dorchester St., 617/268-9300, www.statsboston.com; Mon.-Fri. 11am-1am, Sat.-Sun. 10am-1am

IRISH PUBS
L Street Tavern

How do you like them apples? *Good Will Hunting* may have made it famous outside of Southie, but the L Street Tavern has been a neighborhood staple for decades. At this watering hole you're more likely to find neighbors and the occasional former Boston mayor popping in for a quick pint and a shot of Dr. McGillicuddy's. Everybody may not know your name, but it's small enough that they will by last call.

MAP 7: 658 E. 8th St., 617/268-4335; daily noon-1am

DANCE CLUBS
The Grand

Given how many Bostonians say the Seaport feels more like Miami or Las Vegas than Beantown, it's fitting that at least one of its nightclubs is akin to South Beach or the Strip. The Grand is a see-and-be-seen scene with typically high covers for Boston (sometimes north of $50), bottle service available, and appearances by bigger DJs like Cash Cash. Sure, it can be obnoxious, but even that can be fun for a night on the town.

MAP 7: 58 Seaport Blvd., Suite 300, 617/322-0200, www.thegrandboston. com; Mon. and Thurs. 10pm-2am, Fri.-Sat. 9:30pm-2am; cover varies

COMEDY
Laugh Boston
Newer and cleaner than most improv clubs in town, Laugh Boston brings comedy to the Seaport. Host to national headliners and tour acts like "Sh*t-Faced Shakespeare," the comedy club features cocktails and small bites from its home next to the Boston Convention and Exhibition Center.

MAP 7: 425 Summer St., 617/725-2844, www.laughboston.com; $10-50

Cambridge

Map 8

COCKTAILS
Brick & Mortar
Everyone calls themselves a mixologist lately, but the makers of the chemistry-in-a-glass served at Brick & Mortar seem most deserving of the title. This spot is easy to miss: You'll have to find the blank door and go up a flight of stairs to the second-floor lair. Complex cocktails mix with Bud Light Lime in a can on this menu, but save room for shots—they're not tacky here.

MAP 8: 567 Massachusetts Ave., Cambridge, 617/491-0016, www. brickmortarltd.com; Sun.-Wed. 5pm-1am, Thurs.-Sat. 5pm-2am

The Longfellow Bar
Alden & Harlow is one of Harvard Square's younger and more beloved restaurants, and now it has a cocktail bar upstairs. Shared bar bites like "All Dressed" waffle fries and crab Rangoon nachos are on the menu but so is an impressive mix of libations. Be sure to sip one and take in the restored 130-year-old space.

MAP 8: 40 Brattle St. #3, Cambridge, 617/864-0001, www.longfellowharvard. com; Mon.-Tues. 11:30am-1am, Wed.-Fri. 11:30am-2am, Sat.-Sun. 4pm-1am

CRAFT BEER
Lord Hobo
It looks like a squat biker bar from *Miami Vice* on the outside, but behind the door is a bustling craft beer emporium that draws a blend of hipsters and Cambridge computer geeks. Not only does it produce its own house beer, but also Lord Hobo features 40 taps ranging from domestic classics to European extravagances.

MAP 8: 92 Hampshire St., Cambridge, 617/250-8454, www.lordhobo.com; Mon.-Wed. 4pm-1am, Thurs.-Fri. 4pm-2am, Sat. 11am-2am, Sun. 11am-1am

Miracle of Science Bar & Grill
The food menu is designed after the periodic table, a nod to the brainiacs using said guide at classes at nearby MIT. But you're more likely to find a packed crowd of students vying for a variety of beers on draft or in a bottle and spending the night debating the

world's problems as Cantabrigians do. Grab a pint, and do the same!

MAP 8: 321 Massachusetts Ave., Cambridge, 617/868-2866, www. miracleofscience.us; daily 11am-1am

DIVE BARS
People's Republik

Political headlines make this Russian Communist-themed bar seem timelier than ever, decked out in propaganda, dartboards, and neighbors looking for cheap cocktails and beer. The staff at People's Republik is friendly and is more than happy to point you to the gluten-free beer offerings. Just don't look for political discourse—it ruins the Stoli.

MAP 8: 878 Massachusetts Ave., Cambridge, 617/491-6969, www. peoplesrepublik.com; Sun.-Wed. noon-1am, Thurs.-Sat. noon-2am

State Park

Step away from the glassy, futuristic Kendall Square office buildings and through the screen door into this rustic wood-paneled bar that could just as easily be in Fargo or the boonies of Vermont. This throwback features pinball machines, shots paired with tall cans of beer, delicious cocktail pitchers, and plenty of story material.

MAP 8: 1 Kendall Square, Building 300, Cambridge, 617/848-4355, www.statepark. is; Mon.-Wed. 11am-1am, Thurs.-Fri. 11am-2am, Sat. 10am-2am, Sun. 10am-1am

ARCADE BAR
A4cade

Combine your adult love of speakeasies with your inner child still who still craves Chuck E. Cheese. Hidden behind the freezer door of a grilled cheese restaurant, the fun (and typically crowded) bar is first-come,

first-served for cocktails served alongside Mortal Kombat, pinball, and Skee-ball.

MAP 8: 292 Massachusetts Ave., Cambridge, 617/714-3960, www. a4cade.com; Mon.-Thurs. 5pm-1am, Fri. 5pm-1:30am, Sat. noon-1:30am, Sun. noon-midnight

LOUNGES
Middlesex Lounge

The crowd is diverse, and the DJs keep it loud in this lively Central Square lounge and club. Music often strays into the hip-hop realm, and crowds lap it up—occasionally you'll even see a break-dancer perform. Drinks are reasonable by Boston standards, but keep in mind those follow a cover charge.

MAP 8: 315 Massachusetts Ave., Cambridge, 617/868-7399, www. middlesexlounge.us; Thurs.-Sat. 7pm-2am; $10 cover

DANCE CLUBS
Hong Kong Restaurant

It's a rite of passage for college students to go at least once to Hong Kong in Harvard Square. The Chinese food is reliable and served in huge portions, the scorpion bowls are potent, and the dance floor upstairs is sweaty—all highly valued when you're in college! What better way to work off all those chicken skewers?

MAP 8: 1238 Massachusetts Ave., Cambridge, 617/864-5311, www. hongkongharvard.com; Sun.-Wed. 11:30am-2am, Thurs. 11:30am-2:30am, Fri.-Sat. 11:30am-3am; no cover

Phoenix Landing

It's a sports bar! It's an Irish pub! It's a dance club! It's a bird! It's a plane! OK, it isn't the last two, but Phoenix Landing is a fun night out. Watch parties for the major teams, as well as soccer and rugby, are routine, and live DJs keep this place busy most nights. Since this is Cambridge, "Geeks Who Drink" trivia on Wednesdays is one of the busiest events.

MAP 8: 512 Massachusetts Ave., Cambridge, 617/576-6260, www. phoenixlandingbar.com; Mon.-Wed. 11am-1am, Thurs.-Sat. 11am-2am, Sun. 10am-1am; cover varies

LIVE MUSIC
ROCK
✪ The Sinclair

Part gastropub, part music hall, the Sinclair is up a flight of stairs off a side street in Harvard Square. Grab preshow bites from the kitchen, and be prepared to shake the night away to the musical acts who make their way to the Sinclair's stage. The venue hosts "Downbeat Mondays" each week as well as the occasional emo night and touring indie acts, allowing you to channel your hipster.

MAP 8: 52 Church St., Cambridge, 617/547-5200, www.sinclaircambridge.com; Mon.-Wed. 5pm-1am, Thurs.-Fri. 5pm-2am, Sat. 11am-2am, Sun. 11am-1am; cover varies

The Middle East

Originally a Lebanese restaurant, Middle East now comprises several neighboring venues catering to different types of musical acts. Two restaurant-bars feature live music, while three dedicated concert spaces house rowdier shows that pack in sweaty crowds and club-banging jams each night of the week. Viewed as one of the region's best rock clubs, Middle East has been home to live recordings from acts like the Mighty Mighty Bosstones.

MAP 8: 472-480 Massachusetts Ave., Cambridge, 617/864-3278, www. mideastoffers.com; Sun.-Wed. 11am-1am, Thurs.-Sat. 11am-2am; cover varies

BLUES
The Cantab Lounge

It doesn't look like much from the outside. Honestly, it doesn't look like that much on the inside, either, but the Cantab Lounge is a dive bar for everyone. From poetry slams downstairs to soul revues and other dance music upstairs, there's a lot of entertainment to go with the cheap, strong drinks slung at the bar. Don't worry— I'm sure there's a mixer *somewhere* in your vodka.

MAP 8: 738 Massachusetts Ave., Cambridge, 617/354-2685, www. cantab-lounge.com; Mon.-Wed. 8am-1am, Thurs.-Sat. 8am-2am, Sun. noon-1am; cover varies

AMERICANA
Toad

Toad is refreshing for its live music and lack of cover charge, and dangerous due to its cheap drinks that might leave you kissing a few ah, shall we say *namesakes* of the establishment? You can bring your own vinyl records to play on weekends and have bartenders pour you a craft cocktail or one of their own delightfully creative concoctions.

MAP 8: 1912 Massachusetts Ave., Cambridge, 617/497-4950, www. toadcambridge.com; Mon.-Wed. 8am-1am, Thurs.-Sat. 8am-2am, Sun. noon-1am; no cover

COMEDY
ImprovBoston

Boston's nonprofit improvisational comedy group features performances five days a week from its

Central Square theater. Alumni from ImprovBoston have made it to *Last Comic Standing*, *The Daily Show*, and *John Oliver's Last Week*, to name a few.

Those on longer trips can even drop in and take a class!

MAP 8: 40 Prospect St., Cambridge, 617/576-1253, www.improvboston.com

Greater Boston

Map 9

LIVE MUSIC
Great Scott

Routinely honored as the best music venue in Massachusetts and as one of the best in the country, Great Scott in Allston is the embodiment of Boston's youthful, tipsy club-banging spirit. Local darlings Passion Pit and indie crooners MGMT played here before making it big, and more take to the stage each night hoping to be next.

MAP 9: 1222 Commonwealth Ave., Boston, 617/566-9014, http://greatscottboston.com; daily noon-2am; $5-15 cover

Paradise Rock Club

Don't let the small size deter you: Paradise Rock Club lures both the biggest and more alternative acts in the biz. The venue on the cusp of Boston University's campus (directly on the Green Line) draws a largely student crowd to see bands like U2, R.E.M., and New Found Glory. Arrive early, as good spots to stand are quickly filled with students swaying and sloshing their drinks.

MAP 9: 967 Commonwealth Ave., Boston, 617/562-8800, http://crossroadspresents.com/paradise-rock-club; hours vary; cover varies

COCKTAILS
Pier 6

For drinks that come in plastic, the cocktails at the outdoor bar at Pier 6 are priced high. However, if you turn around to enjoy the incredible view of the Boston skyline, it suddenly seems okay. Immensely popular in warmer months, Pier 6 has a surprisingly good bar menu to go with its spectacular vista best accessed via water taxi from several points downtown.

MAP 9: 1 8th St., Charlestown, 617/337-0054, http://pier6boston.com; Sun.-Thurs. 11am-10pm, Fri.-Sat. 11am-11pm

CRAFT BEER
Warren Tavern

Drop by for a pint, stay for a snack, and experience old Boston (old as in George Washington and Paul Revere used to frequent the place way back when). Dark wood furnishings, friendly bartenders, and affordable fare keep the crowd steady and mixed, as neighbors and tourists both enjoy history with a cheap pint.

MAP 9: 2 Pleasant St., Charlestown, 617/241-8142, http://warrentavern.com; Sun.-Fri. 11am-1am, Sat. 10am-1am

A SLICE OF VEGAS IN BOSTON

Rather than hop on a flight to Vegas or head to Connecticut casinos, Bostonians have been able to hit the slots and blackjack tables in their own backyard since 2018. The $2.6 billion Encore Boston Harbor (1 Broadway, Everett, 857/770-7000, www.encorebostonharbor.com) is a notable curved, bronze addition to the skyline just north of downtown Boston. It features an extensive mix of luxury hotel rooms, restaurants, bars, and a lot of casino gaming (the casino floor is more than twice the size of the resort's sister property in Las Vegas). Gardens and a monumental clean-up have made this formerly contaminated spot on the Mystic River a hot piece of waterfront property. Encore didn't have the easiest road to opening day after Wynn Resorts founder Steve Wynn was accused of a #MeToo scandal; but while his last name remains on the parent company, Wynn is no longer affiliated (the Boston property changed its name from Wynn Boston Harbor to Encore mid-construction after local leaders pressured the company to show it was truly independent of its ex-leader).

NIGHTLIFE

Bringing gaming to Boston's backyard, Encore's massive casino floor, open daily 24 hours, is bright and busy even on weeknights, with people looking to find Lady Luck.

Another way to pass the night here is at Mémoire (Fri.-Sun. 10pm-2am, Mon.-Thurs. hours vary by event), a nightclub that attracts globally famous DJs like DJ Diesel (better known as Shaquille O'Neal) and Steve Aioki.

RESTAURANTS

Notable dining options include Mystique (Mon.-Wed. 4pm-11pm, Thurs. 4pm-midnight, Fri. 4pm-2am, Sat. noon-3pm and 4pm-3am, Sun. noon-3pm and 4pm-11pm, $$), an expansive restaurant overlooking the Mystic River that serves up Asian dishes from sushi to noodles; Rare Steakhouse (daily 4pm-10pm, $$$), where you can find real Kobe beef along with views of the Harborwalk; and Sinatra (daily 4pm-10pm, $$$), an outpost of the Las Vegas restaurant, where Old Blue Eyes gazes down at diners in an elegant, red-hued room that specializes in upscale versions of your favorite Italian dishes.

ACCOMMODATIONS

You can also spend the night in one of the hotel's 671 rooms and suites ($$$) decorated with contemporary art. The 650-foot standard room size is the largest in New England and comes with cozy furnishings, the potential for a skyline view, and the kind of quiet not usually associated with a casino.

Encore Boston Harbor

GETTING THERE

Encore encourages visitors to take advantage of mass transit options to get to the venue. It runs free shuttles from the Wellington and Malden Center MBTA Orange Line stations, every 10-30 minutes 24 hours daily. Trips to the resort are less than 10 minutes from Wellington and under 20 minutes from Malden Center. The free Encore Neighborhood Runner shuttle runs from the MBTA Silver Line's Chelsea Station to the resort every 20 minutes. Trip time is 15-20 minutes. Encore also has a year-round water shuttle service ($12 one-way, credit or debit card only), with climate-controlled indoor cabins that are quite luxurious. It runs every 20-30 minutes 10am-11:40pm from Long Wharf in downtown Boston and the World Trade Center in the Seaport. Encore also offers a premium motor coach service ($7 one way, credit or debit card only) from park-and-ride locations in Millbury, Rockland, and Foxborough in Massachusetts and Londonderry in New Hampshire, every 30 minutes from 11:45am-11:10pm daily.

If you must drive, head about 10 minutes north from downtown Boston on I-93. Signs to the resort are prevalent and take you through Sullivan Square (exit 28). Note parking is limited and pricey ($22 for six hours, $44 for 24 hours), and surrounding streets are often congested.

ARTS AND CULTURE

Boston Brahmins are known for being ardent supporters of the arts. Thanks to their early patronage, the city today is graced with iconic institutions, and no

matter the neighborhood, it's never too difficult to find somewhere to feel a little more highbrow and cultured.

Due to the city's numerous colleges, discount tickets are relatively easy to come by at ticket kiosks throughout the city, which make touring Broadway shows, the Boston Symphony, and other performances more attainable. Boston's theater scene is also increasingly positioning itself to be an incubator and test-run hub for Broadway shows to iron out the kinks before they make their grand debut on the Great White Way.

American Repertory Theater

HIGHLIGHTS

⭐ **BEST THEATER:** The lavish lobby is just an early taste of the opulence to expect at Boston's Wang Theatre, which showcases everything from energetic dance performances to the latest touring Broadway acts (page 144).

⭐ **BEST ART GALLERY:** Let the staff at Galerie d'Orsay assist you in tracking down just the right masterwork for your home—or simply browse the beautiful collection (page 146).

⭐ **BEST WAY TO GET CLOSE TO THE BIGGEST NAMES IN MUSIC:** It may be a national chain, but House of Blues was born in Massachusetts, and this venue in the shadow of Fenway Park manages to feel intimate despite pulling in major acts like Carly Rae Jepsen and Lizzo (page 148).

⭐ **MOST SURREAL NIGHT OUT:** More rave than standard Shakespeare performance, the Donkey Show at the American Repertory Theater presents *A Midsummer Night's Dream* in a far more amusing manner than you'll remember from high school (page 150).

⭐ **BEST ART HOUSE CINEMA:** When the weather is less than ideal for walking around town, pop into Kendall Square Cinema for documentaries, foreign-language films, and obscure indies (page 150).

Wang Theatre

Beacon Hill and the West End

Map 1

CONCERT VENUES

Hatch Memorial Shell

This outdoor concert venue on the Back Bay section of the Charles River Esplanade is most popular on July 4 when it hosts the Boston Pops Independence Day celebration, but it also is home to charity events, summer movie screenings, and concerts with an incredible view of the river and Cambridge skyline all summer long. Bring a blanket, and the Hatch Shell will provide the entertainment.

MAP 1: 47 David G. Mugar Way, 617/626-1250, http://hatchshell.com

TD Garden

From Ariana Grande belting out hits to Celtics slam-dunking to Bruins taking slap shots, a little bit of everything can be expected from the floor of the TD Garden. Boston's biggest arena, the Garden is home to the Celtics NBA franchise as well as the NHL's Boston Bruins. The facility, which seats more 17,000, has hosted the 2004 Democratic National Convention and countless national sporting events, and it's conveniently located directly above Boston's bustling North Station.

MAP 1: 100 Legends Way, 617/624-1050, www.tdgarden.com

Downtown, Chinatown, and the Theater District

Map 3

THEATER AND PERFORMING ARTS

✪ Wang Theatre

Boston's Wang Theatre seats 3,500 and has one of the five largest stages in the country. Originally dubbed "The Met," the theater's lobby was built to resemble Versailles; it's worth arriving early to a performance just to grab a drink and bask in the opulence. After several decades of neglect, the theater was restored (and got its new name) thanks to a generous donation from Dr. An Wang, and today it hosts top touring acts as well as community arts groups.

MAP 3: 270 Tremont St., 617/482-9393, www.bochcenter.org

Boston Opera House

Don't be thrown off by the name: the Boston Opera House got its start in vaudeville and movies. Its opulent decor is a draw for those wishing to connect to the Roaring Twenties, and it is known today more for touring Broadway acts, concerts, and political discussions than operatic productions.

MAP 3: 539 Washington St., 617/259-3400, www.bostonoperahouse.com

Boston Opera House

Charles Playhouse

Boston is one of a select group of cities that have a permanent Blue Man Group production, and the Charles Playhouse has been the troupe's local home since 1995. The venue went through several religious lives—both as a Universalist church and as a synagogue—and was even a speakeasy before venturing into theatrics in the 1950s. It is also home to the long-running murder mystery play *Shear Madness*.

MAP 3: 74 Warrenton St., 617/426-6912, www.charlesplayhouse.com

Cutler Majestic Theatre

Whether you're in the mood for opera or jazz, dance or a touring Broadway musical, there's a good chance you'll find it at some point throughout the year on the Cutler Majestic's impressive stage. The theater's Beaux-Arts architecture has wowed passersby on the outside just as much as the performances have impressed theatergoers since it first opened in 1903.

MAP 3: 219 Tremont St., 617/824-8000, www.cutlermajestic.org

CONCERT VENUES
Orpheum Theatre

Before the Boston Symphony moved to its current home at Symphony Hall in 1900, it played from what was then called the Boston Music Hall. The venue went through a series of name changes before arriving at its current one in 1906. It has served largely as a music hall since the 1970s and features everything from children's acts to alt rock.

MAP 3: 1 Hamilton Pl., 617/482-0106, http://events.crossroadspresents.com

GALLERIES
Boston Athenaeum

Founded in 1807, the Renaissance-style Boston Athenaeum is one of the oldest independent libraries in the country. Requiring membership, the Athenaeum features a collection of rare volumes, art, and primary materials pertaining to the Civil War. John F.

BOSTON ON FILM

Boston has been featured as a backdrop to some of the biggest moments in cinema and television history. From *Cheers* and *Ally McBeal* to *The Departed* and *Good Will Hunting*, Boston is always ready for its close-up. The region's Irish ties and history of organized crime have translated into many films pertaining to South Boston, North End, and Charlestown gangs, such as *The Town* and *Black Mass*, a Whitey Bulger biopic. The *Boston Globe*'s bombshell report on the Catholic Church sex abuse scandal played out in *Spotlight*. Thanks to generous film tax credits, Boston and the state of Massachusetts continue to be used as sets even if the movie isn't supposed to be set in New England, such as the 2016 *Ghostbusters* reboot.

Kennedy, Nathanial Hawthorne, and Louisa May Alcott are but a few of the prominent members to have walked through the arched reading room of this hidden Beacon Hill treasure. Visitors can pay a daily admission fee and take tours ($2 plus admission) of the building's art and architecture and private collections in order to explore the historical setting without annual membership.

MAP 3: 10 ½ Beacon St., 617/227-0270, www.bostonathenaeum.org; Tues. noon-8pm, Wed.-Sat. 10am-4pm; $10 adults (13+), $8 military and students, free for children 12 and under

Boston Athenaeum

Back Bay   Map 4

MUSEUMS

The Mapparium

Just off the Welcome Hall in the Christian Science Publishing House is The Mapparium, a three-story stained glass globe. Built in 1935, The Mapparium gives guests a historical view of what the world was like then, when architects looked to show the Christian Science Monitor's global outreach. Today, guests can have fun with its acoustics and whisper from opposite ends of the room and be able to hear as though they are standing next to each other.

MAP 4: 200 Massachusetts Ave., 617/450-7000, http://marybakereddylibrary.org; daily 10am-5pm; adults $6, seniors, students, and children 6-17 $4

GALLERIES

✪ Galerie D'Orsay

While its premier location on Newbury Street and collection dating back to the 16th century might intimidate, the friendly staff at Galerie d'Orsay make it worth a visit—even if

Gallery NAGA

you aren't in the market to take home a Dalí or Picasso. The gallery hosts exhibitions throughout the year as well as a range of master, impressionist, and modern works for sale.

MAP 4: 33 Newbury St., 617/266-8001, http://galerie-dorsay.com; Mon.-Sat. 10am-6pm, Sun. noon-6pm

Gallery NAGA

Gallery NAGA will catch your eye before you even walk through the door, thanks to its location in the neo-Gothic Church of the Covenant. Open since 1977, the gallery is *the* place to go for contemporary art in Boston and has a special spot in Bostonians' hearts, as the gallery owners prefer to show local artists. Exhibitions range from photography and paintings to furniture.

MAP 4: 67 Newbury St., 617/267-9060, http://gallerynaga.com; Tues.-Sat. 10am-5pm

South End   Map 5

THEATER
Boston Center for the Arts

The BCA might house the headquarters of the Boston Ballet and other local arts organizations throughout the buildings of its South End campus, but it is also home to several stages for its four resident theater companies, including the Commonwealth Shakespeare Company. A go-to for local theater patrons seeking small and mid-sized productions, the BCA offers a prime opportunity to experience the work of some of New England's most talented actors and writers.

MAP 5: 527 Tremont St., 617/266-0800, www.bcaonline.org

Fenway and Kenmore Square

Map 6

THEATER

Huntington Avenue Theatre

The Huntington Avenue Theatre opened in 1925 as America's first civic playhouse. Although its livelihood was in jeopardy after a longtime relationship with Boston University dissolved, the theater and its future were solidified in 2016 with news of an extensive renovation that will enable the Huntington Theatre Company to remain. The space is home to several locally produced shows each season and hosts readings, lectures, and other performances outside the HTC's schedule.

MAP 6: 264 Huntington Ave.,
617/266-0800, www.huntingtontheatre.org

CONCERT VENUES

✪ House of Blues

It may now be a chain, but House of Blues was a Boston institution first, kicking off in Harvard Square and now at home in Fenway. Acts ranging from indie to Top 40 keep the crowds flocking to the House of Blues most nights of the week. Attractive bartenders sling drinks while top talent takes to the stage. Everyone from Katy Perry to Lady Gaga has performed to jammed crowds of local students and hip parents from the burbs looking for a fun night in the city. A restaurant serves American specialties and a weekly gospel brunch.

MAP 6: 15 Lansdowne St., 888/693-2583,
www.houseofblues.com/boston

Symphony Hall

Opened in 1900, Boston's Symphony Hall is considered the top concert hall in the country and one of the best in the world. Home to the Boston Symphony Orchestra and the Boston Pops Orchestra, Symphony Hall's Renaissance architecture and Greek and Roman statues are as much of a draw as the performances on its famous stage. Curiously, Beethoven is the only musician's name found throughout the entire venue, as he was the only composer the original directors could agree was worthy of gracing the space. Free tours are available on select weekdays (check online for schedule and to RSVP). Some $25 tickets are available to those under 40 during the symphony season on a first-come, first-served basis.

MAP 6: 301 Massachusetts Ave.,
617/266-1492, www.bso.org

Symphony Hall

BOSTON POPS

The Boston Pops (www.bso.org) were founded at the pinnacle of Boston Brahmin culture in 1885 as an offshoot of the Boston Symphony Orchestra. Composed of generally non-first-chair players from the BSO, the Pops offered popular music and holiday performances. They have since gone on to sell more commercial recordings than any other orchestra in the world, and they entertain the country each year with their iconic Fourth of July concert on the Charles River Esplanade, which is aired on Bloomberg Television. From holiday classics and patriotic anthems to the music of *Looney Tunes*, the Pops are entertaining to patrons of all ears and ages.

South Boston   Map 7

CONCERT VENUE
Rockland Trust Bank Pavilion

Boston's waterfront amphitheater attracts the world's biggest acts and the city's most ardent live music fans. Everyone from Diana Ross to Sara Bareilles to John Legend has performed on the Pavilion's stage. With 35 on-site concession areas and a VIP tent, concertgoers can enjoy their music with a side of libations and delectable bites.

MAP 7: 290 Northern Ave., 617/728-1600, www.bostonpavilion.net

Cambridge   Map 8

MUSEUMS
Harvard Art Museums

The three museums (the Fogg, the Busch-Reisinger, and the Arthur M. Sackler) that compose the Harvard Art Museums offer a comprehensive collection of Western, European, and Asian art. The system's historic main building underwent an extensive renovation from 2008 until 2014 and now features six additional levels of galleries for the 250,000 pieces in the collection.

MAP 8: 32 Quincy St., Cambridge, 617/495-9400, www.harvardartmuseums.org; daily 10am-5pm; $15 adults, $13 seniors, free for all students and those under 18

Harvard Museum of Natural History

Harvard's natural history museum features permanent galleries with dinosaur fossils and other species as well as a variety of touring exhibits. The

Harvard Art Museums

museum is extremely popular for its Glass Flowers exhibit: Over the span of 50 years, a father-son team from Dresden created 4,200 glass flower models representing more than 830 plant species. This and 15 additional galleries offer a truly one-of-a-kind museum adventure.

MAP 8: 26 Oxford St., Cambridge, 617/495-3045, www.hmnh.harvard.edu; daily 9am-5pm; $15 adults, $13 seniors, $10 non-Harvard students and children

THEATER
✪ American Repertory Theater
Think of the A.R.T. as Broadway's waiting room. Sara Bareilles's *Waitress* workshopped and performed here before moving down to the Great White Way, as have several others. The nonprofit theater is best known for its American works as well as musical theater events, like the wildly popular Donkey Show—a mirrored, feathered, roller-skating take on *A Midsummer Night's Dream*.

MAP 8: 64 Brattle St., Cambridge, 617/547-8300, www.americanrepertorytheater.org

CINEMA
✪ Kendall Square Cinema
Kendall Square may seem dominated by tech and life science companies, but it is also home to one of Greater Boston's leading art house movie theaters. The Kendall Square Cinema is known for showing documentaries, foreign-language flicks, and popular and more obscure independent films as well as occasional film discussions. Reclining seats, fresh popcorn, and beer and wine make this a grown-up approach to a night at the movies.

MAP 8: 355 Binney St., Cambridge, 617/621-1202, www.landmarktheatres.com

Greater Boston   Map 9

THEATER
Coolidge Corner Theatre
In an era dominated by comic book IMAX features, the Coolidge Corner Theatre offers an alternative cinematic experience with art house and independent films. This art deco not-for-profit theater has a bar for patrons wishing to pair wine with a foreign flick. Spaces range from opulent in the 400-person downstairs theater to intimate in one of the upstairs screening rooms that aren't much bigger than home theaters.

MAP 9: 290 Harvard St., Brookline, 617/734-2501, http://coolidge.org

Festivals and Events

WINTER

First Day/First Night

Rather than a ball drop, Boston celebrates the end of the year and the start of a new one with First Night/First Day, a free night-and-day celebration with performances, ice sculptures, and light displays at multiple locations across the city, including a 7pm fireworks display. Bundle up, as these outdoor events are usually frigid in Boston's notorious winter.

Various locations: www.firstnightboston.org

Boston Wine Festival

While the weather in January is still frightful, it's utterly delightful inside the Boston Harbor Hotel, which kicks off its annual Boston Wine Festival in January. The event, which runs into March, is America's longest-running food and wine festival.

Government, North End, and Waterfront: Boston Harbor Hotel, 70 Rowes Wharf, 617/439-7000, www.bhh.com

SPRING

St. Patrick's Day Parade

You won't find an American city with bigger claims to Ireland than Boston, and that's most apparent in March when it seems like all of New England flocks to South Boston (the city's historically Irish enclave) for the annual St. Patrick's Day parade. Arrive early in the morning (in green!) and expect to pay steep cover charges for bars up and down Broadway, but it's the price one pays for the luck of the (Boston)

ironworkers float, St. Patrick's Day Parade

Irish. The parade takes place on the Sunday closest to March 17.

South End: www.southbostonparade.org

Patriots' Day and Marathon Monday

Patriots' Day, the third Monday in April, commemorates the Battles of Lexington and Concord. The two towns celebrate with remembrances and battle reenactments, but the biggest celebration happens in Boston proper, where the holiday is also known as Marathon Monday. The city hosts the Boston Marathon the same day, and hundreds of thousands of people turn out to celebrate the athletes racing the course from Hopkinton to Copley Square. Elite runners typically sprint to the finish down Boylston Street around 10:30am, but Boston starts partying at breakfast and continues to do so well into the night.

Greater Boston: www.baa.org

Boston Calling

The underrated Boston Calling is the area's Lollapalooza-esque music festival. It gets just as many big names with half the headache. Taking place over a spring weekend each year, the multistage concert calls Harvard's Athletic Complex home and has seen the likes of Lorde, the XX, Bon Iver, and Tool. The festival is an all-day and night affair, so comfortable clothing that you aren't afraid to get dirty is advised.

Greater Boston: http://bostoncalling. com

Bunker Hill Day Parade

Since 1786, residents of Charlestown have honored the 1775 Battle of Bunker Hill by having an annual parade through the neighborhood on the Sunday prior to June 17. Thousands show up shortly after noon to see everyone from the mayor to marching bands and minutemen reenactors in this historic, see-and-be-seen event.

Greater Boston: Parade starts at 12:30pm at the intersection of Vine St. and Bunker Hill St. in Charlestown

SUMMER
Boston Pride

June's (ideally) warmer weather also brings Boston Pride, more than a week of celebrations in honor of the LGBTQ community. The Boston Pride parade happens on the second Saturday of Pride Week and weaves through Back Bay, the South End (the city's historically LGBTQ neighborhood), and downtown before wrapping up in a celebration at City Hall Plaza. There are also block parties in Back Bay and the South End that kick off midafternoon following the parade's morning start.

South End: www.bostonpride.org

U.S. and rainbow pride flags

Boston Pops Fireworks Spectacular

Considering its pivotal role in the American Revolution, it's no wonder Boston takes the Fourth of July seriously. The annual Boston Pops Fireworks Spectacular is an evening with headlining musical acts performing alongside the Boston Pops from the Charles River Esplanade, culminating in a pyrotechnic show over the river basin between Cambridge and Boston.

Cambridge: http://bostonpopsjuly4th.org

FALL
Freedom Rally

Labor Day weekend is normally marked by insane traffic from U-Hauls galore as the city's hundreds of thousands of students return to campus for move-in day(s). Things get decidedly more relaxed at Boston Common on the afternoon of the third Saturday in September at the Freedom Rally, the country's second-largest annual assembly demanding marijuana reform (after Seattle's Hempfest).

Beacon Hill and the West End: http://masscann.org/rally

Head of the Charles

The second-to-last weekend of October might be peak foliage season, but it's also time for thousands of elite rowers and even more New England prepsters to flock to Boston for the Head of the Charles, the world's largest two-day regatta. Even if you don't race it's a festive event, with vendors and grandstands dotting the banks from the basin past Harvard Square.

Cambridge: www.hocr.org

RECREATION

From pop-up workouts and solo runs along the Charles River to professional sports franchises, Boston is a city on the move. In addition to the Red Sox at Fenway Park, the city is also home to the New England Patriots, and fans clamor to board the train to Gillette Stadium on Sundays during football season to watch Tom Brady live up to his nickname of "G.O.A.T." (Greatest of all . . . you get the picture). On the other side of town, the TD Garden is home to Bruins and Celtics jerseys, as both teams call the Garden home. The city is a sports and outdoor fanatic's dream, and it never shies away from an opportunity to flaunt its athletic prowess (and ideally its championship victories).

Commonwealth Avenue Mall

HIGHLIGHTS

✪ **MOST INTERACTIVE PARK:** Winding through downtown, the Rose Kennedy Greenway offers fun adventures in nearly every nook and cranny (page 157).

✪ **BEST SKYLINE RUN OR BIKE RIDE:** The tree-lined Charles River Esplanade offers great skyline views as well as a convenient connection to the Paul Dudley White Charles River Bike Path for cardio lovers to extend their jog or ride (pages 160).

✪ **PRIDE OF THE CITY:** The Boston Red Sox play at Fenway Park, the high church of Boston sports—and the top spot in town for a hot dog and beer (page 162).

✪ **BEST WATERFRONT STROLL:** The Harborwalk gives stunning waterfront views while weaving through several of the city's ever-evolving neighborhoods (page 163).

✪ **BEST GREEN SPACE:** Perhaps not as known as Boston Common and the Public Garden, North Point Park is a great spot to hide with a book, a surprising oasis not far from buzzing Kendall Square (page 163).

Harborwalk

SPECTATOR SPORTS
BASKETBALL
Boston Celtics

The Boston Celtics, who play on the famous parquet floor at the TD Garden, are one of the NBA's original teams. With 17 championships under their belt, the Celtics are also the league's most decorated squad. While the Larry Bird era of the 1980s is among the franchise's most popular, the Celtics continue to draw fans in their quest for another banner.

MAP 1: 100 Legends Way, 866/423-5849, www.tdgarden.com/tickets

A statue by sculptor Harry Weber of Boston Bruins legend Bobby Orr lunges outside the TD Garden.

HOCKEY
Boston Bruins

Founded in 1924 by grocery store tycoon Charles Adams, Boston's National Hockey League franchise is the third oldest in the league and was the first American team to join the NHL. The team has notched six Stanley Cup wins and continues to be a hockey powerhouse.

MAP 1: 100 Legends Way, 617/624-2327, www.tdgarden.com/tickets

WALKING AND BIKING TRAILS
Paul Dudley White Charles River Bike Path

The 23-mile (37-km) bike path hugs both the Cambridge and Boston sides of the Charles River and is named for a prominent local cardiologist known for his advocacy of preventative medicine like exercise. Pedal from Science Park to Watertown Square and take in the skylines of several Greater Boston neighborhoods, and take a break or two along the way to observe rowers on the Charles practicing for their next regatta.

MAP 1: Museum of Science at Charles River Dam Rd., between Museum Way (Cambridge) and Nashua St. (Boston)

BOATING
Swan Boats

Dating back to the 1870s and inspired by a German opera where a knight sailed to protect his princess in a boat drawn by a swan, the Boston Public Garden's Swan Boats are less dramatic but still a worthy adventure. Relax on a hot summer day as a leader from the boat crew pedals you and other riders around the garden's lagoon for a 15-minute excursion.

MAP 1: 4 Charles St., 617/522-1966, http://swanboats.com; mid-Apr.-June 20 daily 10am-4pm, June 21-Labor Day daily 10am-5pm; $4 adults, $3.50 seniors, $2.50 children, free for children under 2

ICE-SKATING
Frog Pond

Lacing up and taking to the ice at Frog Pond in Boston Common is one of the

Frog Pond in winter

city's preeminent ways to pass time during the winter months. Whether you're trying to mimic hometown favorite Nancy Kerrigan or simply looking to learn how to skate, Frog Pond accommodates all skill levels during its season from opening (skate) day in mid-November. Skates and lockers are available to rent.

MAP 1: 38 Beacon St., 617/635-2120, www.bostonfrogpond.com; winter Mon. 10am-3:45pm, Tues.-Thurs. 10am-9pm, Fri.-Sat. 10am-10pm, Sun. 10am-9pm; $12 adults, children over 58 inches tall $6, under 58 inches free

Government Center, North End, and Waterfront   Map 2

PARKS
✪ Rose Kennedy Greenway

This linear park is the go-to oasis for first-time visitors to Boston as well as workers in neighboring skyscrapers. The Rose Kennedy Greenway—named after the mother of John F., Robert F., and Ted Kennedy, the latter of whom was a leading force behind the creation of the greenway—was created from land made available after the Big Dig. Today, the park runs from North Station in Boston's West End along the North End and Faneuil Hall parallel to Boston Harbor and eventually makes its way past South Station before culminating at Chinatown Park. The park has been a driving force in establishing a "New Boston" from the city's former grit. Its parks and promenades offer cultural nods to their surrounding areas, like bamboo and Asian art in Chinatown Park. Since the park first opened, the greenway experience has

been enhanced with public art and a seasonal beer and wine garden near Rowes Wharf.

MAP 2: 617/292-0020, www.rosekennedygreenway.org

GUIDED TOURS
Old Town Trolley Tours

Hop aboard for a comprehensive overview of the Hub of the Universe. Old Town Trolley Tours offers a hop-on/hop-off ride to 19 of the city's top sights, with guides giving local trivia along the way. The company even offers a "frightseeing" tour around Halloween. The total tour time is just under two hours and includes tickets for a Boston Harbor Cruise and admission to the Old State House.

MAP 2: www.trolleytours.com/boston; tickets vary and can be purchased in person at most area hotels, but discounts are available online

THE BIG DIG

Rose Kennedy Greenway

Downtown Boston is home to the Rose Kennedy Greenway, a green oasis running between North and South Stations, but it wasn't always so pristine. The Central Artery of I-93 was originally an elevated highway cutting through downtown Boston. It inundated the city with traffic at all hours of the day and cut off the North End and Seaport neighborhoods from the rest of the city. Plans to bury the highway and improve connections to Logan Airport began in 1982, and construction ran from 1991 to 2006. It was the costliest highway project in U.S. history and was seemingly cursed by cost overruns ($24 billion if you count interest), design flaws (a woman was killed by a falling ceiling tile), and delays. Now in ideal condition, the project is seen as the catalyst to the Seaport's explosive growth as well as Logan Airport's, which became much easier to access upon the opening of a new tunnel. Stroll through the expanse of parks and improved transit, and it (almost) seems worth the billions.

NPS Freedom Trail Tour

The National Park Service offers several guided talks and tours along the Freedom Trail. From the history of Faneuil Hall to Boston's Revolution-era reputation for defiance, the NPS guides you through the history of the birth of America. While talks are held year-round, tours are offered on a seasonal basis and are typically free with a ticket obtained through the NPS visitors center in Faneuil Hall.

MAP 2: 4 South Market St., 617/242-5642, www.nps.gov/bost; daily 9am-6pm

HARBOR CRUISES AND WHALE-WATCHING
Boston Harbor Cruises

From city to sea, Boston Harbor Cruises is a one-stop shop. BHC can whisk you from downtown Boston to the gorgeous beaches of Provincetown on the Outer Cape in 90 minutes. Whale-watches, sunset cruises, and historical sightseeing cruises are all ready to leave the port of call at Long Wharf. More of an adventure seeker? Climb aboard *Codzilla*, BHC's high-speed thrill boat.

MAP 2: 1 Long Wharf, 617/227-4231, www.bostonharborcruises.com; Mon.-Sat. 6:30am-10am; prices vary

Classic Harbor Line
Take to Boston Harbor in luxury. Classic Harbor Line offers tours aboard old-style yachts and schooners. Daytime, sunset, and evening cruises are offered and come with outstanding views of the Boston skyline. Brunch and "Champagne City Lights" tours add a dose of romance to these decadent voyages.
MAP 2: 60 Rowes Wharf, 617/951-2460, www.boston-sailing.com; cruises typically $22-70

Downtown, Chinatown, and the Theater District   Map 3

PARKS
Chinatown Park
Just outside Chinatown's *paifang* gateway is Chinatown Park, the first green space to be completed in the greater Rose Kennedy Greenway. What was once a highway off-ramp is now a small park dotted with Asian gardens, water features, and tea and chess

paifang gateway outside of Chinatown Park

tables where visitors can take a break and unwind in a tucked-away corner of the city.
MAP 3: John F. Fitzgerald Surface Rd., 617/292-0020

GUIDED TOURS
Lessons on Liberty Tour
You can walk the Freedom Trail, *or* you could walk the Freedom Trail with a colonist or soldier from the Revolutionary War. Lessons on Liberty boasts its tours are run by historians and not actors, but the guides get in character and deliver an authentic walk down this historic trail. Tours cover a significant portion of the trail but vary depending on weather and group preference.
MAP 3: 148 Tremont St., 857/205-1775, www.lessonsonliberty.com; $14.95 adults, $12.65 students and seniors, $8 children

RECREATION

BACK BAY

PARKS

Commonwealth Avenue Mall

The linear, 32-acre Commonwealth Avenue Mall was designed in the 1800s to be Boston's hat tip to the grand French boulevards on the other side of the Atlantic. The green alley of leafy trees is the narrowest link in Boston's Emerald Necklace of parks and is dotted with sculptures and benches on which to sit and take in the stately mansions lining either side of what locals refer to as "Comm Ave."

MAP 4: Commonwealth Ave. from Arlington St. to Kenmore Square

WALKING AND BIKING TRAILS

✪ Charles River Esplanade

The esplanade along the Charles River is an urban oasis for the outdoor aficionado. Join the many joggers and cyclists each day who run or ride along the tree-lined waterfront paths that offer great views of the skyline and Cambridge. The park features 3 miles (4.8 km) of trails that link in with the greater 23-mile (37-km) **Paul Dudley White Charles River Bike Path,** giving visitors easy access to Boston, Cambridge, and the suburbs.

MAP 4: Accessible via footbridges at Beacon St.'s intersections with Massachusetts Ave., Fairfield St., Dartmouth St., and Arlington St.

Charles River Esplanade

BOSTON BIKE-SHARING

Traffic and parking can be frustrating parts of any visitor's vacation to a big city. Boston's shared bike system is an easy, convenient, and green way to skip the rental car and see all the city has to offer. Some 1,800 bikes are spread among 185 stations in Boston, Cambridge, Brookline, and Somerville. Daily, monthly, and annual passes enable unlimited rides to save you time in getting from attraction to attraction. The 24-hour passes (which include unlimited 2-hour rides) are $10 and single trips are $2.50. Visit Bluebikes (www.bluebikes.com) for details.

GUIDED TOURS

Boston Duck Tours

Make your time in the city quack-tastic with a Duck Tour. Hop on a replica World War II amphibious vehicle and cruise the streets of Boston, hearing historical tidbits and trivia along the way. Before you know it, you'll be heading into the Charles River for a cruise that offers guests one-of-a-kind views of Back Bay, Cambridge, and the downtown skylines. Yes, you even get a chance to drive the boat! MAP 4: 53 Huntington Ave., 617/267-3825, http://bostonducktours.com; 80-minute tours every 30 minutes 9am until 60 minutes before sunset; adults $42.99, seniors $34.99, children $28.99

South End   Map 5

PARKS

Titus Sparrow Park

Located in the northern portion of the South End near the Prudential Center, Titus Sparrow Park is a favorite spot to lounge with a book, bring kids to the playground, or catch a concert series in the summer with friends and a carefully stashed bottle of wine. The Friends of Titus Sparrow Park bring seasonal entertainment and work to maintain the park's greenery for all visitors to enjoy. MAP 5: 200 W. Newton St., www.titussparrowpark.org

WALKING AND BIKING TRAILS

Southwest Corridor Park

The Southwest Corridor could have the alternate title of "the park that almost wasn't." Hundreds of acres from the South End to Jamaica Plain were razed in the 1960s to make way for a 4.6-mile (7.4-km) section of highway to be called the Southwest Expressway. It was met with widespread opposition from a community already unsettled by urban renewal going on elsewhere in the city at the time, and the project was ultimately canceled. Instead, it became a way to realign the Orange

Southwest Corridor Park

THE EMERALD NECKLACE

Boston has more parks than most cities in the United States, thanks in part to the Emerald Necklace. The 1,100-acre series of green spaces is linked by water and parkways from Boston to Brookline and gets its moniker from how Frederick Law Olmsted, the famous American landscape architect who also helped design New York's Central Park (as well as many urban parks in the United States), designed Boston's green space to look like a green necklace hanging from the neck that is the Boston peninsula. Starting with the colonial Boston Common and culminating with the "crown jewel" and "great country park" of Franklin Park in the city's Jamaica Plain neighborhood, the Emerald Necklace is actually incomplete: The Dorchesterway, a planned parkway near Dorchester Bay, was never built—but there are plans to finally construct this missing green link.

Line (then elevated over Washington Street) with a community trail running alongside. It remains popular with neighbors and dogs for an array of outdoor activities.

MAP 5: Starts at Back Bay Station (145 Dartmouth St.), www.swcpc.org

Fenway and Kenmore Square   Map 6

SPECTATOR SPORTS
BASEBALL
✪ Boston Red Sox

Boston would never outwardly say it had a favorite sports team, but the roars from Fenway Park and sheer glee seen throughout the city in the weeks leading up to Opening Day *might* give a hint as to who it would be . . . if there were a favorite. The 86-year "Curse of the Bambino" is no more, as the Red Sox have won four World Series since 2004.

MAP 6: 4 Jersey St., 877/733-7699, www.boston.redsox.mlb.com

South Boston   Map 7

PARKS
Castle Island

Relax amid history at this South Boston respite where Fort Independence has stood since 1634. While you'll run into more joggers and pet owners than minutemen these days, Castle Island is a perfect perch for picnics. Watch planes from around the world soar over you as they take off and land from nearby Logan Airport, or dip your toes in the water at one of the neighborhood beaches. Be sure to save room for treats at Sullivan's, a hamburger shack and neighborhood favorite by Castle Island's parking lot.

MAP 7: 2010 William J. Day Blvd., 617/727-5290

Lawn on D

Kids aren't the only ones with a playground in Boston. This green space in the shadows of the Boston Convention and Exhibition Center (on D Street) features live music, libations, and a glow-in-the-dark swing set. Popular for impromptu gatherings as well as events like movie nights, the Lawn on D has successfully bridged older South Boston with the younger Seaport.

MAP 7: 420 D St., 877/393-3393; Sun.-Thurs. 7am-10pm, Fri.-Sat. 7am-11pm

WALKING AND BIKING TRAILS
✪ Harborwalk

Get cardio with a view. This waterfront path gives visitors views of the downtown skyline and iconic Boston Harbor. Whether you're lacing up to run morning sprints or simply looking to enjoy a picturesque walk en route to the Freedom Trail, the Harborwalk is a choose-your-own experience that takes you by some of the city's most popular attractions.

MAP 7: Various access points along Boston Harbor waterfront

BEACHES
M Street Beach

Sure, it isn't the French Riviera, but skip the Route 3 traffic trying to get to Cape Cod and head to Southie for some of the most convenient sand in town. The 3-mile (4.8-km) stretch fronts Dorchester Bay and offers views of the John F. Kennedy Presidential Library and Boston Harbor islands. Warm weekends bring nearby residents looking to tan, covertly sip alcohol (technically not allowed), and splash in the usually chilly water. Bring lunch to make an afternoon of your visit.

MAP 7: M St. and William J. Day Blvd.

Cambridge   Map 8

PARKS
✪ North Point Park

This 8-acre park near the Charles River Dam is a hidden gem created as part of the Big Dig. Its small islands and canals connect with the neighboring North Point super-development. A favorite of cyclists and pedestrians, North Point is the perfect spot when looking for a secluded green space off the beaten path.

MAP 8: 6 Museum Way, Cambridge, 617/626-1250

Cambridge Common

This guitar pick-shaped park on Harvard Square's northwestern edge is known more for sunbathing and volleyball these days, but it has Revolutionary roots. George Washington stationed troops from the Continental Army here during the Revolutionary War, and the bronze canons and several plaques around the park commemorate its ties to history. This is a quiet spot to unwind after a busy day of touring Harvard and strolling the streets of the nearby square.

MAP 8: 26 Appian Way, Cambridge

NOVEMBER PROJECT

It takes a special kind of dedication to stick to a fitness regimen. It takes a community to stick to the November Project (www.november-project.com). Founders (and Northeastern University rowing alums) Bojan Mandaric and Brogan Graham goaded each other into sticking to workouts even in the dead cold of New England winters, nicknaming their commitment to three weekly workouts the "November Project." Others followed, and a system of high-energy, free workouts was born. Mondays are "Destination Decks" with new locations and workouts determined by a deck of cards, Wednesdays bring stair runs at Harvard Stadium, and Fridays see runs up a steep hill in nearby Brookline. The community has gone global by expanding into cities from Amsterdam to San Francisco. Find out more online.

WALKING AND BIKING TRAILS

Charles River Bike Path

Complete the Charles River Bike Path loop and you've pedaled nearly 28 miles (45 km). In its entirety, the trail follows the Charles River from Boston to the suburbs of Newton, Watertown, Waltham, and into Cambridge, offering riders the best of both city and green views.

MAP 8: 1175A Soldiers Field Rd., Boston, 617/727-4708

Minuteman Bikeway

Want to pedal the path of Paul Revere? The Minuteman Bikeway is a 10-mile (16-km) paved path that closely mimics the route Revere took in 1775 to usher in the American Revolution. It starts at Alewife Station and heads all the way to the towns of Lexington and Bedford, where it connects to an extensive network of suburban bike trails.

MAP 8: Begins at Alewife Station, www.minutemanbikeway.org

CANOEING AND KAYAKING

Paddle Boston

The Charles may have been referred to in song as "That Dirty Water," but today it's clean and inviting. Kendall Square's branch of this boat rental company is the most convenient to central Boston. Rent a single or double kayak and take in the downtown skyline and Charles River Basin.

MAP 8: 15 Broad Canal Way, Cambridge, 617/965-5110, www.paddleboston.com; spring-fall (weather dependent) Mon.-Fri. 10am-7pm, Sat.-Sun. 9am-7pm; $16-22 per hour

GUIDED TOURS

The Hahvahd Tour

Decidedly less stuffy than what you may anticipate an Ivy League college tour would be, The Hahvahd Tour is led by actual Harvard students who spend the 1.25-hour tour taking you by famous landmarks like the *John Harvard* statue (rub it for good luck on your application!), Johnston Gate, and Widener Library. Guides dole out Harvard wisdom, discuss the many famous Harvard alum, and chat about their own personal experiences at the world's most famous university. Tours are offered daily.

MAP 8: 1380 Massachusetts Ave., Cambridge, 855/455-8747 ext. 2, www.trademarktours.com/harvard-tour; $14 adults, $11.50 students, seniors, and children

SPECTATOR SPORTS

FOOTBALL
New England Patriots

It's hard to find something Boston loves more than quarterback Tom Brady and his New England Patriots. The G.O.A.T. and coach Bill Belichick have ushered in an era of six Super Bowl victories, while the Gillette Stadium and its neighboring Patriots Place lifestyle center have reinvented the town of Foxborough. Trains run from South Station to Gillette, so hop aboard to a Patriots victory.

MAP 9: 1 Patriot Pl., Foxborough, 508/543-8200, http://gillettestadium.com

SOCCER
New England Revolution

The Patriots aren't the only reason to head to Foxborough. The New England Revolution Major League Soccer team also plays at Gillette Stadium and, like the Patriots, is also owned by The Kraft Group. The soccer team, one of the 10 original MLS organizations, regularly makes it to the MLS Cup finals but, as of press time, has yet to win the MLS Cup. It may not have the championship banners like other Boston teams, but loyal crowds still flock to their games!

MAP 9: 1 Patriot Pl., Foxborough, 877/438-7387, www.revolutionsoccer.net

PARKS

Arnold Arboretum

The 281-acre Arnold Arboretum of Harvard University is the second-largest park in Boston's Emerald Necklace. The most recent green census of this Jamaica Plain green space counted nearly 15,000 plants.

A favorite for Boston's runners, dog owners, and those just looking for a picturesque picnic, the arboretum is open sunrise to sunset year-round.

MAP 9: 125 Arborway, Boston, 617/524-1718, http://arboretum.harvard.edu; daily sunrise-sunset

Arnold Arboretum

Charlestown Navy Yard

While it may officially be the "Boston Navy Yard" these days, locals (and the National Park Service) have kept the Charlestown moniker for this historic waterfront site popular with runners, bikers, and those just looking for a tranquil spot to relax. Home to the USS *Constitution* and museum ship USS *Cassin Young,* the Navy Yard is easily accessible via water taxi.

MAP 9: 114 16th St., Charlestown, 617/242-5601, www.nps.gov

Jamaica Pond

Another "link" in the Emerald Necklace, Jamaica Pond hugs the border of Brookline and Jamaica Plain and is popular for rowing and sailing. The 1.5-mile (2.4-km) path around the pond's shore is extremely popular with

BOSTON SPORTS TEAMS

In a city as heavily Catholic as Boston, there is still room for the "gods" of the city's professional sports teams: the Boston Red Sox (Major League Baseball), the Boston Bruins (National Hockey League), and the Boston Celtics (National Basketball Association), all of which play within the Boston city limits. The New England Patriots (National Football League) and New England Revolution (Major League Soccer) play at Gillette Stadium in Foxborough, Massachusetts (which is about 30 miles/48 km outside of Boston). Sports are an enormous part of the city's cultural and historical fabric. The Red Sox play at Fenway Park, MLB's oldest ballpark, which is considered the cathedral of the city's sports scene. The Bruins and Celtics play at the TD Garden, the only arena in the NBA with a parquet floor made with oak (a tradition from when the Celtics played at the Boston Garden). Boston fans are enthusiastic, to say the least, and they're happy to share their enthusiasm with visitors.

Boston's runners, as it offers a picturesque moment amid pesky marathon training regimens. You can also cancel out your run a few blocks away at the original J. P. Licks ice cream shop in Jamaica Plain.

MAP 9: 507 Jamaicaway, Jamaica Plain, 617/522-5061

Paul Revere Park

The Big Dig may have helped Boston with its traffic (depending on whom you ask), but it also delivered many parks to the city. Paul Revere Park was the first to open along the Charles River as mitigation for the mammoth infrastructure project. Located between the Freedom Trail and Zakim Bridge, the park includes a performance area, playground, and pedestrian bridge to the nearby North Point Park in Cambridge.

MAP 9: Water St. and N. Washington St., Charlestown, 617/626-1250

BIKING TRAILS
Charlestown Waterfront Bike Path

Head to Charlestown if you're looking for a quick spin on the bike with a view. The just-over-a-mile trail provides a whipping ocean breeze and brush with history as you pedal past the USS *Constitution* and Charlestown Navy Yard. Grab sandwiches and stop for a waterfront picnic to take in the best view of downtown in the entire city.

MAP 9: 1 City Square, Charlestown

SHOPS

It's not difficult to unleash your inner Holly Golightly when shopping in Boston. Beacon Hill boutiques, vintage shops in the South End, and designer flagships in Back Bay afford a litany of ways to ravage your wallet. Newbury Street is the city's historic retail boulevard and features something for all price points and fashion tastes, with haute couture closer to the Public Garden and collegiate, fast fashion chic conglomerating closer to Massachusetts Avenue. Responding to claims in local media that the Seaport's street level vibrancy had all the charm of "a suburban Dallas office park by the sea," developers have worked in recent years to come up with better curated retail. Whether you're looking for the latest from the catwalk or just a good spot to find a Red Sox T-shirt, you won't be disappointed with the retail options in the Hub.

December Thieves

SHOPPING DISTRICTS
BEACON HILL (CHARLES STREET)
Beacon Hill might be synonymous with Boston Brahmins and their palatial townhomes, but this tony neighborhood also features some of the city's best shopping at the base of "the Hill." Charles Street features an eclectic mix of mom-and-pop shops, boutiques, cafés, and delicious dining spots where you sip and nibble away the thought of your next credit card statement.

MAP 1: Charles St. between Beacon St. and Cambridge St./Longfellow Bridge

HIGHLIGHTS

⭐ **BEST WOMEN'S CLOTHING:** Whether it's a unique gift for your friend who wouldn't be caught dead in a Red Sox hat, or a cute dress for a last-minute nice dinner, December Thieves is a great bet for all glamour gals (page 169).

⭐ **BEST HOME GOODS:** It may look like a museum, but RH Boston is actually a furniture showroom, and it's more than okay to touch these comfy masterpieces (page 172).

⭐ **BEST GIFTS:** Travelers should look no further than Topdrawer for the latest in resilient luggage, travel humidifiers, and journals (page 172).

⭐ **BEST BOOKSTORE:** The cozy Trident Booksellers and Café is Boston's indie darling of leading and hard-to-find titles. Pair them with a pastry from the cafés on both levels of this two-story haven for literature (page 172).

⭐ **BEST MARATHON GEAR:** Steps from the Boston Marathon finish line, it only seems apropos for Marathon Sports to be Greater Boston's leading spot for running shoes, Marathon merchandise, and more to make those miles fly by (page 173).

⭐ **BEST DAY SPA:** When you've shopped till you've dropped on Newbury Street, let the talented team at G2O Spa and Salon massage away the pain and pamper you back to a rejuvenated self (page 173).

⭐ **BEST MEN'S CLOTHING:** Put some extra thought into your dapper, sartorial sense by letting the team at Sault New England style you into a new wardrobe that is simultaneously rugged and preppy (page 174).

⭐ **BEST BEAUTY PRODUCTS:** All products at Follain are natural and toxin-free, and likely in part responsible for the many glowing faces around each of its locations in Boston (page 176).

Topdrawer

BACK BAY (NEWBURY STREET)

Newbury Street, Boston's retail flagship, brings out tourists and locals all looking to browse the shops of top designers from around the world as well as smaller brands and local companies. The road gets significantly more decadent as you get closer to the Public Garden, while the initial blocks by Massachusetts Avenue feature eclectic record shops and student-focused fast-fashion brands like Uniqlo.

MAP 4: Newbury St. between Massachusetts Ave. and Arlington St.

SOUTH END (TREMONT STREET AND SHAWMUT AVENUE)

The South End has become a brick-and-mortar equivalent of Etsy in recent years, with independent shops flocking to several of the neighborhood's main thoroughfares. Flower shops, gift emporiums, and one-of-a-kind fashion finds are all within reach. Make an afternoon of it, as the neighborhood is equally known for its fabulous restaurants.

MAP 5: Tremont St., Shawmut Ave., and Harrison Ave. between Dartmouth St. and Berkeley St.

Beacon Hill and the West End

Map 1

CLOTHING

Crush Boutique

Los Angeles style hits Beacon Hill at this women's boutique in the heart of Charles Street. Comfy and chic flowing turtleneck dresses for fall give way to elegant cocktail dresses perfect for a summer party at a fab town house up "the Hill." The mix of casual and elegant makes for a comprehensive and sometimes dangerous shopping experience, as it's hard to leave with just one item.

MAP 1: 131 Charles St., 617/720-0010, www.shopcrushboutique.com; Mon.-Sat. 10am-7pm, Sun. 11am-6pm

North River Outfitter

Consider it the pinnacle of New England prep. Everyone needs a pair of Nantucket red pants and a popped collar on their polo to exude a Brahmin sense of fashion; nowhere is it better to rack up a new look than North River Outfitter. Local favorite fashion lines like Vineyard Vines and Calypso are found on these racks, and kids' and athletic branches of this original venue are located next door and across the street.

MAP 1: 39 Charles St., 617/742-0089, www.northriveroutfitter.com; Mon.-Fri. 10am-7pm, Sat. 10am-6pm, Sun. 11am-6pm

ACCESSORIES

✪ December Thieves

Kitchen gadgets, fashionable handbags, and unique jewelry are but a few of the accessories you'll find yourself lusting after in this gift shop featuring global treasures. Owner and jewelry designer Lana Barakat curates her Beacon Hill shop to feature exclusive lines of candles and skin products to keep you feeling your best long after you've checked out.

MAP 1: 88 Charles St., 617/982-6802, www.decemberthieves.com; Tues.-Fri. 11am-7pm, Sat. 10am-6pm, Sun. noon-5pm

GIFT
Black Ink

Susan and Timothy Corcoran's Beacon Hill paper store lives up to the "unexpected necessities" label hanging over its front door. Arrive looking for a unique birthday card, and walk out with rubber stamps, a concrete tape dispenser, a retro pencil sharpener, and a bevy of other items you never knew you needed.

Black Ink

MAP 1: 101 Charles St., 617/497-1221, www.blackinkboston.com; Mon.-Sat. 10am-7pm, Sun. noon-6pm

Government Center, North End, and Waterfront   Map 2

CLOTHING AND SHOES
LIT Boutique

While the North End might not be known for its shopping scene, LIT Boutique has attracted women from the neighborhood and beyond with its trendy fashion and wardrobe classics. A helpful sales team is more than willing to help you find your style.

MAP 2: 236 Hanover St., 617/391-0086, http://litboutique.com; Mon.-Thurs. 10am-8pm, Fri.-Sat. 10am-9pm, Sun. 11am-7pm

SPAS AND SALONS
Exhale Boston—Battery Wharf

Think of it as the spa mother ship. Exhale in the North End's Battery Wharf offers waterfront choose-your-adventure tranquility. Fitness classes are a rigorous way to accrue endorphins, while a Zen lounge, sauna, and therapy rooms for massages, facials, and other spa services are a more languid way to tend to your inner self.

MAP 2: 2 Battery Wharf, 617/603-3100, www.exhalespa.com; Mon.-Fri. 6am-9pm, Sat. 7:30am-8pm, Sun. 8am-8pm

SHOPPING CENTERS

Faneuil Hall Marketplace

From a plush lobster to take home to the kids to an affordable piece of fast fashion from Uniqlo, the "Cradle of Liberty" also offers a litany of retail options amid its historic backdrop. Looking for a place to rest once you've shopped till you drop? Faneuil Hall has a variety of eateries, including a Cheers location with a replica of the television show's set.

MAP 2: 4 South Market St., 617-523-1300, www.faneuilhallmarketplace.com; spring-fall Mon.-Sat. 10am-9pm, Sun. 11am-7pm, winter Mon.-Thurs. 10am-7pm, Fri.-Sat. 10am-9pm, Sun. noon-6pm

Downtown, Chinatown, and the Theater District   Map 3

CLOTHING AND SHOES

Primark

European fast-fashion chains like H&M and Zara have dominated retail as of late, and Irish brand Primark launched its American foray in Downtown Crossing at the building that once housed Boston's storied Filene's department store. It's hard to go a block in the city without seeing a Primark bag, and it's easy to see why: Clothing, housewares, tech and travel accessories, and more are spread across four floors at prices often lower than H&M.

MAP 3: 10 Summer St., 617-350-5232, www.primark.com; Mon.-Sat. 9am-9:30pm, Sun. 10am-9:30pm

BOOKS

Brattle Book Shop

When you glance at this Downtown Crossing alley lined with rollaway bookcases packed with books, you wouldn't figure it's part of one of the

Brattle Book Shop

country's oldest used-book stores. Founded in 1825, the Brattle Book Shop features used and rare editions inside and discounted volumes outside. J. D. Salinger, Bostonians, and tourists have all passed through its doors on the hunt for elusive pieces of literature or just to have a brief bookish moment.

MAP 3: 9 West St., 617-542-0210, www.brattlebookshop.com; Mon.-Sat. 9am-5:30pm

CLOTHING AND SHOES
Bodega
Walk into an old convenience store, head straight to the soda machine, and stumble into the hippest street-fashion scene in the whole city?! Bodega is a sartorial speakeasy of predominantly male streetwear (though some women's fashion makes the cut) off Massachusetts Avenue. What started as a collaboration between three friends has emerged as one of the most recognizable names in the sneaker scene, offering limited editions by Y3, Adidas, and more. Bodega also offers its own stylish imprint and a slew of urban accessories.

MAP 4: 6 Clearway St., no phone, http://shop.bdgastore.com; Mon.-Wed. 10am-6pm, Thurs.-Sat. 10am-8pm, Sun. noon-6pm

Bodega

GIFT AND HOME
✪ RH Boston
You likely didn't travel to Boston with the hope of taking home a sectional sofa, but a trip to Restoration Hardware's opulent Boston flagship might have you doing just that. Occupying what was the Museum of Natural History, the RH design gallery gives visitors a peek at how every item in the company catalog can be staged to wow all guests to your chic abode.

MAP 4: 234 Berkeley St., 857/239-7202, http://restorationhardware.com; Mon.-Sat. 10am-7pm, Sun. noon-6pm

✪ Topdrawer
Every traveler or traveler-to-be needs a gift from Topdrawer. Intent on providing "tools for nomads," the store focuses on practical gadgets for those on the go. Indestructible luggage, rain gear that stows in a carry-on, and even quirky pens and travel journals line the shelves at this Newbury Street venue perfect for gifts for the wayward soul.

MAP 4: 273 Newbury St., 857/305-3934, http://kolo.com; daily 11am-7pm

BOOKS AND MUSIC
✪ Trident Booksellers and Café
Big-box booksellers might be waning, but don't tell that to Trident Booksellers. The independent company expanded in recent years to add a second floor and new café to its existing shop and restaurant. Featuring a wide range of best sellers and harder-to-find titles, Trident invites patrons to stick around with its late hours and all-day breakfast menu.

MAP 4: 338 Newbury St., 617/267-8688, http://tridentbookscafe.com; daily 8am-midnight

NEWBURY STREET

New England's shopping mecca of Newbury Street brings droves of visitors to Back Bay. Running from Massachusetts Avenue all the way to the Boston Public Garden, the retail hub has everything from quirky Newbury Comics and other eclectic shops closer to Mass Avenue to über-luxe brands like Chanel and Valentino near the Public Garden. Weekends are both the busiest and best times to visit, as shops often run specials and seasonal pedestrian-only access brings musicians and other activities to Boston's retail hub. Unlike its peer luxe retail streets like Fifth Avenue in Manhattan and Rodeo Drive in Beverly Hills, Newbury Street somehow manages to be inviting and intimidating all at once. The cozy brownstones may seem like you're just popping into a friend's small apartment—if that friend

the more eclectic retail end of Newbury Street

happened to also sell a $4,000 Dolce & Gabbana dress in her living room. Grab a coffee near the Hynes MBTA station and spend part of your late morning or early afternoon walking Newbury in its entirety to get the full indie-to-ridiculously wealthy experience. On Newbury, it's just as easy to people-watch as it is to shop till you drop!

Newbury Comics

In the age of streaming music, a place to pick up a CD or, egad, vinyl records is a rarity. Newbury Comics offers just that, on top of its reliable mix of new and vintage comic books and music merchandise and gifts for all tastes and levels of appropriateness. Record signings and friendly staff make the Back Bay flagship a favorite for comic and music lovers alike.

MAP 4: 332 Newbury St., 617/236-4930, http://newburycomics.com; Mon.-Thurs. 10am-9pm, Fri.- Sat. 10am-10pm, Sun. 11am-8pm

SPORTING GOODS

✪ Marathon Sports

As ridiculous as you may feel, the staff at Marathon Sports will make you run up and down the block in a

pair of their shoes before they'll let you walk out the door with the wrong pair. Just over the Boston Marathon finish line on Boylston, Marathon Sports is a temple of sorts for runners due to its hyper-attentive staff and wide range of gear.

MAP 4: 671 Boylston St., 617/267-4774, http://marathonsports.com; Mon.-Wed. and Fri. 10am-7:30pm, Thurs. 10am-8pm, Sat. 10am-8pm, Sun. 11am-6pm

SPAS AND SALONS

✪ G2O Spa and Salon

Two words: Experience Room. G2O Spa and Salon's staff provide every bit of pampering one can imagine, from Swedish massages to a cut-and-color to a simple manicure. The spa's Experience Room is home to herbal-infused steam, a tropical shower, and

Marathon Sports

ice fog to pamper and relax guests both before and after treatments, making a visit to G2O a worthwhile, rejuvenating day trip.

MAP 4: 33 Exeter St., 617/262-2220, http://g2ospasalon.com; Mon.-Tues. 8am-8pm, Wed.-Fri. 8am-9pm, Sat. 8am-6pm, Sun. 10am-6pm

Spa at Mandarin Oriental

Bostonians have come to view the day spa within the Mandarin Oriental hotel in Back Bay as a necessary extravagance. Massages, body scrubs, and "journeys" (think: exfoliation/massage combinations) are but a few of the services offered in this expansive, hushed relaxation center in the heart of the city. Spa suites offer privacy while heat and water facilities include steam rooms, ice showers, and soaking tubs to truly help you unwind.

MAP 4: 776 Boylston St., 617/535-8820, http://mandarinoriental.com; daily 9am-9pm

South End   Map 5

CLOTHING AND SHOES

✪ Sault New England

Despite being on the bustling shopping mecca of Tremont Street, Sault NE feels more like stepping into a rustic cabin in the woods of Vermont. Catering to all things masculine, with sharp Oxford shirts, leather Dopp kits, and a slew of grooming products to care for weathered skin, Sault never fails to jump-start a man's sartorial sense.

MAP 5: 577 Tremont St., 857/239-9434, www.saultne.com; Mon.-Sat. 10am-7pm, Sun. 10am-5pm

Boston Marathon finish line

If there is a silver lining to the horrific events and aftermath of the 2013 Boston Marathon bombing, it is the continuing unity that resonates throughout Greater Boston. "Boston Strong" was created in response to the tragedy that left three dead and injured hundreds. The slogan is found on many pieces of merchandise sold throughout the city, with T-shirts being the most popular. While the One Fund, the original charity created to aid victims, closed in 2015, proceeds from these T-shirts still go to trauma-related charities. You can find the shirts in numerous stores throughout the city or at www.straystrongbostonstrong.org.

GIFT AND HOME

Olives & Grace

This "curtsy to the makers" is a den of unique small-batch gifts from independent brands around the country. From Brooklyn sriracha and taboo greeting cards to organic candles and statement cocktail shakers, owner Sofi Madison's "Best of Boston" store is a must for those looking for a gift to take home that is more thoughtful than a Red Sox cap. Don't worry about your new wares fitting into your carry-on: OG ships to anywhere in the country! **MAP 5:** 623 Tremont St., 617/236-4536, www.olivesandgrace.com; Tues.-Sat. 10am-7pm, Sun.-Mon. 11am-5pm

Olives & Grace

Patch NYC

What started as a crocheted hat collection has blossomed into a brand that has garnered national attention from partnerships with companies like Target, Anthropologie, and West Elm. A funky accessories and decor emporium, Patch is a prime spot in the neighborhood for gifts that you or your special someone will not already have—be it novelty pillows, imprint candles, or a necessary extravagance like a watch.

MAP 5: 46 Waltham St., 617/426-0592, www.patchnyc.com; Wed.-Sat. noon-6pm

SPAS AND SALONS
✪ Follain

If one is to love the skin they're in, they should certainly take a trip to this beauty store promoting healthy, wholesome brands all made in the United States. Founder Tara Foley started her shop after winning a retail business plan competition while pursuing her MBA. Today, Follain carries over 40 brands promoting ultra-performance natural ingredients.

MAP 5: 53 Dartmouth St., 857/284-7078, www.shopfollain.com; Mon.-Sat. 10am-6pm., Sun. noon-5pm

Follain

SPORTING GOODS
Heartbreak Hill Running Company

Even if you don't run the Boston Marathon, you can treat yourself to the same chic athletic wear as the competitors. Named for the infamous hill runners face at the 20-mile mark near Boston College, HHRC offers gait analysis shoe fittings, accessories, and run clubs several nights of the week.

MAP 5: 652 Tremont St., 617/391-0897, www.heartbreakhillrunningcompany.com; Mon.-Thurs. 11am-8pm, Fri. 11am-7pm, Sat. 10am-6pm, Sun. 11am-5pm

GOURMET TREATS
Formaggio Kitchen

Sometimes one of the city's best meals can be a few last-minute items picked up at the market and enjoyed in a park. Formaggio on Shawmut features a variety of meats, cheeses, sweets, and small-batch sandwiches that go quickly at lunchtime. Gift baskets can be made and shipped to give friends back home the same delectable moment you enjoyed in the South End.

MAP 5: 268 Shawmut Ave., 617/350-6996, www.formaggiokitchen.com; 9am-8pm Mon.-Fri., 9am-7pm Sat., 11am-5pm Sun.

Polkadog Bakery

This canine mecca offers handmade treats for your pup—think of it as Magnolia Bakery for the canine crowd. Polkadog became a household name in 2012 when Target came knocking and wanted to feature it as one of its first "Main Street USA" brands. Despite the exposure, the Polkadog team still manages to stick to its locally sourced ingredients when baking treats each day.

MAP 5: 256 Shawmut Ave., 617/338-5155, www.polkadog.com; Mon.-Sat. 9am-8pm, Sun. 10am-6pm

Siena Farms

While it might cost more than a mortgage payment to get *all* the ingredients for a meal at Siena Farms, the produce and flowers are too beautiful to not include at least a few in a snack or to spruce up your hotel room. Carefully selected vegetables come from the company's farm in Sudbury, and kale smoothies taste a little more wholesome when you know the ingredients are locally sourced.

MAP 5: 106 Waltham St., 617/422-0030, www.sienafarms.com; 8am-8pm Mon.-Fri., 11am-7pm Sat.-Sun.

Fenway and Kenmore Square

Map 6

SPORTING GOODS AND MEMORABILIA

Official Red Sox Team Store

You can't head home without scoring some Red Sox swag. Located outside of Fenway Park, the Red Sox Team Store is the official outpost for all your T-shirt, baseball hat, and historical memorabilia needs. While items veer on the pricier side, the vast selection and proximity to home plate (the store is located in the ballpark) make it a must-visit even when the Red Sox aren't in town.

MAP 6: 19 Jersey St., 800/336-9299, www.jerseystreetstore.com; daily 9am-5pm

South Boston

Map 7

CLOTHING AND ACCESSORIES

For Now

In a shopping era of numerous digitally native brands and Etsy shops, For Now brings those online favorites to the brick-and-mortar world of retail. This Seaport shop is meant to be a retail incubator of up-and-coming online brands for men's and women's fashion as well as accessories. For shoppers, it's a great way to score small-batch fashion and never run the risk of showing up to a party in the same thing three other people are wearing.

MAP 7: 68 Seaport Blvd., 857/233-4639, www.itsfornow.com; Mon.-Fri. 10am-7pm, Sat. 10am-6pm, Sun. 11am-5pm

SPORTING GOODS

L.L. Bean

This sleek Seaport store is Boston's first standalone L.L. Bean and the brand's first urban outpost. Smaller than most of the company's other stores, the Seaport store features all the company's popular outdoor gear and apparel, and it's tempting to step in and see if you can score those ever-elusive Bean Boots.

MAP 7: 56 Seaport Blvd., 888/660-1572, www.llbean.com; Mon.-Sat. 9am-8pm, Sun. 10am-6pm

SHOPPING CENTERS

The Current

The Current is a series of modular structures that house various pop-up retailers throughout the year. A previous incarnation included the

She Village series of female-owned pop-up stores, while lately it's been less about theme and more focused on local brands like Sh*t That I Knit, sneaker brand Laced, and CBD company Beam.

MAP 7: 100 Seaport Blvd., www.bostonseaport.xyz; various hours

Cambridge

Map 8

CLOTHING AND SHOES
Drinkwater's

Gentlemen, you'll be a tall glass of water after a few purchases from Drinkwater's. This Porter Square men's boutique offers an expert selection of customized button-down shirts, elegant footwear, and made-to-measure suits to give your wardrobe the dignified look it deserves.

MAP 8: 2067 Massachusetts Ave., Cambridge, 617/547-2067, www.drinkwaterscambridge.com; Mon.-Wed. 10am-7pm, Thurs. 10am-8pm, Fri. 10am-7pm, Sat. 10am-6pm

Mint Julep

This Harvard Square women's boutique is a local staple for everything from designer jeans to a chic summer dress fit for a weekend on the Cape or Nantucket. The wide selection of clothing and accessories from top American and European lines makes Mint Julep a frequent "Best of Boston" winner.

MAP 8: 6 Church St., Cambridge, 617/576-6468, www.shopmintjulep.com; Mon.-Sat. 10am-7pm, Sun. 11am-6pm

BOOKS
Harvard Book Store

Something old, something new, and something spoken can all be obtained in this charming independent bookshop. Top authors from Hillary Clinton to Salman Rushdie and Claire Messud flock to the Harvard Book Store when they have a book to promote. An extensive used section occupies the downstairs while the main level features new titles and great gifts for the bibliophile in your life.

MAP 8: 1256 Massachusetts Ave., Cambridge, 617/661-1515, www.harvard.com; Mon.-Sat. 9am-11pm, Sun. 10am-10pm

GIFT AND HOME
The Coop

Probably the only thing prized in Boston as much as a Red Sox T-shirt is Harvard swag. The Coop in the heart of Harvard Square has the biggest supply of Harvard memorabilia, from T-shirts to mugs to furniture.

Get your Harvard gear at The Coop.

The Coop is also Harvard's official bookstore, so be sure to save time to peruse the stacks and even get a coffee from the on-site café.

MAP 8: 1400 Massachusetts Ave., Cambridge, 617/499-2000, www.thecoop. com; Mon.-Sat. 9am-10pm, Sun. 10am-9pm

L. A. Burdick Handmade Chocolates

This artisanal chocolate shop is a perfect way to give friends back home a taste of Boston—as long as the gifts make it that far! Handcrafted chocolate mice and penguins are delightful treats (and ship anywhere), while classics like bonbons and chocolate bars are sure to please. Save room (and time in line) for hot chocolate during cold months.

MAP 8: 52 Brattle St., Cambridge, 617/491-4340, www.burdickchocolate.com; Sun.-Thurs. 8am-9pm, Fri.-Sat. 8am-10pm

WHERE TO STAY

Boston offers everything from palatial suites overlooking the harbor to affordable hostels in great locations. Considering its size, the city has fewer hotels

Mandarin Oriental

than you would expect, so rates tend to skyrocket.
Booking in advance and knowing peak times of
year (May for graduations, September for college
drop-offs) can save you dollars. While Airbnb and
other home-share services are increasingly popular
for budget travelers in the city, last-minute hotel
deals are often easy to come by during off-peak
travel times. Newer hotels tend to be located along
the waterfront and in the Seaport while posh, established venues ingrained in the city's history are
found in neighborhoods like Back Bay and Beacon
Hill.

CHOOSING WHERE TO STAY
BEACON HILL AND THE WEST END
Visitors looking for a quiet, high-end place to
rest their heads should look no further than the
townhome-lined streets of Beacon Hill. One of
the country's oldest neighborhoods, Beacon Hill's
lodging offerings are primarily smaller boutiques and inns rather than the
convention-sized hotels found elsewhere in the city.

GOVERNMENT CENTER, NORTH END, AND WATERFRONT
Variety prevails in this trio of neighborhoods found on the back half of the
Freedom Trail. From cozy boutiques along Faneuil Hall's perimeter to soaring
glass towers of national hotel chains lining the waterfront, this stretch of the

HIGHLIGHTS

✪ **BEST NIGHT YOU'LL EVER SPEND IN JAIL:** For once, it's okay to be locked up (just with a higher thread count) at the Liberty Hotel, formerly the Charles Street Jail (page 184).

✪ **BEST WATERFRONT VIEWS:** The massive rooms and swanky subterranean spa are enough reason to check in, but the unparalleled views of the water make the Boston Harbor Hotel the city's best bet for seaside lodging (page 185).

✪ **BEST PEOPLE-WATCHING:** Order a Manhattan and sidle up in the Bristol Lounge at the Four Seasons Boston for a peek of the city's see-and-be-seen crowd (page 186).

✪ **BEST INDOOR POOL:** When you're done basking in the waterfront luxury, take a few laps at the InterContinental Boston's indoor pool, overlooking the Rose Kennedy Greenway (page 186).

✪ **BEST BOUTIQUE HOTEL:** Service is extraordinary and rooms are revolutionary—rumor has it Washington slept here—at XV Beacon (page 186).

✪ **BEST BANG FOR YOUR BUCK:** Cost savings doesn't come at the expense of a great location at HI Boston Hostel, in the heart of Boston's Theater District (page 188).

✪ **BEST SPLURGE:** Sometimes you just have to take care of you. There's no better place to do so than in the luxe accommodations and day spa at the Mandarin Oriental in Back Bay (page 189).

✪ **BEST HISTORIC HOTEL:** The lights have been on at the The Newbury (originally home to the city's first Ritz-Carlton) since the Roaring Twenties (page 190).

✪ **BEST SPORTS HOTEL:** The Hotel Commonwealth is the official hotel of the Boston Red Sox, featuring team package deals, baseball suites, and a Fenway Park Suite with a direct view into the park (page 191).

✪ **BEST WAY TO SLEEP LIKE A ROCK STAR:** Channel your inner Aerosmith at The Verb hotel, where guests are treated to a library of more than 500 vinyl albums (page 191).

PRICE KEY

$	Less than $150 per night
$ $	$150-300 per night
$ $ $	More than $300 per night

WHERE TO STAY IF ...

YOU ONLY HAVE A FEW DAYS:
Pack your bags and find a place in Downtown Crossing or the Financial District. These two neighborhoods are at the intersection of most of the city's transit lines, providing convenient commutes to most neighborhoods on a condensed itinerary.

YOU WANT A BOSTON HARBOR VIEW:
Snuggle up to hotels along Atlantic Avenue and in the Seaport, as these neighborhoods afford visitors the best view of Boston's bustling waterway and quick commutes to and from Logan International Airport.

YOU WANT TO FEEL LIKE A FOUNDING FATHER:
Book a room near Faneuil Hall or Government Center, as these centers of Revolutionary history are also home to several of the city's boutique hotels.

YOU'RE ON A BUDGET:
Affordable lodging is often found in the city's quieter Charlestown neighborhood as well as in Theater District hostels.

YOU'RE ON THE QUIET SIDE:
The South End is a charming neighborhood with easy access to Back Bay and downtown but lacking a subway line through its heart, making for quieter streets and an easier night's sleep.

YOU'RE NOT AFRAID OF A LITTLE NOISE:
The Theater District is Boston's loudest and brightest neighborhood, with nightclubs, theater marquees, and several concert venues, but a rise in Seaport nightclubs could make the waterfront enclave another one of Boston's noise centers.

YOU WANT TO HIT A HOME RUN:
Make a reservation at one of the many hotels in Boston's Fenway neighborhood and Kenmore Square to root for the Red Sox and get as close to home plate as you can without being on the official team roster.

YOU WANT TO DO AS THE BRAHMINS DO:
Look to lay your head in Beacon Hill to feel one with Boston aristocracy and get a taste of what life was like when private social clubs and bluebloods dictated the direction of the city.

YOU WANT TO BE CLOSE TO THE IVY LEAGUE:
Explore all options on the other side of the Charles River and look for hotels and alternative lodging in Cambridge. Areas like Kendall Square and Harvard Square will see the largest concentration of visitors to Harvard and MIT.

---

city is a favorite for business travelers and tourists looking to be in the heart of the action with quick commutes to Logan Airport.

DOWNTOWN, CHINATOWN, AND THE THEATER DISTRICT

Experience bright lights in the big city in downtown Boston. Glitzy hotels mingle with affordable hostels amid the marquees of the Theater District, while boutique lodging and larger

global chains for business travelers dot the neighboring Financial District and downtown. (Lodging is limited in Chinatown, and I don't recommend staying here.)

BACK BAY

Some of Boston's priciest rooms are found in historic, glamorous Back Bay. High-end international hotel brands mix with the neighborhood's oldest buildings while several upscale offerings make their mark on the skyline, offering the city's highest concentration of rooms for conventioneers, first-time visitors, and locals looking for a staycation.

SOUTH END

The off-the-beaten-path South End offers smaller-scale hotels and inns for returning visitors looking for a quieter approach to their Boston trip. The neighborhood is ideal for foodies who prefer their stay to be accompanied by quick access to dining and shopping as opposed to historical happenings.

FENWAY AND KENMORE SQUARE

It's easy to make a sports trip truly authentic in one of the several hotels surrounding Fenway Park. From the often affordable, rock-and-roll-themed Verb to the luxurious Hotel Commonwealth, Fenway and Kenmore Square have rooms for all interests.

SOUTH BOSTON

Boston's revitalized Seaport neighborhood is home to some of the city's newest hotels. Glass towers house most national brands as well as a few local offerings like the Seaport Hotel, built to house large groups from the nearby Boston Convention and Exhibition Center. Younger travelers flock to the new Yotel, home to smaller "cabins" and a very popular rooftop bar. Beyond Seaport in Southie, Airbnb is your best bet.

CAMBRIDGE

It may be on the other side of the river, but Red Line subway connectivity as well as easy access to some of the region's best universities make Cambridge an increasingly preferred place to stay, especially for international tourists, business travelers to the Kendall Square tech scene, and college visitors.

CHARLESTOWN AND GREATER BOSTON

Charlestown is slightly removed from the rest of downtown Boston, which can sometimes lead to more affordable rooms and Airbnb offerings. Somewhat quieter than other neighborhoods, Charlestown is great for returning guests with some sense of Boston's layout.

ALTERNATIVE LODGING
AIRBNB, VRBO, AND SHORT-TERM RENTALS

Hotels are increasingly becoming less dominant in metropolitan Boston. Short-term rentals are available through such companies as Airbnb and VRBO, where you can rent a room or entire home or condo for the duration of your stay. Both companies have offerings throughout Greater Boston, both with entire homes and rooms where the owner (and potentially other guests) will be present. Sonder is a newer short-term rental company that provides hotel-style service with its rentals. While you still have access to an entire condo, the stocked kitchens and bathrooms and 24/7 concierge service make your stay feel more like a posh hotel. Short-term rentals in Massachusetts are subject to the same 5.7 percent tax as hotels and can rise even higher depending on the city; Boston's short-term rental tax is 6.5 percent.

AIRPORT HOTELS, RV PARKS, AND CAMPING

If you're only in Boston for a quick layover, or if it is graduation season and rooms are booked, hotels near Boston Logan International Airport are often affordable and surprisingly easy to get to from downtown Boston. The Hyatt Regency Boston Harbor is on airport grounds and is easily accessible to all points along Boston Harbor via water taxi. The Hilton Boston Logan Airport and Embassy Suites are also near the airport and just over 10 minutes to downtown via Blue Line.

There's a place to stay even for outdoorspeople making a trip to Boston. Four of the Boston Harbor Islands (www.bostonharborislands.org; $8 Massachusetts residents, $10 out-of-state residents) offer campsites with views of the Boston skyline and tent sites for up to four adults per party. There is heavy demand, and reservations are recommended (and able to be made up to six months in advance). Boston Minuteman Campground (264 Ayer Rd., Littleton, 978/772-0042, www.minutemancampground. com; $52 for two adults, $10 per extra adult, $4 per child) features RV and tent campsites 33 miles (53 km) northwest of Boston in Minute Man National Historical Park.

Beacon Hill and the West End

Map 1

✪ Liberty Hotel $$

Getting locked up has never been so decadent. Located in the former Charles Street Jail, the Liberty Hotel sprang from the shackles in 2007 and has since reigned as Boston's hippest hotel. Featuring weekly fashion shows along the lobby's soaring catwalks, some of the city's most popular bars and restaurants (incorporated into original cells), and countless rooms with breathtaking views, the Liberty is the best night in jail you'll ever have. MAP 1: 215 Charles St., 617/224-4000, www.libertyhotel.com

Beacon Hill Hotel $$

Live like a posh Beacon Hiller at this neighborhood boutique hotel. BHH's cozy rooms with views over Charles Street and its terrace made perfect for summer cocktails might lead you to extend your reservation. Located steps away from Boston Common and the Public Garden, the hotel names its rooms after friends and family of prior owners. The BHH's staff are hospitable to the point where you may feel as though you are a friend or family member of the current owner! MAP 1: 25 Charles St., 617/723-7575, www. beaconhillhotel.com

CitizenM $$

This Dutch micro-hotel bills itself as "luxury for the wise, not the wealthy." Rooms are certainly on the affordable side by Boston standards, but they also run small: Massive, comfortable king-sized beds often take up half of rooms designed for 1-2 people. Despite being directly over North Station and the TD Garden arena, rooms are quiet. They feature modern furnishings,

Liberty Hotel

free Wi-Fi and movies, walk-in showers, a "MoodPad" to control lights, and views overlooking downtown. The hotel's 1960s-influenced public spaces offer spots to stretch out beyond the cozy guest rooms and include a terrace for weary travelers to unwind with a cocktail or snack from CitizenM's canteen.

MAP 1: 70 Causeway St., 617/861-4360, www.citizenm.com

Government Center, North End, and Waterfront   Map 2

✪ Boston Harbor Hotel $$$

When you're this close to Boston Harbor, you can reenact the Boston Tea Party from your own room. While rooms on the harbor side of this five-star property are a bit pricier than their city-view counterparts, they're worth the expense. Rooms include tablets for reading the daily news and ordering room service. The spa features a pool and hot tub that make a perfect sanctuary during the bitter cold of winter.

MAP 2: 70 Rowes Wharf, 617/439-7000, www.bhh.com

The Bostonian Boston $$$

It's hard to get more in the heart of the action than the Millennium Hotels' Bostonian Boston. Across the street from Faneuil Hall and blocks from the North End and Kennedy Greenway, the hotel offers spacious, modern accommodations with picturesque views of the skyline and some with balcony access and even fireplaces.

MAP 2: 26 North St., 617/523-3600, www. millenniumhotels.com

Battery Wharf Hotel $$

The rooms at the Battery Wharf Hotel are so close to the water, you'll wonder if you woke up aboard a houseboat. Modern rooms with luxurious bathrooms and nearby spa services could make the hotel its own destination. While it is on a far side of the city, water taxis stop at the hotel to whisk you across Boston Harbor to the Seaport, Long Wharf, and elsewhere. MAP 2: 3 Battery Wharf, 617/994-9000, www.batterywharfhotel.com

Downtown, Chinatown, and the Theater District   Map 3

✪ Four Seasons Boston $$$

Ever since the old Ritz moved across the Common to the Theater District, the Four Seasons across from the Public Garden has been old Boston's see-and-be-seen hotel. The Bristol Lounge is Boston society's gold standard for a statement cocktail, while the eighth-floor pool and hot tub provide fitness with a view. Light sleepers, rejoice: Each room's bedroom is separated from the hallway, providing sound, quiet rest each night.

MAP 3: 200 Boylston St., 617/338-4400, http://fourseasons.com/boston

InterContinental Boston (center)

MAP 3: 510 Atlantic Ave., 617/747-1000, www.intercontinentalboston.com

✪ InterContinental Boston $$$

While the InterContinental might look like a typical waterfront upscale chain hotel on the outside, everything on the inside is personalized to painstaking detail. Rooms have rich, dark furniture with luxurious bathrooms, and the second-floor spa overlooks the Kennedy Greenway and features a heated pool and treatment rooms. Save time in warmer weather for alfresco cocktails from the hotel's perch on the Harborwalk and take in the nearby Boston Tea Party Museum.

✪ XV Beacon $$$

Tucked away just past the corner of Beacon and Park Streets, XV Beacon is the city's most under-the-radar luxury hotel. Each of its fabulously decorated rooms features a fireplace and a nod to Boston's history with portraits of George Washington (rumored to be a guest in one of the hotel's prior lives) and plush bedding. Head to the rooftop deck for a cocktail and one of the city's most fabulous views of Boston Common and beyond.

MAP 3: 15 Beacon St., 617/670-1500, www. xvbeacon.com

THE OLDEST HOTEL IN THE UNITED STATES

Omni Parker House

Opened in 1855, Boston's Omni Parker House is the oldest continuously operating hotel in the United States. The history inside its doors is as captivating as that of the Freedom Trail outside. John F. Kennedy used the hotel as a base for both his candidacy for Congress and his bachelor party. Everyone from Malcolm X to Emeril Lagasse has been on the hotel's payroll. Ho Chi Minh was a pastry chef at the hotel, which is also the birthplace of the Boston cream pie and the Parker House roll.

Marriott Vacation Club Pulse at Custom House $$$

Even Boston locals are sometimes surprised to learn the Custom House Tower is a hotel. Originally used to inspect and register cargo for ships docking at nearby Long Wharf, the building is now a luxury hotel with incredible views of Boston Harbor that only get better the higher your room is. Rooms manage to be spacious and comfortable while retaining their historical charm—all while conveniently located steps away from the subway. MAP 3: 3 McKinley Square, 617/310-6300, www.marriottvacationclub.com

Ritz-Carlton Boston $$$

The developer behind much of downtown Boston's revitalization opened Boston's second Ritz in 2001 across Boston Common from the original, which dated back to 1927. The older property changed affiliations in 2007, making this the only Ritz in town. While locals bemoan the loss of the original, this one boasts more modern, luxurious rooms with views of the Common and State House, spa and fitness services, and a hotel bar known to attract Boston's modern Brahmins. MAP 3: 10 Avery St., 617/574-7100, www.ritzcarlton.com

Godfrey Hotel $$

One of Boston's newer boutique hotels, the Godfrey opened in 2016 and quickly gained a local following for its Asian-influenced restaurant and lobby coffee shop. Its modern design, rooms equipped with smartphone-to-TV streaming, and comfy bedding keep visitors coming back. MAP 3: 505 Washington St., 617/804-2000, www.godfreyhotelboston.com

The Langham, Boston $$

Before the Federal Reserve Bank of Boston moved to the waterfront, it was housed here. Today, the building is better known for its hotel, which flaunts "British elegance" and cozy, opulent rooms, particularly after a renovation in 2019 shut the complex down for a facelift. The sleek lobby features high-backed chairs clustered for a secluded yet still see-and-be-seen afternoon tea. Be sure to request rooms overlooking Post Office Square, and schedule time for the Saturday all-you-can-eat chocolate bar.

MAP 3: 250 Franklin St., 617/451-1900, www.langhamhotels.com

Moxy Boston Downtown $$

Old Boston blends with hip accommodations at this Theater District "micro-hotel" aimed at younger travelers looking to spend more of their budget on sightseeing than a spacious hotel room. Check in from an app—or at the lobby cocktail bar that doubles as a front desk—and enjoy modern, clean rooms that err on the smaller side but feature modern furnishings and (on higher floors) incredible views of downtown and Cambridge. Be sure to check out the rooftop bar for a lively scene and the best views of the city from the hotel.

MAP 3: 240 Tremont St., 617/793-4200, www.marriott.com

Revere Hotel $$

This boutique hotel might be named in honor of a certain revolutionary midnight rider, but everything else is decidedly modern. Impeccably designed rooms feature cushy beds, modern artwork of some key players in the American Revolution, rich lighting, and balcony access. Quench your thirst at the hotel's lobby bar, on-site lounge, and seasonal poolside bar and raise a toast to the Founding Fathers.

MAP 3: 200 Stuart St., 617/482-1800, www.reverehotel.com

W Boston $$

Whether you're a visitor or a local looking for a weekend home away from home, the W Boston is a great way to feel hip among history. Its lobby includes a vast bar churning out seasonal cocktails late into the evening while DJs drop by to spin new beats. Upstairs, Spanish artist Antonio Moras was commissioned to create murals for suites, while all rooms feature the brand's signature bath products and modern design.

MAP 3: 100 Stuart St., 617/261-8700, www.wboston.com

✪ HI Boston Hostel $

This hostel combines convenience with value. Mere steps from Boston Common, Chinatown, and the Theater District, HI Boston offers free tours, Wi-Fi, and breakfast. Private rooms (book well in advance) offer free DirecTV and en suite bathrooms, while four- and six-person dorms are also available. The first-floor bistro and café keep the lobby buzzing, and a pool table and games are great for breaking the ice with fellow travelers.

MAP 3: 19 Stuart St., 617/536-9455, www.bostonhostel.org

Boston Park Plaza $

Boston is getting more expensive by the day, but the Park Plaza maintains its reputation for an economical, clean stay. Its 1,060 rooms certainly vary in size and price, but the hotel has been modernized with an open lobby and more tech-savvy rooms. Boston Park Plaza is a block from the Public Garden and has several restaurants—and,

the main lobby at Boston Park Plaza

thanks to the closing of an upscale gym chain in its basement, easily the nicest hotel fitness center in the city.
MAP 3: 50 Park Plaza, 617/426-2000, http://bostonparkplaza.com

Omni Parker House $

Rooms skew on the smaller side at the Omni Parker House, but they also reign as some of the city's most convenient, as the Freedom Trail starts blocks away. The hotel's history is rich: Ho Chi Minh worked as a baker, Malcolm X was a busboy, and Charles Dickens took residency in the hotel in the 1800s. The hotel even originated some of Boston's most notable delicacies: the Boston cream pie and scrod!
MAP 3: 60 School St., 617/227-8600, www.omnihotels.com

Back Bay   Map 4

✪ Mandarin Oriental $$$

Arguably Boston's most exclusive hotel, the Mandarin Oriental in Back Bay is also one of its most convenient. Located in the Prudential Center, MO Boston and its 148 rooms and suites offer guests easy access to the city's historic sites while being a welcome retreat with delicious dining, a lavish spa, and über-high thread counts. Back Bay rooms have better views, while a quieter stay is guaranteed on the residential end.
MAP 4: 776 Boylston St., 617/535-8888, http://mandarinoriental.com

Four Seasons Hotel One Dalton Street $$$

The soaring, 61-story Four Seasons One Dalton tower is an addition to Boston's skyline and its luxury hotel scene. Putting Boston on an exclusive

189

list of global cities with two Four Seasons hotels within city limits, the One Dalton property opened in 2019 and has modern, chic rooms with views of the nearby Christian Science Plaza. A wellness floor includes a lap pool, spa, and 24-hour gym to work off the delicious food offered at its three dining options, including globally acclaimed Zuma.

MAP 4: 1 Dalton St., 617/377-4888, www.fourseasons.com

Inn at St. Botolph $$$

Live like a local from one of the suites in this chic brownstone on tree-lined St. Botolph Street. Conveniently nestled between Back Bay and the South End, the inn is steps from the Prudential Center and Tremont Street restaurants and shopping. Fireplaces in larger rooms and discounts to the hotel's partner restaurants make the inn a romantic haven for those looking for a quieter approach to Boston.

MAP 4: 99 St. Botolph St., 617/236-8099, www.innatstbotolph.com

✪ The Newbury $$

The Newbury, renovated in 2019, is still a bastion of old Boston luxury. Many of its 273 rooms and suites feature incredible views of the Public Garden, so request ahead. Staff are ready to cater to any whim. Rooms with fireplaces come with seasonal fireplace butlers, while all rooms have bath attendants to personalize bubbles dependent on aches and pains or merely fragrance preference. A rooftop restaurant is the pinnacle of power dining, while the bar downstairs brings back the see-and-be-seen scene of this grand dame's early years of the Roaring Twenties, when the hotel began life as the original Ritz-Carlton in town.

MAP 4: 1 Newbury St., 617/536-5700

The Colonnade Hotel $$

Centrally located across the street from the Prudential Center and atop the MBTA E Line, the Colonnade offers luxury accommodations to tourists, business travelers, and visitors to nearby colleges. Rooms feature extremely fast Internet, streaming capability on large televisions, and pet accessories for four-legged guests (both the barking and meowing kind). The Colonnade's crown jewel, though, is its rooftop pool, a Boston summer favorite free of charge to guests.

MAP 4: 120 Huntington Ave., 617/424-7000, http://colonnadehotel.com

Fairmont Copley Plaza $$

Designed by Henry Janeway Hardenbergh, the Fairmont Copley Plaza is the shorter sister of Manhattan's Plaza Hotel. Renovated in 2012 as part of its centennial celebration, the hotel may be modernized but still retains elements of its historic, Brahmin past. Carly Copley, the hotel's canine ambassador, greets guests at the front door before they whisk through the Versailles-style hall of mirrors en route to check-in. Guests can enjoy cozy lodging with utmost convenience: The hotel is walkable from two rapid transit lines.

MAP 4: 138 St. James Ave., 617/267-5300, http://fairmont.com

Lenox Hotel $$

Steps from the Boston Marathon finish line and other top tourist attractions, the Lenox is one of Boston's favorite boutique hotels. Its lobby is a sophisticated spot to relax around the fireplace, while the rooms upstairs are cozy and classic with nightly turndown service and fireplace attendants for certain suites. The Judy Garland Suite, named for the celebrity-in-residence who spent time here in 1968, offers stunning views, a marble master bath, and even a red ruby slipper.

MAP 4: 61 Exeter St., 617/536-5300, http://lenoxhotel.com

South End
Map 5

Staypineapple Boston $$
Economical travelers will find this a welcome sanctuary in the heart of the South End. Located above Trophy Room, a popular LGBTQ-friendly restaurant and bar, Staypineapple Boston offers clean, modern rooms at a fraction of the cost of a Back Bay boutique hotel. Each of the 56 guest rooms is smoke-free and has free Wi-Fi. Mere blocks from Back Bay Station and bustling Copley Square, the property is a convenient pick for visitors.
MAP 5: 26 Chandler St., 617/482-3450, www.chandlerinn.com

The Revolution Hotel $
Affordability and luxury aren't mutually exclusive at this South End hotel aimed at stylish travelers and Boston's revolutionary history of firsts. The property features well-decorated "Bath: In Room" and "Bath: Down the Hall" guest rooms sized better for sleeping than lingering. Pillow and spiritual menus afford guests a variety of pillows and religious texts at their beck and call.
MAP 5: 40 Berkeley St., 617/848-9200, www.therevolutionhotel.com

Fenway and Kenmore Square
Map 6

✪ Hotel Commonwealth $$$
After a $50 million makeover in 2015, the 245-room Hotel Commonwealth appeals to all bases. The new Fenway Park Suite was built in partnership with the Boston Red Sox and features a balcony with original seats from Fenway and, yes, direct views into the legendary ballpark. Classic Commonwealth rooms overlooking Kenmore Square are large by Boston standards and were given a refresh in the renovation, while newer rooms are on the Fenway side (guests take note—these rooms also overlook the bustling Massachusetts Turnpike but are largely soundproof).
MAP 6: 500 Commonwealth Ave., 617/933-5000, www.hotelcommonwealth.com

✪ The Verb $$
This isn't your grandparents' motor lodge. The Verb was born when an old Howard Johnson was renovated into 93 hip, contemporary rooms in the heart of Fenway. Decorated throughout with music memorabilia, the hotel

features a see-and-be-seen pool during the summer, and the small lobby houses attentive staff and a coffee cart with Twinkies and other snacks.

MAP 6: 1271 Boylston St., 617/566-4500, www.theverbhotel.com

Hotel Buckminster $

Bargains are increasingly hard to find at Boston's notoriously expensive hotels, but the Hotel Buckminster affords guests decent, simply furnished rooms at an incredible location. The hotel is a block away from the MBTA Kenmore Station (serving the Green Line) and ideal for those visiting students at nearby Boston University or attending a summer concert at Fenway Park. Book directly through the hotel and receive a $10 dining credit.

MAP 6: 645 Beacon St., 617/236-7050, www.bostonhotelbuckminster.com

South Boston   Map 7

Envoy Hotel $$

The Envoy brings modern flair to the shores of Fort Point Channel. Its lobby features sleek lounge areas and a high-definition touchscreen virtual billiards table alongside the decadent Outlook Kitchen and Bar. Guests flock to the cozy, upscale rooms with city and water views (ask to be on the Fort Point Channel side), while locals and tourists alike will spend hours waiting for a chance to sip cocktails at the Envoy's über-popular rooftop bar.

MAP 7: 70 Sleeper St., 617/338-3030, www.theenvoyhotel.com

Seaport Boston Hotel $$

Amid the countless convention hotels spread across the city, the Seaport's original hotel is also its most local. The independent Seaport Hotel was the first in the neighborhood when it opened in 1998 and has been updated consistently, keeping top billing in local rankings. Extremely hospitable team members, a pillow library (because why shouldn't your head get pampered, too?), three delicious dining options, and chicly decorated rooms make the Seaport a stylish way to stay in a truly Boston property.

MAP 7: 1 Seaport Ln., 617/385-4000, www.seaportboston.com

Westin Boston Waterfront $$

Conventioneers in town for an event at the adjacent Boston Convention and Exhibition Center will appreciate this on-site hotel. Connected to the event hall and offering harbor views (which get better on higher floors), the Westin is surprisingly more personable than a typical chain. A large, leafy lobby offers ample work nooks. One of Boston's improv comedy theaters (Laugh Boston), a coffee bar, and one of the city's favorite parks (Lawn on D) are all here as well.

MAP 7: 425 Summer St., 617/532-4600, www.westinbostonwaterfront.com

Yotel $$

Just because room is sparse in the city doesn't mean efficient spaces should be any less chic. Yotel is a European brand that opened its 360-"cabin" hotel in the summer of 2017 and has quickly become a favorite among younger travelers. Featuring a popular rooftop bar that also plays movies in the summer, an on-site MBTA station, and monsoon showers in every room,

Yotel proves smaller doesn't come at the cost of convenience or luxury. **MAP 7:** 65 Seaport Blvd., 617/377-4747, www.yotel.com

Cambridge

Map 8

Charles Hotel $$$

This Harvard Square hotel offers views of the Charles River as well as an easy commute to nearby colleges and downtown Boston, making it a favorite for visiting speakers and parents alike. Tech-savvy rooms, an on-site spa and library, as well as several dining and drinking options make the Charles a destination in itself.
MAP 8: 1 Bennett St., Cambridge, 617/864-1200, www.charleshotel.com

Charles Hotel

Hotel Marlowe $$

The posh Hotel Marlowe gives guests a boutique hotel experience with incredible views of the Charles River and downtown Boston. Guests are treated to an evening wine reception and can embrace the great outdoors with the hotel's loaner bikes and kayaks. Looking for extra company in your room? The hotel even offers "Guppy Love," a goldfish program where they'll bring a finned friend to your room—don't worry, they'll feed him!
MAP 8: 25 Edwin H. Land Blvd., Cambridge, 617/868-8000, www. hotelmarlowe.com

The Kendall Hotel $$

Crimson isn't limited to Harvard, but the red at the Kendall Hotel has a different meaning. This boutique hotel is located in the historic Engine 7 Firehouse and is decorated in a theme to match. The hotel's 77 rooms and suites are like stepping into a folk painting, and guests are treated to a breakfast buffet each morning. Steps from the Kendall/MIT MBTA stop, the hotel is easily accessible to all points in the city.
MAP 8: 350 Main St., Cambridge, 617/577-1300, www.kendallhotel.com

Greater Boston

Residence Inn Boston Harbor on Tudor Wharf $$

The Residence Inn is an excellent, economical way to be a part of the action but from a comfortable distance. Located at the Tudor Wharf marina with skyline views, this all-suite hotel is a short walk from the North End and several transit lines. If you're thinking of a longer stay in Boston, this is a great way to have the comforts of home while you visit.

MAP 9: 34-44 Charles River Ave., Boston, 617/242-9000, www.marriott.com

DAY TRIPS

Greater Boston spans from the tides of the Atlantic Ocean to the rolling terrain of central Massachusetts. History manages to weave its way into all the nooks and crannies of the bustling region, making for road (and boat) trips that can't be missed.

Fast ferries depart from Long Wharf downtown and the World Trade Center in the Seaport to whisk passengers to the Outer Cape in 90 minutes. The eclectic Provincetown has been a historic haven for LGBTQ travelers for decades. More mainstream tourists are beginning to realize that the retail and nightlife along Commercial Street, coupled with the town's dune-laden beaches, make for an incredible vacation. From cozy inns to crowded dance floors, the town is a convenient choose-your-own adventure.

Provincetown

Hop aboard a seasonal Salem ferry from Long Wharf and get spellbound by Salem, the North Shore town with an infamous past. While Halloween and landmarks associated with the witch trials of the 1600s dominate most visitor itineraries, it's also home to many of the region's top seafood restaurants and the Peabody Essex Museum, which has one of the country's largest collections of Asian art.

Road warriors can take comfort in the relative ease of getting to major attractions throughout the metro region via Boston's system of highways. Plymouth, accessible via I-93 and Route 3 south of the city (as though you are driving to Cape Cod), is a history buff's dream, connecting visitors to early America at Plimoth Plantation and Plymouth Rock. Lexington and Concord, accessed via Route 2 to the west from Cambridge, bring the Revolutionary War to life at Minute Man National Historical Park while also revealing the region's literary

HIGHLIGHTS

✪ **BEST QUICK SUMMER RETREAT:** Grab a picnic or plan for a Thursday clambake dinner and spend a chunk of your day at Spectacle Island, filled with hiking, beaches, and outdoor summer treats (page 200).

✪ **BEST PARK WITH A PAST:** Relive Revere's Midnight Ride and the birth of a nation at Minute Man National Historical Park, commemorating the opening battle of the American Revolution (page 201).

✪ **BEST FRIGHT:** Salem's Witch House is the only structure in town still standing with ties to the infamous witch trials (page 206).

✪ **BEST SURPRISE:** Salem's Peabody Essex Museum is one of the world's top art museums (page 208).

✪ **BEST HISTORY:** Plymouth may have landed in the history books, but the Pilgrim Monument and Provincetown Museum tells the tale of the Pilgrims' first stop in what became the United States (page 209).

Salem's Witch House

Day Trips

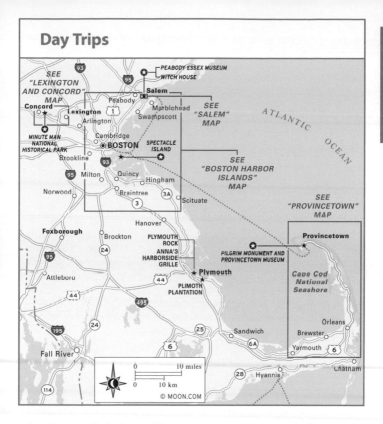

SEE "LEXINGTON AND CONCORD" MAP

PEABODY ESSEX MUSEUM
WITCH HOUSE

Salem

SEE "SALEM" MAP

ATLANTIC OCEAN

Peabody

Concord
Lexington
Arlington
Marblehead
Swampscott

MINUTE MAN NATIONAL HISTORICAL PARK

Cambridge
BOSTON

SPECTACLE ISLAND

SEE "BOSTON HARBOR ISLANDS" MAP

Brookline

Milton
Quincy
Hingham

SEE "PROVINCETOWN" MAP

Norwood
Braintree

Provincetown

Scituate

Hanover

PILGRIM MONUMENT AND PROVINCETOWN MUSEUM

Foxborough

Brockton

PLYMOUTH ROCK
ANNA'S HARBORSIDE GRILLE

Cape Cod National Seashore

Attleboro

Plymouth

PLIMOTH PLANTATION

Fall River

Orleans

Sandwich
Brewster

Yarmouth

Hyannis
Chatham

0   10 miles
0   10 km
© MOON.COM

foundation with the home of Louisa May Alcott and Walden Pond, the natural muse of Henry David Thoreau.

If you're more about the great outdoors and the high seas, Boston Harbor Cruises is the best connection to the Boston Harbor Islands, a network of barrier islands scattered throughout the harbor. Home to hilly trails, breathtaking views of the ocean and Boston skyline, and even summer camping and clambakes, the Boston Harbor Islands connect one to nature with just a 20 minute boat ride.

PLANNING YOUR TIME

Whether you're a first-time visitor with a few days to fill your itinerary

or a returning guest looking to see a different side to Greater Boston, there are several excursions a short ride away from the city. Each destination can be explored in a day or less, but some, like Provincetown, might leave you wanting to book a room and stick around for added time. Lexington and Concord to the northwest can be explored in as little as a morning or afternoon, depending on if you just wish to wander Minute Man National Historical Park or stick around and venture into both towns. The Boston Harbor Islands have a similar time frame, though travel time is dictated by ferry schedules. Salem and Provincetown can take the longest to reach if traveling by car, whereas taking a ferry to each town can cut down on travel time by avoiding notoriously congested Massachusetts highways, especially the Provincetown fast ferries in comparison to driving the entire length of Cape Cod.

Travel via car, although unnecessary with the exception of visiting Lexington and Concord, can provide the most freedom, should you decide to stop in other New England towns along the way to places like Salem and Provincetown. Plan for at least one night in Provincetown if you decide to travel by car, as the drive alone can take several hours during peak summer travel times.

All day trips, with the exception of the Boston Harbor Islands, are accessible via highway, albeit in different directions. Lexington and Concord, to the northwest, are quickly reached via Route 2 from Cambridge. Salem is reached by taking I-93 north and then continuing north on I-95. The easiest way to Provincetown is via the 90-minute fast ferries from Long Wharf or the World Trade Center in the Seaport, but you can drive by taking I-93 south to Route 3 south and then Route 6 east once you cross the bridge onto Cape Cod. The Boston Harbor Islands are only accessible via Boston Harbor Cruises ferries.

It would be difficult to combine trips unless you have a rental car, which would permit Lexington, Concord, and Salem to be accessed, as all are convenient to I-95.

Traffic is always a problem in Boston, but it's particularly awful 3pm-7pm on weekdays. The southern highways to Cape Cod are congested on summer weekends; utilize public transportation and ferries when possible. Salem is congested during the month of October, and the Boston Harbor Islands get crowded during the summer. Provincetown is extremely busy during the summer, especially during the week of July 4, July's Bear Week, Carnival in August, and Halloween.

While most of the region is compact and has the same weather, Provincetown is an outlier and can sometimes have sunny, breezy days while Boston experiences thunderstorms, and vice versa. Be sure to check the weather before venturing to the Outer Cape.

Boston Harbor Islands

The 34 islands that make up Boston Harbor Islands National Recreation Area offer a collection of hiking trails, sandy beaches, and incredible views of Boston's skyline. Ferry service in warmer weather whisks you from Long Wharf to island adventures and fun in the sun. Summer jazz concerts, beach yoga seminars, and Civil War-era forts are just a few of the ways you can pass time on the islands, so plan most of your day around a visit.

GEORGES ISLAND

Georges Island has a storied past, as during the Civil War it housed a prison for Confederate soldiers. The tale of the Lady in Black, rumored to have been hanged on the island after she failed to break her husband out of

Boston Harbor Islands

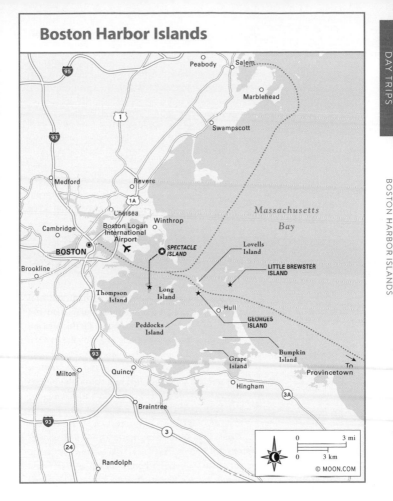

the prison, makes this island perfect for ghost hunters. She is said to reside amid the archways of Fort Warren, a Civil War-era fort that was utilized through World War II before being decommissioned in 1947. The fort also features a museum and guided tours. Spend a few hours on the island to picnic and take a scenic walk.

GETTING THERE

Boston Harbor Cruises (www. bostonharborcruises.com) operates a Boston Harbor Islands ferry from Long Wharf to Georges Island from early May to Columbus Day. Tickets are $19.95 for adults, $14.95 for seniors, and $12.95 for children. Families of four can get a group rate of $49. The ferry takes approximately 40 minutes and can get windy and chilly in the early and later part of the season, so bring a jacket if planning to stay outside on the deck.

✪ SPECTACLE ISLAND

The 105-acre Spectacle Island is a nature lover's best friend, with 5 miles (8 km) of hiking trails, high hills with 360-degree views of the harbor and skyline, and equally as picturesque beaches. Once you disembark from the ferry, head up the pier onto the island, where you'll be greeted with a visitors center and refreshment stand perfect for grabbing lunch to take to the peak of the hike. Learn about the island and then head out from the trailhead near the visitor stand. The hike is a choose-your-own-adventure between a gradual incline and a very steep direct trail to North Drumlin, the highest point in Boston Harbor. A gazebo and panoramic views of downtown and the entire harbor await at the top. A sandy (and lifeguarded) beach is close to the pier and is a great place to cool off in the typically chilly waters of Boston Harbor. Thursday night clambakes are popular in the summer and require reservations via Boston Harbor Cruises. Clambake tickets ($99 adults, $70 children) include round-trip ferry travel, the clambake, lawn games, water, and soft drinks.

GETTING THERE

Boston Harbor Cruises (www.bostonharborcruises.com) operates a Boston Harbor Islands ferry from Long Wharf to Spectacle Island from early May to Columbus Day. Tickets are $19.95 for adults, $14.95 for seniors, and $12.95 for children. Families of four can get a group rate of $49. The ferry takes approximately 20 minutes and can get windy and chilly in the early and later part of the season, so bring a jacket if planning to stay outside on the deck. Thursday clambake ferries leave Long Wharf at 6:30pm and return to Boston at 9pm.

Spectacle Island in Boston Harbor

LITTLE BREWSTER ISLAND

The rocky outer island of Little Brewster is one of the farthest from downtown Boston. It's also home to the first lighthouse in America: The original was built in 1716 while the current one dates to 1783. The Coast Guard still operates the light, which has a beam that can be viewed as far as 27 miles (43 km) away. The only way to visit the island is if you take part in a three-hour Boston Light Climbing Tour that features a park ranger-guided tour on the island's history and geography. The height-averse might be deterred from climbing to the top of the lighthouse, but the one of a kind views (and photo opportunities) are worth confronting those towering fears. Bring a picnic with you, as concessions are not offered on the island. The island is not ADA accessible.

GETTING THERE

Ferry service to Little Brewster Island is only offered as part of the greater **Boston Harbor Lighthouse Tour** (www.bostonharborislands.org/little-brewster-island). Tours are offered on Saturdays in warmer months at 1pm from mid-June until the beginning of October. The entire tour, including round-trip travel, lasts two hours. Tickets are $35 for adults, $30 for seniors, and $25 for children.

Lexington and Concord

The site of the first battle of the American Revolution, the suburbs of Lexington and Concord are a must-visit for history buffs. A rental car is needed to make the 30-minute drive up Route 2 from downtown. Visit Minute Man National Historical Park to see where Paul Revere was captured on his midnight ride and to take in Battle Green in Lexington and the Wayside in Concord. Nearby Walden Pond in Concord is an added literary excursion, while the town's Monument Square is a great place to grab a bite before heading back to the city.

LEXINGTON
SIGHTS
✪ Minute Man National Historical Park

It's more than the Revolutionary War at this national park. **Minute Man National Historical Park** (3113 Marrett Rd., Concord, 978/369-6993, www.nps.gov/mima) honors the Battles of Lexington and Concord, the site of the first shots of the American Revolution. It also is home to Wayside, which was the home to three iconic American authors: Margaret Sidney, Louisa May Alcott, and Nathaniel Hawthorne. Historical reenactments take place on Patriots' Day in April each year, while guided ranger tours run daily during the summer and into October. There are several paths one can take through Minute Man National Historical Park, but it is best to orientate oneself with the history of the battlegrounds at the Minute Man Visitor Center. Located at the eastern side of the park, the center features a theater to view an introductory film that depicts Revere's ride and each of the significant battles at Lexington Green, the Battle Road, and North

Lexington and Concord

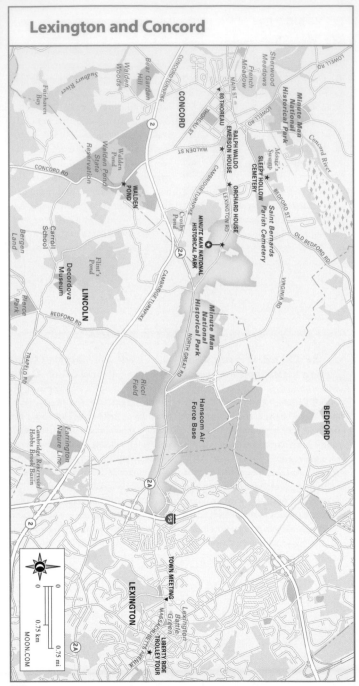

THE BATTLES OF LEXINGTON AND CONCORD

It was the shot heard 'round the world. The April 19, 1775, Battles of Lexington and Concord launched the American Revolution. While tension had been rising between the 13 colonies and their mother country, Great Britain, for years, it was the night of Paul Revere's Midnight Ride when British troops moved across the region to seize colonial arms stores. Colonists and the troops had a confrontation in Lexington, and the fighting escalated into battle. The scrappy militia of 700 prevailed, and the "Redcoats" retreated. It took years of fighting for the colonies to gain their independence in 1783.

Bridge. The visitors center is on the historic Battle Road just west of Lexington. Visitors can walk the Battle Road from the visitors center toward North Bridge, but history buffs who favor a chronological visit will likely prefer to begin where the "shot heard 'round the world" was fired at North Bridge (where there is another visitors center, albeit without the film presentation) and walk the Battle Road to Lexington.

Liberty Ride Trolley Tour

Rather than worry about hitting all the top sights in Lexington and Concord on your own, hop aboard a **Liberty Ride Trolley Tour** (1875 Massachusetts Ave., Lexington, 781/862-1450, www.tourlexington.us, $28 adults, $25 seniors, $12 students). The trolley departs from Lexington and features an in-character guide doling out historical and literary facts as you go down Battle Road. From the start of the war and the literature that also sprang from the area, you'll

a trail in Minute Man National Historical Park

realize just how important the two towns are to the fabric of America.

RESTAURANTS

Town Meeting (2027 Massachusetts Ave., Lexington, 781/301-6660, www.innathastingspark.com, restaurant Mon. 7am-10:30am, Tues.-Fri. 7am-10:30am, 11:30am-2:30pm, and 5:30pm-9pm, Sat. 7am-1pm and 5pm-9:30pm, Sun. 8am-2:30pm, $24-46) gives even the snootiest of palates in Boston a reason to book it to the burbs, as this Relais & Chateaux property (part of the Inn at Hastings Park) is viewed as one of Boston's best. Upscale New England fare is plated in innovative ways, à la the roasted cod with lobster-chorizo broth. Order an Uber so you're able to relax with several of the wine and cocktail offerings. Note the bar stays open until 11pm Tuesday-Saturday.

The North End is not the lone spot in Greater Boston for delectable Italian fare. The dining room noise and crowds at **Il Casale Cucina Campana and Bar** (1727 Massachusetts Ave., Lexington, 781/538-5846, www.ilcasalelexington.com, Mon.-Thurs. 5pm-9:30pm, Fri.-Sat. 5pm-10pm, Sun. 1pm-8pm, $22-30) should be seen as a positive: The food here is that good. Begin with a burrata cheese first course, meander through grilled Spanish octopus and fried artichoke antipasti, and segue into house-made pastas for a culinary walk through Italy.

GETTING THERE

A rental car is needed to get to Lexington, which is accessed via a 30-minute drive west from Boston on Route 2. Zipcar users will find cars throughout Boston. Most major rental car companies have locations throughout the city, particularly near Long Wharf, Back Bay Station and the Prudential Center, and in Harvard Square.

CONCORD

SIGHTS

Walden Pond

Walden Pond (915 Walden St., Concord, 978/369-3254, www.mass.gov, daily 7am-7pm, admission free, parking $8 Massachusetts residents, $15 out-of-state visitors) is part of the 335-acre Walden Pond State Reservation and has captivated nature lovers and the literary-minded thanks to Henry David Thoreau depicting his time living in a cabin on the north side of the body of water in *Walden*. More popular with dogs and their human companions these days than the Romantics, Walden Pond still inspires those looking to be the brains behind the next great American novel. Go on a leisurely stroll around the pond's nearly 2-mile (3.2-km) perimeter, boat on the water (there are no rentals on-site, but there is a boat ramp if you want to bring your own), or visit a replica of Thoreau's cabin.

Walden Pond

Orchard House

One of the most iconic novels in American literature was both written and set in this historic home in Concord. Orchard House (399 Lexington Rd., Concord, 978/369-4118, www.louisamayalcott.org, Nov.-Mar. Mon.-Fri. 11am-3pm, Sat. 10am-4:30pm, Sun. 1pm-4:30pm, Apr.-Oct. Mon.-Sat. 10am-4:30pm, Sun. 11am-4:30pm, adults $10, seniors and students $8, children $5) was the longtime home of the Alcott family, including daughter Louisa May Alcott. She penned *Little Women* in the clapboard home on a desk built for her by her father. The novel, based on the activities of her sisters, is still widely read 150 years after its first printing. The home has been preserved to include many Alcott family belongings and looks largely the same as it did when the family lived there. It is open for guided tours daily with the exception of major holidays.

Sleepy Hollow Cemetery

Concord was home to a litany of America's leading thinkers and authors and is also home to several of their final resting places. Sleepy Hollow Cemetery (34 Bedford St., Concord, 978/318-3233, daily 7am-7pm) is of particular importance as it includes "Author's Ridge," a hill that is home to the graves of Louisa May Alcott, Ralph Waldo Emerson, Nathaniel Hawthorne, and Henry David Thoreau. Each of the writers lived in the area, and their legacy makes the cemetery a pertinent pilgrimage for bibliophiles, who often leave notes in remembrance of their favorite writers.

Ralph Waldo Emerson House

Concord's early stake in literary history is partially owed to resident Ralph Waldo Emerson, who made it the center of the American Transcendentalist movement. The philosopher moved into this home (28 Cambridge Turnpike, Concord, 978/369-2236, www.ralphwaldoemersonhouse.org, mid-Apr.-Oct. Thurs.-Sat. 10am-4:30pm, Sun. 1pm-4:30pm, adults $10, seniors/children/students $8, children under 7 free), which he named "Bush," shortly after marrying his wife Lydia in 1835. Emerson lived in the home for the rest of his life, entertaining the likes of Louisa May Alcott and Henry David Thoreau and writing seminal works like *Self-Reliance*. The house today is open to the public as a museum and remains largely the same as it was following a renovation in 1873.

a replica of Henry David Thoreau's cabin at Walden Pond

RESTAURANTS

Even a minuteman deserves refined farm-to-table cuisine, and 80 Thoreau (80 Thoreau St., Concord, 978/318-0008, www.80thoreau.com, Mon.-Tues. 5:30pm-10:30pm, Wed.-Thurs. 5:30pm-10.45pm, Fri.-Sat 5pm-11:30pm, $26-32) serves just that in a shabby-chic dining room five minutes from Henry David Thoreau's cabin on

Walden Pond. From bar burgers to seasonal entrées paired with an über-expensive bottle of wine, this venue is almost as much of a destination as the cabin up the road.

Take the whole family to Helen's Restaurant (17 Main St., Concord, 978/369-9885, www.helensrestaurantconcord.com, Mon.-Sat. 7am-9pm, Sun. 7am-8pm, $5-12) after a morning or afternoon at Minute Man National Historical Park. Simple, standard, no-fuss diner fare usually runs under $10 (apart from a few organic offerings). Counter service and a cash-only atmosphere make Helen's a true step back in time in this historic town.

GETTING THERE

A rental car is needed to get to Concord, which is accessed via a 30-minute drive west from Boston on Route 2. Zipcar users will find cars throughout Boston. Most major rental car companies have locations throughout the city, particularly near Long Wharf, Back Bay Station and the Prudential Center, and in Harvard Square.

Salem

For locals, Salem is primarily a charming seaside town on the North Shore, but the town's sordid past and the legacy of its infamous witch trials attract one million visitors a year. Halloween is the best (and most crowded) time to visit. The Witch House is certain to satisfy your fright fix, and the Peabody Essex Museum, with its vast collection of Asian art, is well worth a visit. Ferry service from downtown Boston to Salem is the easiest way to commute for an afternoon and evening on the North Shore, but a rental car offers more freedom with time. Be sure to pack a copy of *The Crucible* to read on your ride into town!

SIGHTS
✪ Witch House

Witch House (310 ½ Essex St., Salem, 978/744-8815, www.thewitchhouse.org, mid-Mar.-mid-Nov. daily 10am-5pm, mid-Nov.-mid-Mar. Thurs.-Sun. noon-4pm, $10.25 adults, $8.25 seniors, $6.25 children) is Salem's only remaining structure with direct ties to the Salem witch trials. While it is unclear exactly when the 17th-century home was built, it is known that Judge Jonathan Corwin, who looked into accusations of devilish deeds during the height of the trials, purchased the home in 1675, 17 years before the notorious witchcraft trials. Despite his legal standing, Corwin's own mother-in-law was accused of witchcraft by a servant. Tour the home and gain insight to the trials and the Corwin family history.

House of the Seven Gables

The impervious gray clapboard of Salem's House of the Seven Gables (115 Derby St., Salem, 978/744-0991, www.7gables.org, hours vary, adults $16, seniors/college students $15, teenagers $13, children $11) sticks out for, obviously, its numerous gables and claim to literary history. The mansion, built in the 1600s, inspired Nathaniel Hawthorne to pen *The House of the*

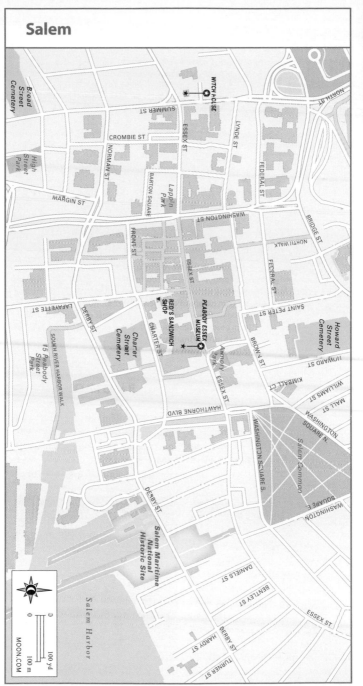

Salem

Broad Street Cemetery

High Street Park

WITCH HOUSE

SUMMER ST

ESSEX ST

CROMBIE ST

LYNDE ST

NORMAN ST

FEDERAL ST

BARTON SQUARE

Lappin Park

MARGIN ST

WASHINGTON ST

FRONT ST

ESSEX ST

BRIDGE ST

NORTH WALK

FEDERAL ST

LAFAYETTE ST

DERBY ST

RED'S SANDWICH SHOP

PEABODY ESSEX MUSEUM

SAINT PETER ST

Howard Street Cemetery

Charter Street Cemetery

CHARTER ST

HOWARD ST

15 Peabody Harbor Walk

SOUTH RIVER HARBOR WALK

Armory Park

ESSEX ST

BROWN ST

KIMBALL CT

WILLIAMS ST

MALL ST

WASHINGTON SQUARE N

HAWTHORNE BLVD

WASHINGTON SQUARE S.

Salem Common

DERBY ST

WASHINGTON SQUARE E.

Salem Maritime National Historic Site

DANIELS ST

BENTLEY ST

ESSEX ST

HARDY ST

TURNER ST

ABBY ST

Salem Harbor

0 100 yd

0 100 m

MOON.COM

SALEM WITCH TRIALS

While the Salem witch trials are heavily depicted on stage, in film, and in literature, it is sometimes easy to forget there is fact at the root of all the fiction. The hearings and prosecutions of people accused of witchcraft in colonial New England spanned from early 1692 to 1693. Ultimately, 20 people were executed for their alleged ties to witchcraft. An additional five, including two infants, died in prison.

The hysteria surrounding the trials at the time has since been regarded as a lesson in American history of the dangers of isolationism, extremism, and a faulty legal system. Historians view the events as steering the burgeoning country away from a theocratic system. The victims were commemorated at the 300th anniversary of the trials in 1992, and all were officially exonerated by the Massachusetts legislature in 2001.

Seven Gables, his Gothic follow-up to *The Scarlet Letter.* The home is open to the public, who can take a tour that features a secret passageway and important history of Hawthorne and Salem.

❸ Peabody Essex Museum

Salem's **Peabody Essex Museum** (161 Essex St., Salem, 978/745-9500, www. pem.org, Tues.-Sun. 10am-5pm, adults $20, seniors $18, students $12, children free) dates to 1799. It was founded by a society of the town's captains who had sailed beyond the Cape of Good Hope and Cape Horn and returned with artifacts from Africa, Asia, and beyond. Today, the museum houses one of America's most extensive collections of Asian art. Ranked as one of the country's best and fastest-growing

the Peabody Essex Museum

museums, the Peabody Essex has 1.3 million pieces in its vast collection.

RESTAURANTS

Sometimes all you want out of a quaint town is simple fare, and **Red's Sandwich Shop** (15 Central St., Salem, 978/745-3527, www. redssandwichshop.com, Mon.-Sat. 5am-3pm, Sun. 6am-1pm, $5-12) is happy to oblige. This no-frills venue offers plenty of delicious diner staples for under $10. Friendly waiters are more than happy to give ideas to fill out your itinerary after one of the many omelets or a lunch special.

It's criminal to be this close to the sea and not taste some of its fruits. **Turners Seafood** (43 Church St., Salem, 978/745-7665, www.turners-seafood.com, Sun.-Thurs. 11:30am-9pm, Fri.-Sat. 11:30am-10pm, $17-30) is one spot where it's okay to skip the clam chowder, because the lobster bisque can't be beat. Cocktails in the bar coupled with hearty seafood staples like fried clams and scallops are a great way to pregame for a haunted tour later in the evening.

The seafood at **Finz Seafood and Grill** (76 Wharf St., Salem, 978/744-8485, www.hipfinz.com, Sun.-Thurs. 11:30am-10pm, Fri.-Sat. 11:30am-11pm, $23-30) seems particularly fresh because the restaurant is essentially on

Salem Harbor. Finz offers refined surf and turf offerings, including steamed lobsters and steaks. An outdoor patio on which to enjoy the creative cocktail menu keeps things lively in warmer months, while the venue's location makes it a perfect stop during a downtown shopping excursion.

GETTING THERE

Salem is easily reached via **Boston Harbor Cruises** ferry service (www.bostonharborcruises.com, $45 round-trip adults, $35 children) from Long Wharf to Salem Harbor. Commuter rail service is offered between Boston's North Station and Salem. Road warriors can drive to Salem via I-93 and I-95 from downtown Boston.

Provincetown

The Kennedys and their Camelot lore put Cape Cod on the map; however, unlike the rest of the region, eclectic Provincetown isn't exactly known for Nantucket red shorts and other preppy paraphernalia. Home to quaint inns, myriad nightlife options, and numerous galleries, this funky town at the tip of the Cape is a haven for artists, writers, and the LGBTQ community. Easily accessible from Boston via 90-minute fast ferry from mid-May through the fall, P-town is also home to two of America's top beaches.

SIGHTS
✪ Pilgrim Monument and Provincetown Museum

Before the Pilgrims made landfall in Plymouth, they spent five weeks in what became Provincetown. That period is commemorated by the 252-foot **Pilgrim Monument and Provincetown Museum** (1 High Pole Rd., Provincetown, 508/487-1310, www.pilgrim-monument.org, daily 9am-7pm, adults $14, seniors $11, children $6). The tallest structure in P-town, the monument was completed in 1910 and dedicated by President William Taft. While it was largely panned by Bostonians at its opening, today it's treasured by sightseers looking to climb to the top for expansive views of the Atlantic Ocean and Cape Cod Bay. Whether you're looking for cardio with a view or just a way to burn off that extra lobster roll you had down the street at Canteen, a half hour or so climbing to the top of the monument and touring the museum is a small, wonderful slice of history to add to an otherwise raucous time in P-town.

Provincetown Beaches

Two of America's top-rated beaches, **Race Point** and **Herring Cove** (508/487-1256, www.capecodonline.com/beaches/provincetown), are in Provincetown. Herring Cove, the busier of the two, offers warmer water closer to Cape Cod Bay and is the more ideal if you're looking for sand between your toes while you watch an incredible sunset (it's actually one of the few East Coast beaches where you can catch the setting sun). Walk away from the crowds and you'll stumble onto "hidden" Herring Cove beach, where nude sunbathers tend to tan. Race Point, on the Atlantic side of the

Provincetown

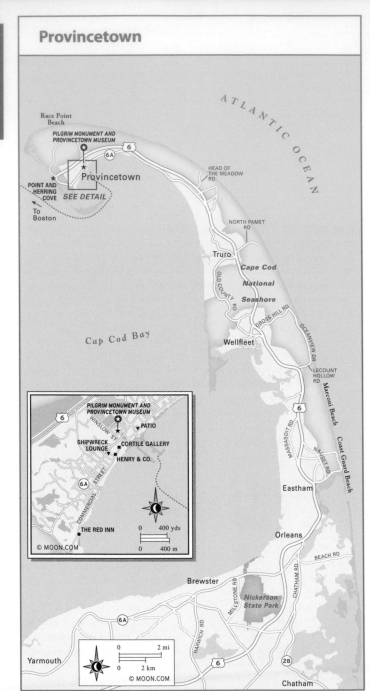

ATLANTIC OCEAN

Race Point Beach

PILGRIM MONUMENT AND PROVINCETOWN MUSEUM

6
6A

Provincetown

SEE DETAIL

POINT AND HERRING COVE

To Boston

HEAD OF THE MEADOW RD

NORTH PAMET RD

Truro

Cape Cod

National

Seashore

OLD COUNTY RD

GROSS HILL RD

OCEANVIEW DR

Wellfleet

Cap Cod Bay

LECOUNT HOLLOW RD

Marconi Beach

MASSASOIT RD

NAUSET RD

Coast Guard Beach

Eastham

PILGRIM MONUMENT AND PROVINCETOWN MUSEUM

PATIO

6

WINSLOW ST

SHIPWRECK LOUNGE

CORTILE GALLERY

HENRY & CO.

COMMERCIAL STREET

6A

THE RED INN

0   400 yds
0   400 m

© MOON.COM

Orleans

BEACH RD

CHATHAM RD

Brewster

MILLSTONE RD

Nickerson State Park

HARWICH RD

Yarmouth

0   2 mi
0   2 km

© MOON.COM

6

28

Chatham

Race Point beach in Provincetown

Cape, is more secluded and is where you'll find several sunset bonfires. The dunes separate parking areas from the sizable stretch of beach, and bike trails run off from the parking lot. While the crashing waves and scenery are beautiful, beachgoers should take caution: Sharks do occasionally appear off the coast. Grab lunch in town to bring with you before visiting either beach, as food offerings (and cell phone service) are sparse.

RESTAURANTS

The cozy outdoor dining area of **Patio** (328 Commercial St., Provincetown, 508/487-4003, www.ptownpatio. com, Sun.-Thurs. 11am-10pm, Fri.-Sat. 11am-11pm, $16-26) is an ideal summer hot spot when you're in the mood for nicer fare with a potent cocktail (which your waiter will ensure remains bottomless). While the raw bar and lobster dishes dominate the menu, seafood-averse guests will still have plenty of American dishes to choose from.

Not exactly fast-casual but not full-service either, **The Canteen** (225 Commercial St., Provincetown, 508/487-3800, www.thecanteenptown. com, daily 8am-10pm, $8-22) has amassed a following thanks to the frozen rosé (frosé) machine. The counter service offers delicious local fare like lobster rolls served up hot or cold, fish oil-fried Brussels sprouts, and fish-and-chips. Enjoy all on Canteen's back patio and beachfront dining area, and stick around for a few more

The Canteen

rounds at the beachy outdoor bar in the back, too.

Take a break from seafood and imbibe in some beer and burgers at **Local 186** (186 Commercial St., Provincetown, 508/487-7555, www.local186.com, Sun.-Thurs. noon-10pm, Fri.-Sat. noon-10:30pm, $14-26), which has a loyal clientele who clamber into the restored home on Commercial Street for an extensive list of gourmet beef creations. Get yours served French-style (fried onions) or as surf-and-turf (with poached lobster), or create your own and sit back and people-watch as the eclectic community whizzes by on the bustling thoroughfare.

NIGHTLIFE

Getting "wrek't" at the **Shipwreck Lounge** (10 Carver St., 508/487-9005, www.ptownlounge.com, summer daily 6pm-1am, spring and fall Thurs.-Sun. 5pm-1am, winter hours vary) is a popular pastime; this is a place for cocktails and catching up. It's also a popular spot just to grab a drink heading either to or from one of Commercial Street's dance clubs.

Billed as America's oldest gay bar, the **Atlantic House** (4-6 Masonic Pl., 508/487-3169, daily noon-1am)—or

Atlantic House

"A House"—offers history, an uneven dance floor (watch your step!), and potent albeit tiny cocktails. If the dance floor isn't mobbed, you can enjoy porthole windows, lanterns, and the stone fireplace. It's one of the few gay bars with a maritime aesthetic, likely a holdover from the town's whaling origins. Note it's cash-only here.

Whatever your mood, the **Crown & Anchor** (247 Commercial St., 508/487-1430, Wed.-Fri. 6pm-1am, Sat.-Sun. noon-1am) is the venue for you. The property, billed as Provincetown's largest entertainment complex, includes a wide array of attractions across several beachfront buildings. There's a seafood restaurant closest to Commercial Street that turns into a piano bar in the evenings, multiple dance clubs closer to the waterfront, a theater for comedy, cabaret, and drag queen shows (among others), and even an inn if you don't want to sleep too far from all the excitement. Belt out Broadway hits, sip vodka sodas and lip-sync along to Cher at Wave Bar, or sweat the night away with EDM throbbing on the perpetually crowded Paramount dance floor—the Crown & Anchor might actually have it all.

GALLERIES

Cortile Gallery (230 Commercial St., Provincetown, 508/487-4200, www.cortilegallery.com, July-Sept. daily 10:30am-10:30pm, Oct.-Dec. and Apr.-June daily 11am-5pm) houses one of the largest contemporary local art collections in the greater Provincetown artist colony. Oils, glass, sculptures, and photography are but a few of the works on display in this rich two-level space. Looking for more? Request to be taken to the gallery's studio down the street for more selections.

Step into a quaint West End home,

and you'll find yourself surrounded by the paintings, sculpture, and furniture of local artist **Adam Peck Gallery** (142 Commercial St., Provincetown, 508/274-8298, www.adampeckgallery. com, summer Sun.-Thurs. 10:30am-5pm, Fri.-Sat. 10:30am-5pm and 7pm-9pm, fall-spring hours vary). His simple, clean pieces often feature homes, lighthouses, and other Cape staples, making him a favorite in many a local beach house.

SHOPS

While Commercial Street is lined with venues to buy a kitschy T-shirt, a proper haberdasher is harder to come by. **Henry & Co.** (210 Commercial St., Provincetown, 508/487-6215, www.henryptown.com, Memorial Day-Labor Day daily 10am-11pm, off-season hours vary) brings a mix of casual and refined fashion and shoes perfect for all occasions both on your vacation and back home. Friendly staff help with sizes and aren't shy about giving a gentle style nudge to get you into something you might not normally pick for your closet. You can thank them later.

Anyone can get a plain-Jane Cape Cod T-shirt, but Paul Nesbit's **Mate Provincetown Inc.** (349 Commercial St., Provincetown, 415/407-4352, www.mateprovincetowninc.com, daily 10am-8pm) offers truly unique gifts and apparel inspired by the quirky town it calls home. Mate features "Townie" T-shirts, Pilgrim Monument screen-printed designs, and other gifts that can only come from this special town at the tip of the Cape.

HOTELS

Just before you reach the end of Commercial Street in P-town's West End, you'll come across a vividly red house on the left. **The Red Inn** (15 Commercial St., Provincetown, 508/487-7334, www.theredinn. com, $194-650) has been around since 1805 (and housed President Theodore Roosevelt during a 1907 visit). Significantly renovated since, The Red Inn's guest rooms and suites offer some of the town's most luxurious waterfront accommodations. The inn's restaurant and back patio are extremely popular no matter the time of day and are great options if you feel like dining and imbibing closer to your room.

Billing itself as Provincetown's first boutique inn, **Salt House Inn** (6 Conwell St., Provincetown, 508/487-1911, www.salthouseinn.com, $195-320) has gathered national acclaim for its well-appointed, minimalist rooms. Accommodations are on the smaller side but feature luxurious amenities and come with breakfast in the lobby. Splurge on the Loft, a high-beamed space complete with a claw-foot tub in the middle of the room.

Salt House Inn

GETTING THERE

The easiest way to reach Provincetown is via the **Bay State Cruises** (www. baystatecruisecompany.com) or

Boston Harbor Cruises (www. bostonharborcruises.com) fast ferries that depart from Boston's World Trade Center and Long Wharf, respectively. Both charge $93 for a round-trip fare or $61 one-way for adults. Children are $68 round-trip or $39 one-way. The ferry trip takes 90 minutes. Cape Air flies from Boston Logan International Airport to Provincetown, and those with rental cars can reach the Outer Cape in 2-3 hours (depending on traffic) via Routes 3 and 6.

GETTING AROUND

Provincetown is an extremely walkable town and mainly concentrated around the main thoroughfares of Bradford and Commercial Streets. To get around with greater ease, bike rentals are easily available near the ferry dock at Arnold's Bike Rentals (329 Commercial St., 508/487-0844, www.provincetownbikes.com) or Provincetown Bike Rentals (136 Bradford St., 774/447-4539, www. ptownbikes.com) for around $25 for 24 hours or just under $100 for a week. Uber and Lyft are available but often come with a long wait. Most locals either use Cape Cab (www. capecabtaxi.com, 508/487-2222) or hail down Ptown Pedicabs (508/487-0660, www.ptownpedicabs.com) during busy summer months.

Plymouth

Boston may lay claim as one of America's founding cities, but nowhere can have the same kind of bragging rights as Plymouth. The waterfront town on Boston's South Shore was founded in 1620 with the arrival of British settlers (aka the Pilgrims) from the *Mayflower*. It is the birthplace of New England, one of the first settlements in what became the United States, and has celebrated Thanksgiving long before anyone else, as it is the site of the first Thanksgiving feast. Today, the tourist hot spot is home to several historical attractions, waterfront restaurants, and incredible views of Cape Cod Bay.

SIGHTS

Plimoth Plantation

Head to Plimoth Plantation (137 Warren Ave., Plymouth, 508/746-1622, www.plimoth.org, daily 9am-5pm, $30 adults, $28 seniors, $18 children ages 5-12, free to those 4 and under, outdoor portions open only in warmer months) for a hands-on account of what life in Massachusetts was like for the early settlers who came to be known as the Pilgrims. The nonprofit living history museum was founded in 1947 and uses re-creations based on records and artifacts passed down from the actual settlers. Historical interpreters are on hand to answer questions from their modern visitors and reenact life in the replica village. You can easily self-guide a visit through the plantation, as historical interpreters you meet along the way can answer any questions you have while interacting with history.

Plymouth Rock

When one studies Plymouth Rock (79 Water St., Plymouth, 508/747-5360, daily 24 hours, free) in history books, it might be easy to conjure images of a soaring cliff upon which the Pilgrims arrived in what became Massachusetts. Instead, visitors today are greeted by a caged stone about the size of a large coffee table. Plymouth Rock has been a symbol for the founding of America but was split in two pieces in 1774, with one piece carried to the town square to gin up support for American independence while the other piece was chipped away at by neighbors. The symbolic piece used for political moves was returned to its current resting place in 1880 and is open for public viewing.

Plymouth Rock

RESTAURANTS

Head to Plymouth Harbor for the history and stick around for the delicious Greek and American cuisine of **Anna's Harborside Grille** (145 Water St., Plymouth, 508/591-7372, www.annasharborsidegrille.com, daily 11:30am-1am, $16-27). Meze platters and lamb kebabs blend with baked scallops and waterfront views at this popular seaside venue, perfect for happy hour or a leisurely meal after being immersed in Pilgrim history.

For those looking for a more romantic time in Plymouth, the **1620 Wine Bar** (170 Water St., Plymouth, 508/746-3532, www.1620winery.com, Wed.-Thurs. 4pm-10pm, Fri. 4pm-11pm, Sat. noon-11pm, Sun. noon-8pm, $24-32) pours delectable varietals with waterfront views. Charcuterie and tapas pair with any of the vintner's selections, while live music heard both inside and outside adds to the atmosphere.

When hunger cravings are calling for New England classic surf-and-turf, look no further than **East Bay Grille** (173 Water St., Plymouth, 508/503-8739, www.eastbaygrille.com, daily 11am-10:30pm, $22-34). This spacious restaurant on the harbor may seem built for summer with its expansive patio and summery cocktail menu, but its grilled seafood and steak dishes draw large crowds year-round. Live music and other performances carry on at East Bay throughout the year, promising diners a lively pairing to whatever they select from the menu.

GETTING THERE

A rental car is needed to get to Plymouth, which is accessed via a 30-minute drive south on I-93 and Route 3. Zipcar users will find cars throughout the city. Most major rental car companies have locations throughout the city, particularly near Long Wharf, Back Bay Station and the Prudential Center, and in Harvard Square. **Plymouth & Brockton Street Railway Co.** (www.p-b.com) operates bus service between South Station in Boston and Plymouth, while limited commuter rail service runs daily between South Station and Plymouth on the Kingston/Plymouth line.

BACKGROUND

The Landscape

GEOGRAPHY

You could say Boston is America's original seaside town that grew up. Nestled north of Cape Cod at the convergence of the Charles River with the Atlantic Ocean, Boston is the only U.S. state capital with an oceanic coastline.

Boston Harbor

The rolling hills of Boston make the city's elevation range from 330 feet (101 m) above sea level at Bellevue Hill in the West Roxbury neighborhood to directly at sea level along the shore. The city was once even hillier. Beacon Hill remains, but the city (and its original form on the Shawmut Peninsula) was once composed of five hills: the "Trimountaine" (consisting of Beacon Hill, Pemberton Hill, and Mt. Vernon) as well as Copp's Hill and Fort Hill. The trio of hills is where some think Boston's original nickname of "The City Upon a Hill" came from (the real reason is under *Colonialism* in the *History* section later in this chapter), but it's actually just where Tremont Street got its name. The non-Beacon hills were eventually shaved down (and even Beacon Hill was to a lesser extent) to take the city from a small peninsula of fewer than 800 acres to the 89-square-mile (231-sq-km) metropolis of today.

The Charles cleaves Boston proper from neighboring cities of Cambridge and Watertown as well as the neighborhood of Charlestown, which is part of Boston. The only landmasses directly east of the city (before reaching Europe) are the Boston Harbor Islands. The Mystic River separates Charlestown from the neighboring towns of Chelsea and Everett. Boston Harbor also separates East Boston from the rest of the city. The Neponset River to the south separates southern Boston neighborhoods like Milton from the neighboring city of Quincy.

CLIMATE

Boston has a reputation for being cold, and it often lives up to the expectation. It's not uncommon to get a surprise blizzard in April, but some joke that the three months of summer make the remaining nine volatile months of the year worth it.

Boston does get all four seasons, which account for year-round tourism from guests with a variety of weather preferences. On average, Boston gets over 22 days of snow each year, with average annual accumulation reaching nearly 44 inches. The city broke its seasonal snowfall record in 2015 with a whopping 108.6 inches of snow. By comparison, the city's average rainfall is only 44 inches.

July and August tend to be the hottest months of the year, with average high temperatures reaching 81-82°F (27-28°C). January and February tend to be the coldest, with average high temperatures of 36°F (2°C) and 39°F (4°C), respectively.

While most buildings have heat, air-conditioning is not always a guarantee, so be sure to ask ahead of time when booking a hotel for a stay in warmer months.

ENVIRONMENTAL ISSUES

Greater Boston is seen as one of the greenest places in the United States, and park advocates and politicians fight down to the most painstaking of details to sustain the enormous concentration of parks. The work is paying off, as city leaders have embraced sustainability in their Imagine Boston 2030 long-term growth strategy.

In the wake of President Donald Trump removing the United States from the Paris Agreement, Boston mayor Martin Walsh announced in June 2017 the city will remain committed to the global environmental pact's standards. Pre-Paris, the city committed to reducing greenhouse gas emissions by 25 percent by 2020, a goal it reached in 2014. The city now is committed to reducing these emissions by 80 percent by 2050 and becoming carbon-neutral the same year. While the city is prone to the impact of rising sea levels, particularly in areas like the Seaport and Fort Point, many developers have embraced sustainable building practices to curtail such vulnerability.

History

ANCIENT CIVILIZATION

The Shawmut Peninsula was the original name for what later became the "Boston Neck," a narrow isthmus that connected the mainland with the peninsula. The construction of the Boston subway (America's first) uncovered Native American fishweirs that carbon dating revealed to have been constructed as far back as 5,200 years before present. During the Big Dig, archaeologists removed items up to 7,000 years old from below Boston's surface.

EARLY HISTORY

The Plymouth Colony was founded in 1620, and John Winthrop arrived 10 years later with 11 ships in what would become Salem. Lack of resources there pushed the settlers farther south to what is today Charlestown. They moved farther in to "Trimountaine" due to its access to fresh water and later renamed it (and officially incorporated it as) Boston, after a town in England, in 1630.

COLONIALISM

Boston's first colonists felt their land was so special that it was the product of a divine pact with God; thus, John Winthrop labeled it the "City Upon a Hill." The belief made the early days particularly charged with morality and the punishment of those who strayed from it. Concurrently with Boston's early Puritanism, the city's embrace of education was born, with Harvard being founded in 1636.

THE BOSTON MASSACRE AND REVOLUTIONARY WAR

Bostonians were certainly not fond of the Stamp Act of 1765, which taxed American colonists on every piece of paper they used. Massachusetts Bay Colony governor Francis Bernard and British officials in Boston wrote letters describing a growing mob sentiment in Boston (believed to be exaggerated), and London responded by sending thousands of British troops to the city in 1768.

Around the same period, the idea of "No Taxation Without Representation" was born to chide the mother country over its passage of laws influencing American colonists despite the colonists not having a seat in Parliament. Boston was a hotbed of discontent by this point, and it proved to be a catalyst for the American Revolution when British soldiers fired into a crowd of unarmed protestors outside the British custom house (today's Old State House) on March 5, 1770. Five people died, and the colonies lurched toward open rebellion. Three years later, Bostonians again protested the meaning behind a new tax, this time one on tea. Members of the Sons of Liberty dressed as Native Americans snuck aboard three ships and dumped 342 tea chests into the harbor as protest of the Tea Act of 1773, which they felt further raised the British government's sphere of influence over the colonies.

The British government responded by shutting down Boston's port and stripping Massachusetts of its ability

In the years leading up to the American Revolution, Paul Revere was employed as a messenger to carry news, documents, and messages from Boston to places as far away as Philadelphia. On the night of April 18, 1775, Revere was instructed to carry news to Lexington, Massachusetts, with word that British troops were going to march northwest to the town intending to arrest Samuel Adams and John Hancock (later proven to be false information) before likely continuing to Concord to seize stored military goods. Revere told a friend to show two lanterns in the tower of the Old North Church if the troops were leaving "by sea" across the Charles River to Cambridge instead of "by land" across the Boston Neck.

Upon seeing the "by sea" signal in the church tower, Revere set off on horse from nearby Charlestown shortly after 11pm. Narrowly avoiding British capture just outside Charlestown, Revere changed his path and warned people from Medford to eventually Lexington that the Redcoats were coming. He was eventually detained and questioned by British soldiers outside Lexington before being released as the first shots of the American Revolution were fired.

to elect its own leaders and self-govern. The king was essentially in control of appointing leaders in Boston. Other colonies feared the style of leadership would spread, and they formed the First Continental Congress and walked further toward war. Britain sent more troops into Massachusetts to capture rebels. The first shots of the American Revolution were fired in 1775 at the Battle of Lexington and Concord. The British suffered heavy losses in Boston and at the Battle of Bunker Hill as a result of getting trapped in the city due to the narrow isthmus of the Boston Neck. The British evacuation after this "Siege of Boston" is celebrated today throughout the city as Evacuation Day.

EARLY STATEHOOD

The tight British control over Boston toward the end of colonial days had stagnated the city and sent many elsewhere in pursuit of better economic conditions. Once the American Revolution was over, the city mounted a comeback. By 1800, Boston was a booming port city and more socially progressive than other parts of the country due to Massachusetts's

abolishment of slavery within its borders in 1783. Despite the growth, the town was never formally incorporated as a city until 1822. The 1800s led to vast infrastructure improvements, from railways to roads and even sewers, adding to the region's commerce sector and producing mill towns like Lowell to the north.

The idea of the "Boston Brahmin," the city's term for its early aristocracy, was also born in the 19th century. The wealthy, philanthropic families were largely cloistered on Beacon Hill and often held themselves to early Puritan ideals of morality. The 19th century was also when Boston's Irish population arrived, a direct result of the Irish potato famine.

CIVIL WAR AND THE TURN OF THE 20TH CENTURY

Massachusetts abolished slavery in 1783, and its deep-rooted abolitionist sentiment spread elsewhere in the fledgling country. William Lloyd Garrison founded *The Liberator,* an abolitionist newspaper, in 1831 and ran it for 35 years through the end of the Civil War in 1865, finally ceasing publication upon the passage of the 13th Amendment. The abolitionist sentiment was spread by the many Bostonians and other antislavery New Englanders who uprooted themselves to the Kansas Territory, as the Kansas-Nebraska Act enabled the area to choose whether or not to allow slavery.

The city offered significant financial support and other resources in support of the Union during the Civil War, and the 54th Regiment Massachusetts Voluntary Infantry became the first African American regiment organized by the Union following the 1863 Emancipation Proclamation.

As the war came to a close, actor John Wilkes Booth stayed at the Parker House Hotel, where it is believed he plotted to kidnap President Abraham Lincoln and hold him as ransom in exchange for Confederate prisoners of war. The kidnapping attempt never came to fruition, but he later assassinated Lincoln while the president attended a play at Ford's Theatre in Washington.

Post-Civil War Boston flourished. While the city experienced the Great Boston Fire of 1872, which destroyed 776 buildings in what is present-day downtown, the area also made significant cultural and academic strides. The Massachusetts Institute of Technology opened on the Boston side of the Charles in 1865 (it moved to its current site in June 1916), and a vaudeville theater scene exploded in 1883 and ran through the 1950s in what is now Government Center. The city also became home to the first subway system in America when the Tremont Street Subway (today's Green Line) opened in 1897.

URBAN DECAY, BUSING, AND RENEWAL

Post-World War II Boston was a different story. Boston proper was in a downturn by the middle of the 20th century. The city's manufacturing sector was heading to different parts of the country in pursuit of cheaper labor, and the economic pillars of modern Boston (higher education, banking, and health care) were not yet significant to the U.S. economy. City leaders looked to change the course of Boston by enacting urban renewal programs, which razed neighborhoods and replaced them with new high-rise developments. While thousands of Bostonians were displaced from their homes, the backlash eventually put a halt to the measures, saving areas like Back Bay and the South End from the wrecking ball.

The city's financial industry became more prominent in the 1970s thanks to loosened regulations. Health care and higher education also grew in their significance to the economy, further boosting the city's profile and that of its many hospitals and universities. But the city was again dealt a setback as a result of social turmoil in response to a 1974 ruling by federal judge Wendell Arthur Garrity, who ordered city schools to integrate by way of busing. Racial tensions exploded, as students from the largely white and Irish South Boston were bused to the predominantly African American Roxbury and vice versa. Violence, and even death, ensued, but the busing system remained in effect until 2013.

CONTEMPORARY TIMES

Boston and its economy have hummed along in recent years. While the Big Dig made downtown a massive infrastructure headache from 1991 until its completion in 2006, the result is seen as the catalyst for much of the city's growth and new neighborhoods. The project opened up the waterfront along Atlantic Avenue downtown as well as the Fort Point and Seaport neighborhoods. As a result, companies like General Electric and Reebok have moved into the city center, and new transit lines, like the Silver Line, have made access to Logan International Airport easier.

Many of Boston's old banking companies have been gobbled up by bigger, out-of-state national companies, but the city has taken on a new identity as a hub of "eds and meds" (colleges and health care) as well as one for tech and life science companies. Interest in living in the city again has come from all age groups, and leaders are working to improve city transit, as the growing population has things becoming increasingly congested. Significant time and resources are being put forward to accommodate the interest, both in housing and in better trains to get residents, old and new, where they need to be in an efficient manner.

Local Culture

Visitors from other cities might balk at Boston referring to itself as the "Hub of the Universe," but there are historical ties to the nickname. Oliver Wendell Holmes is responsible for the phrase due to a series of articles he wrote in 1858 referring to the Massachusetts State House as the "hub of the solar system," cheekily (and arrogantly, of course) implying Boston was the center of all intellectual and commercial activity at the time. The dome of the State House, at that point copper instead of today's gold, was prominently featured in most artistic depictions of the city, so it is believed to be why Holmes felt it stood as the center of global life at the time.

DIVERSITY

Historically, the demographic dominance of Boston's Irish Catholic population has given the area a homogenous feel, but signs of change are beginning to appear. Boston was nearly 95 percent Caucasian in 1950, but that number dropped to 49.5 percent in 2000, the first time in the city's history that it was majority-minority. The Irish population is still the city's largest ethnic group, with nearly 16 percent of the population. Italians are second with more than 8 percent. Boston's Asian population is growing in areas like Chinatown and elsewhere, thanks to both existing families and immigrants drawn to the area's jobs and institutes of higher learning. The city is also home to a sizable Hispanic population in areas like East Boston.

SUBCULTURES

Boston's hipster scene is not as pronounced as in other cities, but areas like Cambridge, Somerville, and Allston/Brighton have historically

BOSTON LINGO

You might start to hear things like "where did you pahk the cah?" and "chowdah!" as soon as you get off the plane at Logan, but these are just the beginning of Boston lingo. You might say we have our own language up here, so here's a handy guide to top terms you may not know the true meaning of:

- **Bubbler:** water fountain
- **Comm Ave:** Commonwealth Avenue
- **Frappe:** a milk shake
- **The Hill:** Beacon Hill
- **Mass Ave:** Massachusetts Avenue
- **Packie:** a liquor store
- **The T:** the local subway
- **Wicked:** Very, as in "wicked cool" or "wicked pissah" (aka very drunk)

been draws to more indie crowds thanks to cheaper costs of living and music scenes. Rising home prices and gentrification have led to changes in these neighborhoods, however.

The LGBTQ scene has and still is significantly concentrated in the South End, where many annual Boston Pride events take place each year. The neighborhood is similarly reflected in largely independent retailers and restaurants, but soaring real estate costs have pushed some of this population farther south into Dorchester in areas like Savin Hill.

RELIGION

Boston might have the reputation as an all-Catholic city, but the reality might surprise you. While 57 percent of the city identified as Christian, there was a narrow margin between Catholics and Protestants, with 29 percent identifying as the former and 25 percent as the latter. Some 33 percent claim no religious affiliation, and 10 percent identify with other religions. Greater Boston does have a sizable Jewish population, but many reside in surrounding towns like Brookline, Newton, or Cambridge.

LITERATURE

Boston's nickname of the "Athens of America" was coined by a cofounder of the North American Review, the country's first literary magazine. The city's reputation as a literary hub came from it producing some of the country's greatest writers and concepts. Transcendentalism, American Romanticism, and American Realism are all seen as originating in Boston.

The Boston Public Library's central branch in Copley Square and Walden Pond in Concord are two of Greater Boston's biggest literary landmarks; the Brattle Book Shop downtown and Harvard Book Store in Cambridge are also draws for those looking to take a piece of Boston literature home with them.

Those with more time to dig deeper into the region's important stake in American literature should spend more time in Concord to explore Louisa May Alcott's family home, Orchard House, where she penned *Little Women*. The nearby Ralph Waldo Emerson House is also open for visitors in warmer months, while Sleepy Hollow Cemetery is the final resting place for many early American authors.

Books like *The Bostonians* by Henry James give a peek into Brahmin culture, while Margaret Atwood's *The Handmaid's Tale* hypothesizes how the city might unfold in a dark, dystopian future. Hop on the T, and it's hard not to find someone perusing the latest Dennis Lehane offering, with *Mystic River* being his most famous on the national level.

VISUAL ARTS

Most of Boston's most famous visual artists hail from earlier centuries, like John Singleton Copley (whom the square of the same name honors). Copley's portraits of New England (and later European) elite garnered his reputation as one of colonial America's most prominent artists. Boston-born Lilla Cabot Perry was the mentee of Claude Monet and is known for her Impressionist works. The minimalist and abstract painter and sculptor Frank Stella is New York-based, but he was born just north of Boston in Malden, Massachusetts.

The only thing that might be close in number to Boston's parks is its museums. The Museum of Fine Arts features the city's most comprehensive art collection (with the most galleries). The nearby Isabella Stewart Gardner Museum and the Institute of Contemporary Art are the city's other two leading museums with significant focus on the visual arts. Galleries also line Newbury Street in Back Bay and Harrison Avenue in the South End. On the first Friday of each month, the South End galleries stay open late and allow guests to meet the artists.

MUSIC AND DANCE

Boston's music scene is one for all ears. The Boston Symphony Orchestra, the Handel and Haydn Society, and the Boston Pops are but a few of the classically tuned acts to perform from such renowned facilities as Symphony Hall, Jordan Hall, and the Berklee Performance Center. Boy-band aficionados will enjoy walking the same streets that produced New Kids On The Block, while the rock crowd will appreciate that both Aerosmith and Boston hail from, well, Boston.

The city's indie and live music scene is largely concentrated in Allston/Brighton music venues like Paradise Rock Club, Great Scott, and Brighton Music Hall, as well as The Middle East and The Sinclair in Cambridge. Up-and-coming music talent can often be spotted in venues surrounding Berklee College of Music—at one point, that included John Mayer. Each spring, the Boston Calling music festival brings a litany of top-charting and indie artists to several stages in Harvard's athletic fields in Allston.

FOOD

Boston may be synonymous with seafood, but the city's dining scene has grown far beyond "lobstah rolls." Of course, the city is best known for its lobster, clam chowder, fish-and-chips (most often cod or scrod with piping-hot french fries if done right), raw oysters, and steamed and fried clams.

The city's dining scene has transformed since the late 1980s, as stuffier fine dining has given way to more experimental kitchens and the rise of celebrity chefs. Todd English (Figs) and Ming Tsai (Blue Dragon) are the two biggest culinary names you'll see from Boston on the television, but other celeb chefs like Barbara Lynch (No. 9 Park and B&G Oysters), Lydia Shire (Scampo), and Ken Oringer (Toro and Uni) arguably have the venues that are better-known (and preferred) among locals.

Boston's cuisine has also gone global and farm-to-table. The North End is the Italian quarter of the city, while Chinatown is home to a variety of top Asian fare. A surge in international tourists and students has resulted in more restaurants and cuisines, making any global taste significantly more accessible than in the past.

Haymarket has been the long-time farmers market in town, but the debut of the Boston Public Market next door has added more upscale and indoor offerings. While the gentrified iteration may lack some of the gritty luster of Haymarket, it's wonderful when the weather is inclement.

ESSENTIALS

Transportation

GETTING THERE

AIR

When landing at **Boston Logan International Airport** (1 Harborside Dr., Boston, 800/235-6426, www.massport.com), named for military officer and politico General Edward Lawrence Logan, it might feel like you're coming in on an aircraft carrier, as the airport is surrounded by water on three sides, making for some nail-biting landings for first-time visitors who don't realize it's perfectly normal the water is getting so close to the plane.

Boston ferry

Most visitors will fly into Logan for its convenience to downtown Boston and its global connectivity. The airport is one of the most convenient for all U.S. cities, situated a mere 3 miles (8 km) northeast of downtown Boston, only a 15-minute drive in ideal traffic conditions or a 5-minute subway ride from the on-site Blue Line stop to Aquarium Station downtown. The facility has been and will continue to be under construction for some time to modernize terminals at what is one of the country's busiest airports. Flights are operated daily to Europe, Asia, the Middle East, and South America as well as to numerous North American destinations.

Travelers to the South Shore and western suburbs sometimes prefer to fly into **T. F. Green Airport** (2000 Post Rd., Warwick, RI, 401/737-8222, www.pvdairport.com) outside Providence, Rhode Island, and visitors to points north may prefer to fly into **Manchester-Boston Regional Airport** (1 Airport Rd., Manchester, NH, 603/624-6539, www.flymanchester.com) in Manchester,

New Hampshire. JetBlue also provides flights to Florida and New York from Worcester Regional Airport in Worcester, Massachusetts.

CAR

Boston's downtown roads can irk drivers due to their lack of grid pattern (locals claim they follow the old cow paths from the city's early days). There are, however, highways that easily get visitors in and out of the city when there is no traffic. Boston is the eastern terminus of I-90 (known as the Massachusetts Turnpike within state lines). I-93 and I-95 run north-south. I-93 is relatively short, running from Canton, Massachusetts, south of the city to St. Johnsbury, Vermont, where it meets I-91. I-95 runs from Florida to Maine and is used heavily by Bostonians looking to travel to Rhode Island or to points north of the city.

RAIL

Boston is the northern terminus of Amtrak's Northeast Corridor (800/272-7245, www.amtrak.com), the southern terminus of the rail operator's Downeaster rail line, and the western terminus of its Lake Shore Limited line from Chicago. Coupled with the MBTA's commuter rail network, Boston is conveniently serviced by trains, whether you're coming from within New England or from the other side of the United States.

Trains serve all four of Greater Boston's train hubs: Route 128, Back Bay, South Station, and North Station. Keep in mind that North Station is used for only Downeaster and northern commuter rail services.

Northeast Regional/Acela: The Amtrak Northeast Regional and Acela lines provide local and high-speed service, respectively, to New York and Washington, DC. Business class is offered on the Northeast Regional, while the Acela has business-class and first-class service. Trains depart South Station and make local stops at Back Bay and Route 128 Stations.

Downeaster: The Amtrak Downeaster line serves travelers heading north to New Hampshire and coastal Maine. The train makes stops in cities like Dover, New Hampshire, and Portland, Maine. Trains depart from North Station.

Lake Shore Limited: This service is an overnight train to Chicago, making stops in cities like Albany and Buffalo in New York and Detroit, Michigan. Trains depart South Station and make a local stop at Back Bay Station.

BUS

Bus service to New York and other points around the country is a popular alternative mode of transportation for those looking to save money. Greyhound (800/231-2222, www.greyhound.com), BoltBus (877/265-8287, www.boltbus.com), and Peter Pan Bus Lines (800/343-9999, www.peterpanbus.com) are popular options to get around the Northeast, with buses offering Wi-Fi and power outlets at all seats.

The Lucky Star Bus (888/881-0887, www.luckystarbus.com) is a bus line popular with college students, as the bus offers affordable fares from South Station in Boston to New York's Chinatown.

BOAT

More than 300,000 people take to the seas each year utilizing the major cruise lines that operate from the Flynn Cruiseport on the eastern edge of the Seaport neighborhood. The Cunard Line (800/728-6273, www.

cunard.com) offers transatlantic cruises from Hamburg, Germany, via the U.K. to Boston, as well as return trips to Southampton, England.

Norwegian Cruise Line (866/234-7350, www.ncl.com) offers cruises to Bermuda, the Caribbean, and Canada from Boston. Royal Caribbean (800/256-6649, www.royalcaribbean.com) offers similar services.

GETTING AROUND
PUBLIC TRANSPORTATION (THE "T")

The Massachusetts Bay Transportation Authority (the MBTA) is the most comprehensive way to ride your way through Greater Boston. Plan your trips through the MBTA's mobile app or website (www.mbta.com), or just go old school and consult maps for the system, found throughout the city and in all of its stations. Passengers pay via cash, CharlieCard, or CharlieTicket on board buses and light rail and at fare machines at subway stations. Subway fares are $2.40 with a CharlieCard and $2.90 with CharlieTicket or cash. Bus fare is $1.70 with a CharlieCard and $2 with CharlieTicket or cash. A seven-day unlimited bus/subway pass is available on a CharlieCard or CharlieTicket for $22.50. CharlieTickets are easily purchased at all pay machines, while CharlieCards, though cheaper, are a bit more difficult to track down, as you have to get them from a station attendant or at the Downtown Crossing Station MBTA store. Monthly passes are $90.

The MBTA also offers unlimited weekend commuter rail passes for $10.

Bus fare is applied to both regular city buses as well as the Silver Line bus rapid transit lines through the South End, Seaport, and Chelsea. The system typically runs 5am-1am, with some buses and trains running outside that time frame (check schedules online).

Subway

Conventional subway service is centered on the Red, Orange, Blue, and Green Lines. There is also a Mattapan light rail line, which is a spur of the Red Line from its Ashmont southern terminus. The Red Line runs north-south, from Alewife Station in Cambridge to two southern endpoints: Ashmont Station in Dorchester and Braintree Station in the suburb of Braintree. The Orange Line runs north-south from Oak Grove Station in Malden to Forest Hills Station in Boston's Jamaica Plain neighborhood. The Blue runs east-west from Bowdoin Station in downtown Boston to Wonderland Station in Revere. The Green Line also runs east-west, from Lechmere Station in Cambridge to several western endpoints, depending on which of the four branches you take.

Rail

Commuter rail service is provided by the MBTA but sold in different fare classes from subway and bus services. Commuter rail service is spread across 13 lines (three have two branches, and one is a special line to Gillette Stadium in Foxborough). Northern commuter rail lines operate from North Station while southern lines operate from South Station. The two stations are not connected via rail, but there has been a political push to link them through a multibillion-dollar North-South Rail Link.

Bus

The MBTA's bus network is among the country's largest, with 172 routes spread across traditional bus service and more frequent bus rapid transit on the Silver Line. Transfers from the subway are free if using a CharlieCard, but transfers to the subway require a difference in fare.

TAXI AND RIDE-SHARING

While ride-share companies have drastically changed Boston's taxi industry, cabs are still convenient ways to get into the city from Logan Airport as well as from popular destinations and hotels with taxi stands. **Metro Cab** (617/782-5500, www.boston-cab.com) and **Boston Cab Association** (617/536-5010, www.bostoncab.us) are the two most popular companies. Taxi rates are $2.60 for the first 1/7 of a mile and .40 for each additional 1/7 of a mile. The passenger pays a $2.75 toll for all trips from Boston to Logan Airport and North Shore communities.

The city also has **Uber** (www.uber.com) and **Lyft** (www.lyft.com) for ride-share alternatives, with both companies allowed to pick up at Logan Airport. All ride-share pickups and drop-offs 10am-4am from Logan Airport occur within the central parking garage and not at the front door of the terminal. Drop-offs 4am-10am occur by the various terminals, but pickups are still in the central parking garage.

CAR

The easiest way to rent a car in Boston is through **Zipcar** (www.zipcar.com), where cars are rented by the hour with gas and insurance included. These cars can be picked up at several locations throughout Greater Boston, ranging from single street-level parking spaces to garages in high-rise towers. Advance registration is required, as renters are sent an access card used to open and lock cars.

The Massachusetts Turnpike is a tolled road, as are several other highways throughout Greater Boston. Tollbooths have been dismantled in favor of automated collection from overhead cameras that take photos of license plates and send bills to addresses or rental car companies. Tolls are paid at http://massdot.state.ma.us. Reduced rates are offered with an E-Z Pass, which can be ordered online; the passes are also fairly common in rental cars.

FERRY AND WATER TAXI

Several private ferry companies operate on behalf of the MBTA to provide water transportation to commuters throughout Boston Harbor. Hingham, Hull, and Salem all see ferry service to Long Wharf in downtown Boston, with some making stops at Logan Airport. Intra-harbor water taxi service is offered by **Boston Harbor Cruises** (www.bostonharborcruises.com), which makes stops at several spots along the waterfront.

Travel Tips

Boston is a vibrant, fun city to visit, and it is always fun to explore at your own pace, but there are a few things to remember before embarking on your travels. Smoking is not allowed in bars, restaurants, nightclubs, or indoors. Even restaurant terraces ban smoking. E-cigarettes are sometimes allowed.

The drinking age in the United States is 21, and it is strictly enforced in Boston due to the high population of college students. Identification is routinely asked for at restaurants and bars. Be advised some grocery stores, liquor stores, and sports venues do not allow drinking if you present an out-of-state ID and are under the age of 25. All bars and nightclubs close no later than 2am.

Massachusetts voted to legalize marijuana for recreational use in 2016, but the rollout has been slow. Adults aged 21 or older can buy up to 1 ounce of marijuana from a store. Use of marijuana on public or federal lands is not allowed. Most recreational stores operate outside Boston city limits.

ACCESS FOR TRAVELERS WITH DISABILITIES

While some older Boston attractions and subway stations lack accessibility, most are in the process of adhering to federal standards. Boston is primarily flat and easy to maneuver in tourist-heavy areas like Back Bay, the Seaport, and the waterfront, but travelers with disabilities may find Beacon Hill challenging beyond Charles Street. All MBTA buses are accessible, and portable bridge plates are available at all Red, Blue, and Orange Line stations if

needed to close the gap between the station platform and a railcar. Service animals are allowed on all MBTA vehicles.

TRAVELING WITH CHILDREN

Boston is an extremely family-friendly destination. Children will enjoy countless activities, from the Swan Boats in the Boston Public Garden to the Boston Children's Museum. Even the Freedom Trail and historical museums provide interactive approaches to history, perfect for keeping young minds busy. Most museums and attractions offer discounted rates for children, and some offer family rates.

In the event of inclement weather, plan a trip to the Boston Children's Museum, as it is a great way to stay busy for hours while it downpours outside. Whale-watches and the Boston Tea Party Ships & Museum are fun attractions during nicer weather, as they both require time outdoors.

SENIOR TRAVELERS

Mature travelers to Boston are welcomed with open arms and frequent discounts! Mention you're a senior citizen, and many hotels will offer reduced rates. Proof of AARP membership is sometimes required, while other properties will occasionally just offer the discount.

Museums, movie theaters, and even some transportation options offer special senior rates.

LGBTQ TRAVELERS

Massachusetts is extremely progressive and very hospitable to the LGBTQ community. Boston hosts its annual Boston Pride (www.bostonpride.org) each June, and Provincetown on the Outer Cape is widely regarded as the top LGBTQ destination in the country.

In 2004, Massachusetts became the first U.S. state to legalize gay marriage. Both Boston and Provincetown (easily accessible via 90-minute ferry) are popular gay wedding destinations, and all local venues are friendly to hosting them.

INTERNATIONAL TRAVELERS

International travelers visiting the United States are required to show a valid passport upon arrival. In some cases, a visa will also be required. For a list of those countries exempt from U.S. visa requirements, visit http://travel.state.gov/visa.

Canadian tourism is significant in the Boston area, and these neighbors to the north are welcomed without a visa requirement, but a passport or other approved travel document is still required.

Travelers entering the United States via car, train, or airplane are subject to additional questioning from customs agents pertaining, but not limited to, one's final destination (have your lodging address ready), the purpose of the visit, and length of stay. Cross-border transportation of fruit and vegetables is sometimes prohibited. For more information, visit www.cbp.gov.

Health and Safety

HOSPITALS AND EMERGENCY SERVICES

In cases requiring immediate, non-emergency medical attention, there are several urgent care facilities in the city. Partners Urgent Care (https://partnersurgentcare.org) offers several facilities throughout Greater Boston, and appointments can be made over the phone.

The city has several leading hospitals, but the most central emergency room will likely be that at Massachusetts General Hospital (55 Fruit St., Boston, 617/726-2000, www.massgeneral.org).

In cases of an immediate emergency, dial 911.

PHARMACIES

Boston has a high number of CVS Pharmacy locations (www.cvs.com, 800/746-7287), as the national company is based in nearby Woonsocket, Rhode Island. Many locations are 24/7.

Downtown Crossing is also home to a Walgreens flagship (24 School St., Boston, 617/372-8156, www.walgreens.com, 6am-midnight daily).

CRIME

Boston has come a long way from its prior reputation as a town of organized crime. Today, it is one of America's safest cities, but it is still important to exercise caution.

All tourist-heavy areas are extremely safe, but keep valuables secure from occasional pickpockets. Nighttime remains safe, although the Theater District and areas around train stations can attract more panhandlers at that time. Street crime and occasional gang fights happen on the extreme western edges of the South End leading into the Roxbury neighborhood, but these acts are never random or aimed at tourists.

Information and Services

VISITORS CENTERS

If you're looking for physical maps, guided tours, souvenirs, or further information, head to the **Boston Common Visitor Center** (139 Tremont St., Boston, 617/536-4100, www.bostonusa.com, Mon.-Fri. 8:30am-5pm, Sat.-Sun. 9am-5pm), perfect for travelers about to embark on the Freedom Trail; in Back Bay, visit the **Copley Place Visitor Information Center** (100 Huntington Ave., Boston, 617/536-4100, www.bostonusa.com, Mon.-Fri. 9am-5pm, Sat.-Sun. 10am-6pm) in the Copley Place Mall at the Dartmouth Street entrance.

POST OFFICE

Tucked behind South Station, the **Fort Point Post Office** (25 Dorchester Ave., Boston, 617/654-5302, www.usps.com, daily 6am-11:59pm) is a massive facility offering a variety of shipping options, both domestic and international, and is open late.

RESOURCES

Suggested Reading

HISTORY

Botticelli, Jim. *Dirty Old Boston: Four Decades of a City in Transition.* Boston: Union Park Press, 2014. This visual history provides hundreds of photos revealing Boston's gritty past and how it has transformed into the city of today.

Lukas, J. Anthony. *Common Ground: A Turbulent Decade in the Lives of Three American Families.* New York: Vintage, 1986. The Boston busing crisis ripped open a wound of racial tension in the city that some argue still exists. This depiction follows three families as they navigate the turmoil, beginning the evening of Martin Luther King Jr.'s assassination.

Most, Doug. *The Race Underground: Boston, New York, and the Incredible Rivalry That Built America's First Subway.* New York: St. Martin's Griffin, 2015. Subways have as much of a story as the people who ride them. This book depicts the race between the Big Apple and Beantown to have bragging rights of launching America's first subway.

NOTABLE AUTHORS

Hawthorne, Nathaniel. *The Scarlet Letter.* New York: Dover Publications, 1994. It's the required high school reading everyone skips, but Hawthorne's portrayal of Hester Prynne is a must-read to grasp Massachusetts's Puritan roots.

Lehane, Dennis. *Shutter Island: A Novel.* New York: William Morrow Paperbacks, 2009. The Boston Harbor Islands are more than just the bucolic pieces of green space you see today. Lehane's gripping novel, inspired by an actual hospital that used to operate from Long Island, was made into a film starring Leonardo DiCaprio.

Mezrich, Ben. *The Accidental Billionaires: The Founding of Facebook.* New York: Anchor, 2010. Boston's tech scene birthed Facebook, and popular local author Mezrich details the sordid past you may not know behind your favorite piece of social media.

Thoreau, Henry David. *Walden, or Life in the Woods.* New York: Castle, 2007. Experience the birth of the Transcendental movement in this real-life depiction of Thoreau's two years in a cabin on the edge of Walden Pond in Concord.

CONTEMPORARY WORKS

Boser, Ulrich. *The Gardner Heist: The True Story of the World's Largest Unsolved Art Theft.* New York:

Harper Paperbacks, 2010. The Isabella Stewart Gardner Museum was robbed late one night in March of 1990, when thieves disguised as police pilfered over $600 million in art, including Rembrandts. The crime remains unsolved, and Boser details the painstaking (and ongoing) process to track down the stolen art.

Lehr, Dick, and Gerard O'Neill. *Black Mass: Whitey Bulger, The FBI, And A Devil's Deal*. New York: PubliAffairs, 2012. Two Boston Globe reporters relate the history behind two South Boston brothers who took very different paths: Whitey Bulger, one of the most infamous gangsters in U.S. history, and his brother Billy, who served as the president of the Massachusetts Senate.

Internet Resources

PERIODICALS

The Boston Globe
www.bostonglobe.com
Boston's largest daily newspaper features local news as well as award-winning investigative pieces from its Spotlight team of reporters.

Boston Herald
www.bostonherald.com
Boston's tabloid newspaper delivers quick rundowns of local and national news with a typically conservative slant.

Boston Magazine
www.bostonmagazine.com
This glossy, monthly lifestyle magazine covers Boston culture and society.

DigBoston
www.digboston.com
This free weekly alternative publication covers culture, business, and general news and has restaurant and bar listings.

GENERAL INFORMATION

Greater Boston Convention & Visitors Bureau
www.bostonusa.com
Find out about events, conventions, and other city happenings.

PARKS AND RECREATION

Boston Parks and Recreation
www.cityofboston.gov/parks
This resource has information on the more than 2,300 acres of parks spread throughout Boston.

Department of Conservation & Recreation
www.mass.gov/dcr
This is Massachusetts' state-wide online guide to its more than 450,000 parks and natural resources.

TRANSPORTATION

Bay State Cruises
www.baystatecruisecompany.com
This company focuses primarily on Provincetown fast ferry service from Boston's Seaport neighborhood but

also features inner Boston Harbor ferry service.

Boston Airports
www.massport.com
Massport is the owner and operator of several New England airports, including Boston Logan International Airport.

Boston Harbor Cruises
www.bostonharborcruises.com
This comprehensive company features a Provincetown fast ferry, whale-watching cruises, commuter ferries, and other water transportation from its hub at Long Wharf in downtown Boston.

Massachusetts Bay Transportation Authority
www.mbta.com
Greater Boston's transit agency has online travel guides, service updates, and fare information.

Index

I

JKL

M

Restaurants

Nightlife

Shops

Hotels

Photo Credits

MAP SYMBOLS

■	Sights	◉	National Capital	▲	Mountain	═══ Major Hwy
■	Restaurants	◉	State Capital	✛	Natural Feature	Road/Hwy
■	Nightlife	○	City/Town	⚲	Waterfall	Pedestrian Friendly
■	Arts and Culture	★	Point of Interest	♠	Park	- - - - - Trail
■	Sports and Activities	•	Accommodation	▲	Archaeological Site	✕✕✕✕✕ Stairs
■	Shops	▼	Restaurant/Bar	🄃	Trailhead	·········· Ferry
■	Hotels	•	Other Location	🅿	Parking Area	⌐⌐⌐⌐ Railroad

CONVERSION TABLES

°C = (°F - 32) / 1.8
°F = (°C x 1.8) + 32
1 inch = 2.54 centimeters (cm)
1 foot = 0.304 meters (m)
1 yard = 0.914 meters
1 mile = 1.6093 kilometers (km)
1 km = 0.6214 miles
1 fathom = 1.8288 m
1 chain = 20.1168 m
1 furlong = 201.168 m
1 acre = 0.4047 hectares
1 sq km = 100 hectares
1 sq mile = 2.59 square km
1 ounce = 28.35 grams
1 pound = 0.4536 kilograms
1 short ton = 0.90718 metric ton
1 short ton = 2,000 pounds
1 long ton = 1.016 metric tons
1 long ton = 2,240 pounds
1 metric ton = 1,000 kilograms
1 quart = 0.94635 liters
1 US gallon = 3.7854 liters
1 Imperial gallon = 4.5459 liters
1 nautical mile = 1.852 km

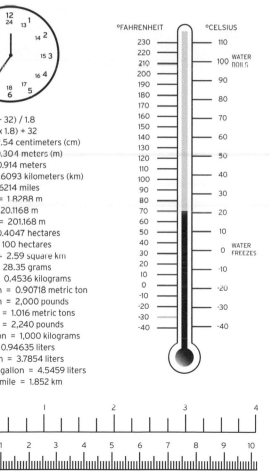

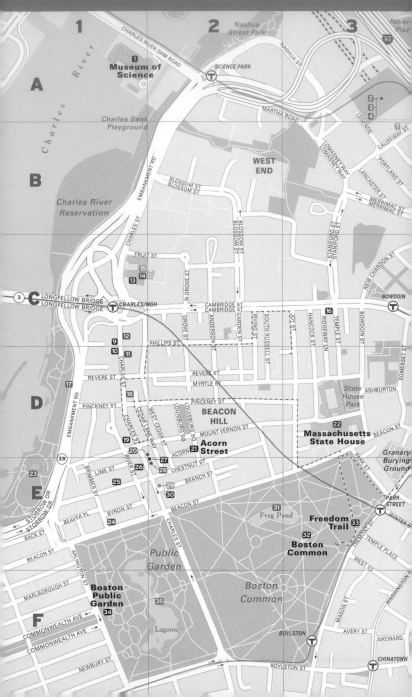

1   2   3

Nashua Street Park

93   Rever Plaz

CHARLES RIVER DAM ROAD

SCIENCE PARK

1 Museum of Science

CAUSEWAY ST

2
3
4

7

LEGENDS

A

Charles River

MARTHA ROAD

PORTLAND ST

NASHUA ST

LOMASNEY WAY
LOMASNEY WAY

LANCASTER ST

MERRIMAC ST
MERRIMAC ST

Charles Bank Playground

EMBANKMENT RD

WEST END

BLOSSOM ST
BLOSSOM ST

STANIFORD ST
STANIFORD ST

NEW CHARDON ST

B

Charles River Reservation

BLOSSOM ST
BLOSSOM ST

BOWDOIN

FRUIT ST

N GROVE ST

CHARLES ST

15
14
13

3   LONGFELLOW BRIDGE
LONGFELLOW BRIDGE

CHARLES/MGH

CAMBRIDGE ST
CAMBRIDGE ST

IRVING ST

SOUTH RUSSELL ST

JOY ST

16

HANCOCK ST

RIDGEWAY LN

TEMPLE ST

BOWDOIN ST

SOMERSET ST

C

GROVE ST

ANDERSON ST

GARDEN ST

PHILLIPS ST

9   12
10
11

REVERE ST

CHARLES ST

REVERE ST

MYRTLE ST

State House Park

ASHBURTON

17

PINCKNEY ST

18

PINCKNEY ST

BEACON HILL

LOUISBURG SQ

MOUNT VERNON ST

BEACON ST

D

EMBANKMENT RD

CHARLES ST

WEST CEDAR ST

CEDAR LANE WAY

22 Massachusetts State House

28

19

20

27

ACORN ST

21 Acorn Street

Granary Burying Ground

PARK ST

23

RIVER ST

26

28

CHESTNUT ST

BRANCH ST

PARK STREET

WINTER S

E

STORROW DR
STORROW DR

BRIMMER ST

LIME ST

25

29

30

BEACON ST

31 Frog Pond

32 Boston Common

33 Freedom Trail

TREMONT ST

TEMPLE PLACE

BACK ST

BEAVER PL

BYRON ST

24

Public Garden

Boston Common

WEST ST

MASON ST

WASHINGTON ST

BEACON ST

MARLBOROUGH ST

Boston Public Garden

35

34

Lagoon

BOYLSTON

AVERY ST

HAYWARD

F

COMMONWEALTH AVE
COMMONWEALTH AVE

ARLINGTON ST

NEWBURY ST

BOYLSTON ST

CHINATOWN

FREEDOM TRAIL

BLACK HERITAGE TRAIL

SIGHTS

1	A1	Museum of Science
21	D2	Acorn Street
22	D3	Massachusetts State House
32	E3	Boston Common
33	E3	Freedom Trail
34	F1	Boston Public Garden

RESTAURANTS

5	A4	A&D Burgers
9	C1	Savenor's Market
10	D1	J. P. Licks
13	C1	Scampo
16	C3	Tip Tap Room
19	D1	Tatte Bakery & Café
25	E1	75 Chestnut
26	E1	The Paramount
27	D2	Toscano
30	E2	Beacon Hill Bistro

NIGHTLIFE

6	A4	Night Shift Brewing
8	B4	Ward 8
12	C1	Beacon Hill Pub
14	C1	Alibi
24	E1	Cheers

ARTS AND CULTURE

2	A3	TD Garden
23	E1	Hatch Memorial Shell

RECREATION

3	A3	Boston Celtics
4	A3	Boston Bruins
17	D1	Paul Dudley White Charles River Bike Path
31	E2	Frog Pond
35	F2	Swan Boats

SHOPS

11	D1	Crush Boutique
18	D1	Black Ink
20	D1	December Thieves
28	E2	North River Outfitter

HOTELS

7	B3	CitizenM
15	C1	Liberty Hotel
29	E2	Beacon Hill Hotel

0		200 yds
0		200 m

DISTANCE ACROSS MAP
Approximate: 1.5 mi or 2.5 km
© MOON.COM

SIGHTS

3	A5	Old North Church	28	D5	Faneuil Hall Marketplace
17	B5	Paul Revere House			
22	C4	New England Holocaust Memorial	36	D6	New England Aquarium

RESTAURANTS

1	A4	Tony & Elaine's	15	B5	Mike's Pastry
2	A4	The Original Regina Pizzeria	16	B5	The Daily Catch
6	A6	Il Molo	18	B5	Giacomo's
7	B5	Neptune Oyster	19	B5	Mamma Maria
9	B5	Rigoletto Ristorante	20	C4	Boston Public Market
12	B5	Bricco Panetteria	21	C4	Haymarket
13	B5	Bricco	31	D5	Kamakura
14	B5	Modern Pastry	40	F6	James Hook & Co.

NIGHTLIFE

8	B5	Improv Asylum	26	D5	Sam Adams Downtown Boston Taproom
10	B5	Parla			
23	C4	Bell In Hand	30	D5	Ned Devine's Pub
24	C4	Durty Nelly's	32	D5	The Black Rose
			35	D6	The Landing

RECREATION

27	D5	NPS Freedom Trail Tour	37	E6	Rose Kennedy Greenway
33	D6	Old Town Trolley Tours	39	E6	Classic Harbor Line
34	D6	Boston Harbor Cruises			

SHOPS

| 4 | A6 | Exhale Boston– Battery Wharf | 29 | D5 | Faneuil Hall Marketplace |
| 11 | B5 | LIT Boutique | | | |

HOTELS

| 5 | A6 | Battery Wharf Hotel | 38 | E6 | Boston Harbor Hotel |
| 25 | C5 | The Bostonian Boston | | | |

0   150 yds
0   150 m

DISTANCE ACROSS MAP
Approximate: 1.4mi or 2.2km
© MOON.COM

- - - - - **FREEDOM TRAIL**
- - - - - **BLACK HERITAGE TRAIL**

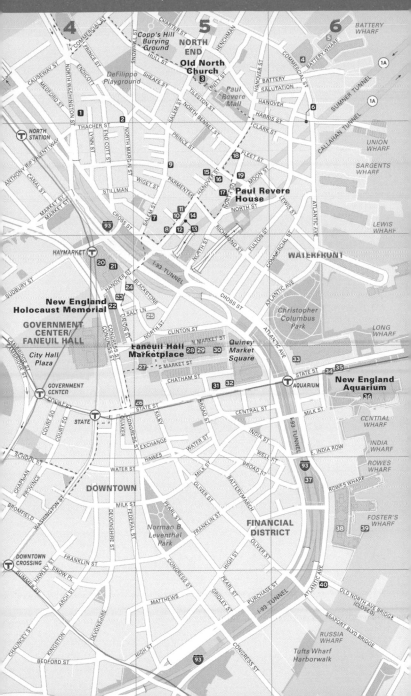

4 **5** **6**

BATTERY WHARF

CHARTER ST

HENCHMAN ST

COMMERCIAL ST

Copp's Hill
Burying
Ground

NORTH
END

Old North
Church
3

PRINCE ST

SNOWHILL ST

HULL ST

SHEAFE ST

TILESTON ST

Paul
Revere
Mall

BATTERY
SALUTATION

HANOVER ST

DeFilippo
Playground

COMMERCIAL ST

SUMNER TUNNEL

1A

1A

UNION
WHARF

SARGENTS
WHARF

CAUSEWAY ST

MEDFORD ST

NORTH WASHINGTON ST

ENDICOTT ST

THACHER ST

1

2

LYNN ST

ENDICOTT ST

SALEM ST

NORTH MARGIN ST

NORTH BENNETT ST

PRINCE ST

HANOVER ST

HARRIS ST

CLARK ST

6

CALLAHAN TUNNEL

NORTH
STATION

T

9

FLEET ST

18

PARMENTER ST

WIGET ST

STILLMAN ST

15

16

17

19

Paul Revere
House

MOON ST

LEWIS ST

ATLANTIC AVE

LEWIS
WHARF

ANTHONY TIP VALENTI WAY

CANAL ST

MARKET ST

MARKET ST

CROSS ST

93

SALEM ST

11

10

14

7

8

12

13

NORTH ST

RICHMOND ST

FULTON ST

COMMERCIAL ST

WATERFRONT

HAYMARKET

T

20

21

HANOVER ST

BLACKSTONE ST

I-93 TUNNEL

CROSS ST

ATLANTIC AVE

Christopher
Columbus
Park

LONG
WHARF

SUDBURY ST

24

23

22

New England
Holocaust Memorial

SALT LN

25

DUTTON ST

NORTH ST

GOVERNMENT
CENTER/
FANEUIL HALL

CONGRESS ST

CLINTON ST

N MARKET ST

Faneuil Hall
Marketplace

28 29

30

Quincy
Market
Square

ATLANTIC AVE

33

City Hall
Plaza

27

S MARKET ST

CHATHAM ST

31 32

T

AQUARIUM

STATE ST

34 35

New England
Aquarium

36

CAMBRIDGE ST

CAMBRIDGE ST

GOVERNMENT
CENTER

T

COURT ST

COURT SQ

COURT SQ

STATE

T

26

STATE ST

QUAKER LN

KILBY ST

BROAD ST

CENTRAL ST

CENTRAL
WHARF

SCHOOL ST

CHAPMAN PL

PROVINCE ST

WATER ST

EXCHANGE ST

WATER ST

HAWES ST

INDIA ST

INDIA
WHARF

ROWES
WHARF

I-93 TUNNEL

E. INDIA ROW

BROMFIELD ST

WASHINGTON ST

DOWNTOWN

MILK ST

DEVONSHIRE ST

FEDERAL ST

Norman B.
Leventhal
Park

PEARL ST

MILK ST

OLIVER ST

FRANKLIN ST

BATTERYMARCH ST

WELL ST

BROAD ST

FINANCIAL
DISTRICT

OLIVER ST

93

37

ROWES WHARF

FOSTER'S
WHARF

38

39

FRANKLIN ST

DOWNTOWN
CROSSING

T

SUMMER ST

HAWLEY ST

SNOW PL

ARCH ST

CONGRESS ST

HIGH ST

PEARL ST

GRIDLEY ST

PURCHASE ST

ATLANTIC AVE

40

OLD NORTH AVE BRIDGE
(CLOSED)

CHAUNCEY ST

KINGSTON ST

BEDFORD ST

DEVONSHIRE ST

MATTHEWS ST

HIGH ST

CONGRESS ST

93

SEAPORT BLVD BRIDGE

L-93 TUNNEL

RUSSIA
WHARF

Tufts Wharf
Harborwalk

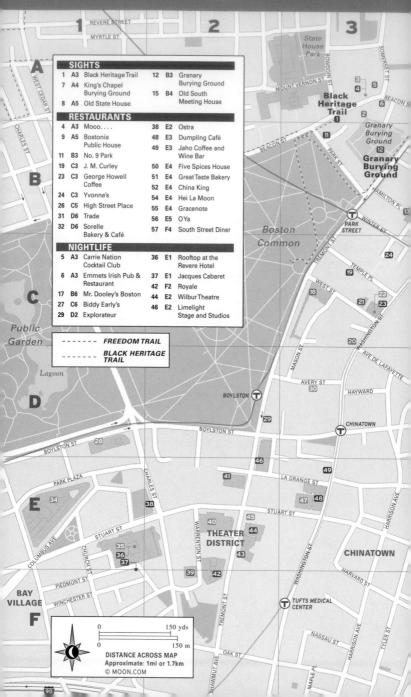

SIGHTS

1	A3	Black Heritage Trail
7	A4	King's Chapel Burying Ground
8	A5	Old State House
12	B3	Granary Burying Ground
15	B4	Old South Meeting House

RESTAURANTS

4	A3	Mooo....
9	A5	Bostonia Public House
11	B3	No. 9 Park
19	C3	J. M. Curley
23	C3	George Howell Coffee
24	C3	Yvonne's
26	C5	High Street Place
31	D6	Trade
32	D6	Sorelle Bakery & Café
38	E2	Ostra
48	E3	Dumpling Café
49	E3	Jaho Coffee and Wine Bar
50	E4	Five Spices House
51	E4	Great Taste Bakery
52	E4	China King
54	E4	Hei La Moon
55	E4	Gracenote
56	E5	O Ya
57	F4	South Street Diner

NIGHTLIFE

5	A3	Carrie Nation Cocktail Club
6	A3	Emmets Irish Pub & Restaurant
17	B6	Mr. Dooley's Boston
27	C6	Biddy Early's
29	D2	Explorateur
36	E1	Rooftop at the Revere Hotel
37	E1	Jacques Cabaret
42	F2	Royale
44	E2	Wilbur Theatre
46	E2	Limelight Stage and Studios

- - - - - FREEDOM TRAIL

- - - - - BLACK HERITAGE TRAIL

0   150 yds
0   150 m

DISTANCE ACROSS MAP
Approximate: 1mi or 1.7km
© MOON.COM

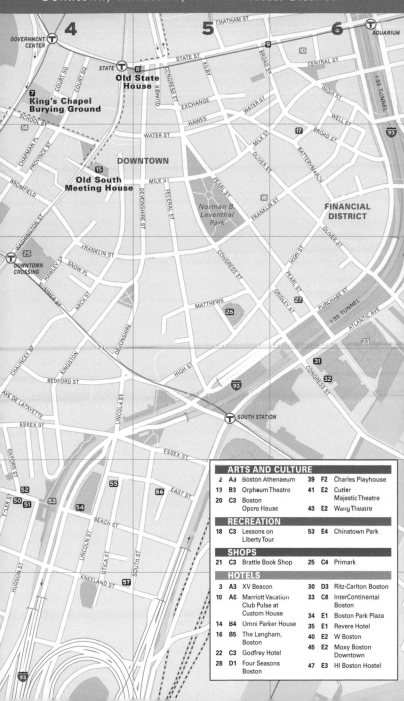

ARTS AND CULTURE

2	A3	Boston Athenaeum	39	F2	Charles Playhouse
13	B3	Orpheum Theatre	41	E2	Cutler Majestic Theatre
20	C3	Boston Opera House	43	E2	Wang Theatre

RECREATION

18	C3	Lessons on Liberty Tour	53	E4	Chinatown Park

SHOPS

21	C3	Brattle Book Shop	25	C4	Primark

HOTELS

3	A3	XV Beacon	30	D3	Ritz-Carlton Boston
10	A6	Marriott Vacation Club Pulse at Custom House	33	C6	InterContinental Boston
14	B4	Omni Parker House	34	E1	Boston Park Plaza
16	B5	The Langham, Boston	35	E1	Revere Hotel
22	C3	Godfrey Hotel	40	E2	W Boston
28	D1	Four Seasons Boston	45	E2	Moxy Boston Downtown
			47	E3	HI Boston Hostel

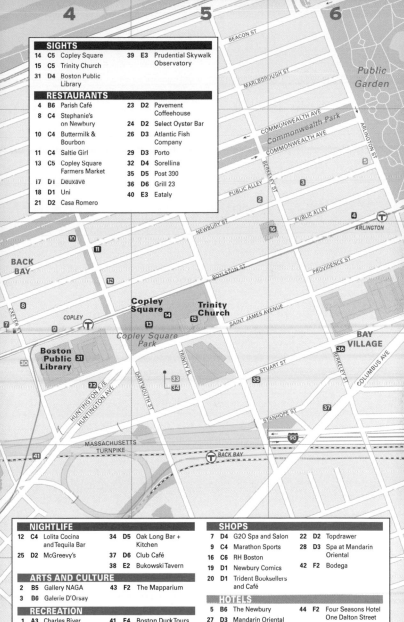

SIGHTS

14	C5	Copley Square
15	C5	Trinity Church
31	D4	Boston Public Library
39	E3	Prudential Skywalk Observatory

RESTAURANTS

4	B6	Parish Café
8	C4	Stephanie's on Newbury
10	C4	Buttermilk & Bourbon
11	C4	Saltie Girl
13	C5	Copley Square Farmers Market
17	D1	Deuxave
18	D1	Uni
21	D2	Casa Romero
23	D2	Pavement Coffeehouse
24	D2	Select Oyster Bar
26	D3	Atlantic Fish Company
29	D3	Porto
32	D4	Sorellina
35	D5	Post 390
36	D6	Grill 23
40	E3	Eataly

NIGHTLIFE

12	C4	Lolita Cocina and Tequila Bar
25	D2	McGreevy's
34	D5	Oak Long Bar + Kitchen
37	D6	Club Café
38	E2	Bukowski Tavern

ARTS AND CULTURE

2	B5	Gallery NAGA
3	B6	Galerie D'Orsay
43	F2	The Mapparium

RECREATION

1	A3	Charles River Esplanade
6	C3	Commonwealth Avenue Mall
41	E4	Boston Duck Tours

SHOPS

7	D4	G2O Spa and Salon
9	C4	Marathon Sports
16	C6	RH Boston
19	D1	Newbury Comics
20	D1	Trident Booksellers and Café
22	D2	Topdrawer
28	D3	Spa at Mandarin Oriental
42	F2	Bodega

HOTELS

5	B6	The Newbury
27	D3	Mandarin Oriental
30	D4	Lenox Hotel
33	D5	Fairmont Copley Plaza
44	F2	Four Seasons Hotel One Dalton Street
45	F3	The Colonnade Hotel
46	F3	Inn at St. Botolph

1

2

3

A

MASSACHUSETTS TURNPIKE

90

BACK BAY

1

7

B

Christian Science Plaza

BELVIDERE ST

PRUDENTIAL

HUNTINGTON AVE
HUNTINGTON AVE

W. NEWTON ST

PUBLIC ALLEY

SAINT BOTOLPH ST

FOLLEN ST

6

WEST CANTON ST

YARMOUTH ST

HOLYOKE ST

COLUMBUS AVE

DARTMOUTH ST

DARTMOUTH PL

8

C

PUBLIC ALLEY

SAINT BOTOLPH ST

CUMBERLAND

BLACKWOOD

DURHAM

Titus Sparrow Park

18

19

BRADDOCK PARK

W. NEWTON ST

GREENWICH PARK

PEMBROKE ST

W. NEWTON ST

W. BROOKLINE ST

WARREN AVE

DARTMOUTH ST

20

D

ALBEMARLE

MASSACHUSETTS AVE

WELLINGTON

CLAREMONT PARK

38

37

36

35

MASSACHUSETTS AVE

WORCESTER ST

RUTLAND SQ

PUBLIC ALLEY

CONCORD SQ

RUTLAND ST

TREMONT ST

39

SAN JUAN ST

WEST NEWTON STREET

WEST HAVEN ST

SOUTH END

E

COLUMBUS AVENUE

NORTHAMPTON ST

WEST SPRINGFIELD STREET

WEST CONCORD ST

NEWLAND PLACE

WORCESTER ST

SHAWMUT AVE

NEWLAND ST

45

46

Blackstone Square

W. NEWTON ST

F

LENOX STREET

CAMDEN STREET

NORTHAMPTON ST

S. EAST SPRINGFIELD ST

MASSACHUSETTS AVE

WASHINGTON ST

EAST CONCORD ST

WORCESTER SQ

PUBLIC ALLEY

49

48

DISTANCE ACROSS MAP
Approximate: 1.2 mi or 1.8 km

0   100 yds
0   100 m

© MOON.COM

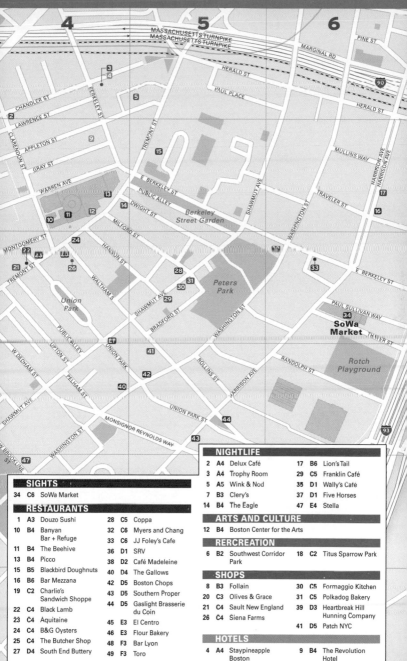

SIGHTS

34	C6	SoWa Market

RESTAURANTS

1	A3	Douzo Sushi
10	B4	Banyan Bar + Refuge
11	B4	The Beehive
13	B4	Picco
15	B5	Blackbird Doughnuts
16	B6	Bar Mezzana
19	C2	Charlie's Sandwich Shoppe
22	C4	Black Lamb
23	C4	Aquitaine
24	C4	B&G Oysters
25	C4	The Butcher Shop
27	D4	South End Buttery
28	C5	Coppa
32	C6	Myers and Chang
33	C6	JJ Foley's Cafe
36	D1	SRV
38	D2	Café Madeleine
40	D4	The Gallows
42	D5	Boston Chops
43	D5	Southern Proper
44	D5	Gaslight Brasserie du Coin
45	E3	El Centro
46	E3	Flour Bakery
48	F3	Bar Lyon
49	F3	Toro

NIGHTLIFE

2	A4	Delux Café	17	B6	Lion's Tail
3	A4	Trophy Room	29	C5	Franklin Café
5	A5	Wink & Nod	35	D1	Wally's Café
7	B3	Clery's	37	D1	Five Horses
14	B4	The Eagle	47	E4	Stella

ARTS AND CULTURE

12	B4	Boston Center for the Arts

RERCREATION

6	B2	Southwest Corridor Park	18	C2	Titus Sparrow Park

SHOPS

8	B3	Follain	30	C5	Formaggio Kitchen
20	C3	Olives & Grace	31	C5	Polkadog Bakery
21	C4	Sault New England	39	D3	Heartbreak Hill Running Company
26	C4	Siena Farms	41	D5	Patch NYC

HOTELS

4	A4	Staypineapple Boston	9	B4	The Revolution Hotel

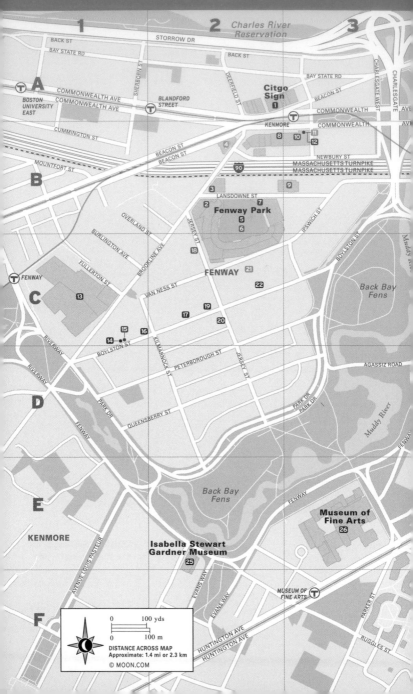

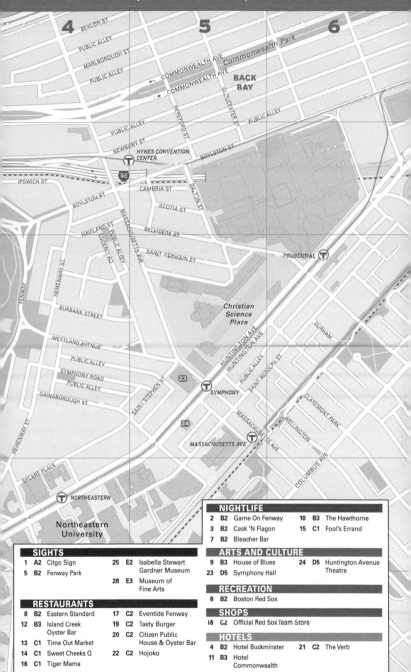

SIGHTS

1	A2	Citgo Sign	25	E2	Isabella Stewart Gardner Museum
5	B2	Fenway Park	26	E3	Museum of Fine Arts

RESTAURANTS

8	B2	Eastern Standard	17	C2	Eventide Fenway
12	B3	Island Creek Oyster Bar	19	C2	Tasty Burger
13	C1	Time Out Market	20	C2	Citizen Public House & Oyster Bar
14	C1	Sweet Cheeks Q	22	C2	Hojoko
16	C1	Tiger Mama			

NIGHTLIFE

2	B2	Game On Fenway	10	B3	The Hawthorne
3	B2	Cask 'N Flagon	15	C1	Fool's Errand
7	B2	Bleacher Bar			

ARTS AND CULTURE

9	B3	House of Blues	24	D5	Huntington Avenue Theatre
23	D5	Symphony Hall			

RECREATION

6	B2	Boston Red Sox

SHOPS

18	C2	Official Red Sox Team Store

HOTELS

4	B2	Hotel Buckminster	21	C2	The Verb
11	B3	Hotel Commonwealth			

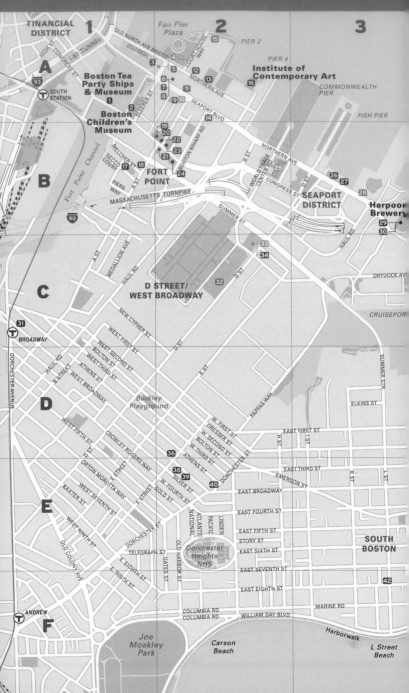

FINANCIAL DISTRICT 1

Fan Pier Plaza 2

3

HIGH ST
CONGRESS ST
I-93 TUNNEL
OLD NORTH AVE BRIDGE (CLOSED)

A

93

SOUTH STATION

Boston Tea Party Ships & Museum 1

2

3

4

5

6

7

8

9

10

11

12

13

14

15

COURT HOUSE WAY

NORTHERN AVE

SLEEPER ST

SEAPORT BLVD

PIER 2

PIER 4

Institute of Contemporary Art 16

COMMONWEALTH PIER

FISH PIER

Boston Children's Museum

B

Fort Point Channel

WELCHER ST

NECCO COURT 17 18

FORT POINT

PIERS A ST

PIERS WAY

19
20
22
23
21
24

BOSTON WHARF RD

NORTHERN AVE

B ST

WORLD TRADE CENTER RD

CONGRESS ST

25

D ST

26 27

SEAPORT DISTRICT

28

Harpoor Brewery

29
30

90

Massachusetts Turnpike

SUMMER ST

HAUL RD

33
34

DRYDOCK AV

C

MEDALLION AVE

HAUL RD

A ST

D STREET/ WEST BROADWAY

32

D ST

NEW CYPHER ST

CRUISEPOR

SUMMER STR

31

BROADWAY

WEST FIRST ST

D ST

E ST

WEST SECOND ST

BOLTON ST

WEST THIRD ST

PAPPAS WAY

ELKINS ST

DORCHESTER AVENUE

D

HAUL RD

B STREET

ATHENS ST

WEST BROADWAY

Buckley Playground

W. FIRST ST
DRESSER ST
W. SECOND ST
BOLTON ST
W. THIRD ST

DORCHESTER ST

EAST FIRST ST

H ST
J ST
I ST

EAST THIRD ST

EMERSON ST

WEST FIFTH ST

CROWLEY ROGERS WAY

F STREET

36

W. FOURTH ST

SILVER ST
38
39
GOLD ST
40

ATHENS ST

K ST

E

ORTON MOROTTA WAY

WEST SEVENTH ST

BAXTER ST

DORCHESTER ST

Dorchester Heights NHS

ATLANTIC
NATIONAL
PACIFIC
LINDEN

EAST BROADWAY

EAST FOURTH ST

EAST FIFTH ST

STORY ST

EAST SIXTH ST

SOUTH BOSTON

WEST NINTH ST

OLD COLONY AVE

TELEGRAPH ST

E. EIGHTH ST

GATES ST

OLD HARBOR ST

EAST SEVENTH ST

EAST EIGHTH ST

42

E. NINTH ST

MARINE RD

F

ANDREW

COLUMBIA RD
COLUMBIA RD

WILLIAM DAY BLVD

Harborwalk

Joe Moakley Park

Carson Beach

L Street Beach

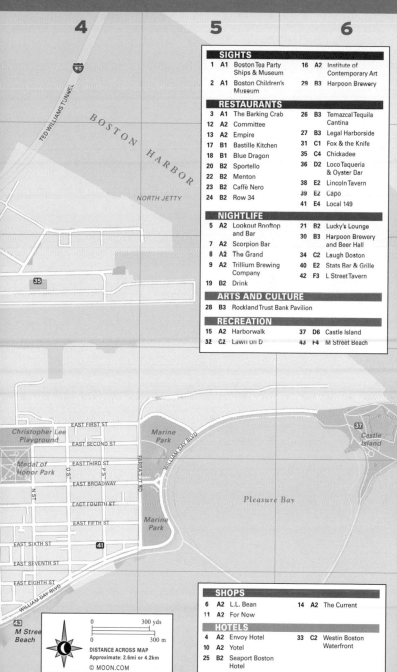

SIGHTS

1	A1	Boston Tea Party Ships & Museum
2	A1	Boston Children's Museum
16	A2	Institute of Contemporary Art
29	B3	Harpoon Brewery

RESTAURANTS

3	A1	The Barking Crab
12	A2	Committee
13	A2	Empire
17	B1	Bastille Kitchen
18	B1	Blue Dragon
20	B2	Sportello
22	B2	Menton
23	B2	Caffè Nero
24	B2	Row 34
26	B3	Temazcal Tequila Cantina
27	B3	Legal Harborside
31	C1	Fox & the Knife
35	C4	Chickadee
36	D2	Loco Taqueria & Oyster Bar
38	E2	Lincoln Tavern
39	E2	Capo
41	E4	Local 149

NIGHTLIFE

5	A2	Lookout Rooftop and Bar
7	A2	Scorpion Bar
8	A2	The Grand
9	A2	Trillium Brewing Company
19	B2	Drink
21	B2	Lucky's Lounge
30	B3	Harpoon Brewery and Beer Hall
34	C2	Laugh Boston
40	E2	Stats Bar & Grille
42	F3	L Street Tavern

ARTS AND CULTURE

28	B3	Rockland Trust Bank Pavilion

RECREATION

15	A2	Harborwalk
32	C2	Lawn on D
37	D6	Castle Island
43	F4	M Street Beach

BOSTON HARBOR

NORTH JETTY

TED WILLIAMS TUNNEL

EAST FIRST ST
EAST SECOND ST
EAST THIRD ST
EAST BROADWAY
EAST FOURTH ST
EAST FIFTH ST
EAST SIXTH ST
EAST SEVENTH ST
EAST EIGHTH ST
WILLIAM DAY BLVD

Christopher Lee Playground
Medal of Honor Park
Marine Park
FARRAGUT RD
WILLIAM DAY BLVD
Castle Island
Pleasure Bay

M Street Beach

0   300 yds
0   300 m
DISTANCE ACROSS MAP
Approximate: 2.6mi or 4.2km
© MOON.COM

SHOPS

6	A2	L.L. Bean
11	A2	For Now
14	A2	The Current

HOTELS

4	A2	Envoy Hotel
10	A2	Yotel
25	B2	Seaport Boston Hotel
33	C2	Westin Boston Waterfront

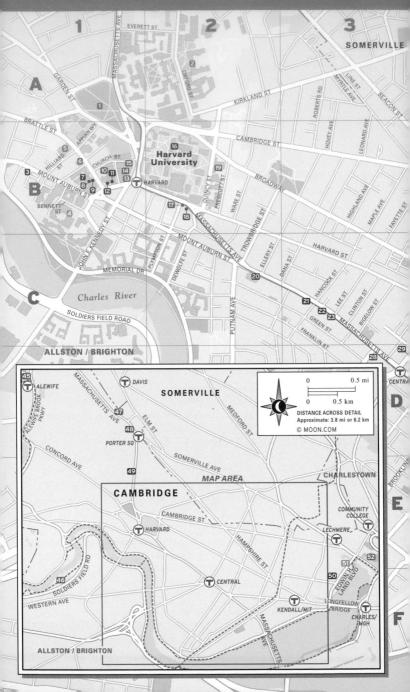

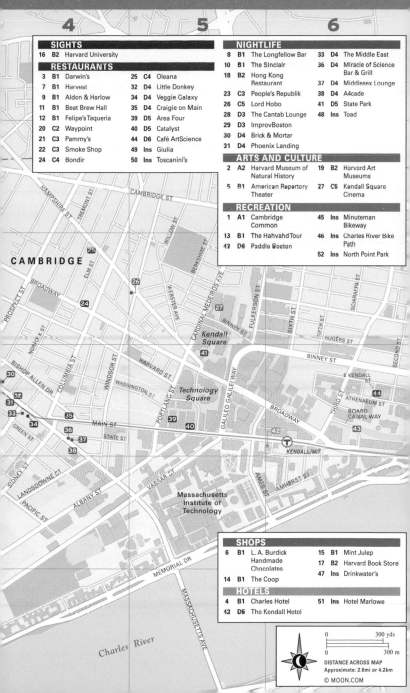

SIGHTS

| 16 | B2 | Harvard University |

RESTAURANTS

3	B1	Darwin's		25	C4	Oleana
7	B1	Harvest		32	D4	Little Donkey
9	B1	Alden & Harlow		34	D4	Veggie Galaxy
11	B1	Beat Brew Hall		35	D4	Craigie on Main
12	B1	Felipe's Taqueria		39	D5	Area Four
20	C2	Waypoint		40	D5	Catalyst
21	C3	Pammy's		44	D6	Café ArtScience
22	C3	Smoke Shop		49	Ins	Giulia
24	C4	Bondir		50	Ins	Toscanini's

NIGHTLIFE

8	B1	The Longfellow Bar		33	D4	The Middle East
10	B1	The Sinclair		36	D4	Miracle of Science Bar & Grill
18	B2	Hong Kong Restaurant		37	D4	Middlesex Lounge
23	C3	People's Republik		38	D4	A4cade
26	C5	Lord Hobo		41	D5	State Park
28	D3	The Cantab Lounge		48	Ins	Toad
29	D3	ImprovBoston
30	D4	Brick & Mortar
31	D4	Phoenix Landing

ARTS AND CULTURE

| 2 | A2 | Harvard Museum of Natural History | | 19 | B2 | Harvard Art Museums |
| 5 | B1 | American Repertory Theater | | 27 | C5 | Kendall Square Cinema |

RECREATION

1	A1	Cambridge Common		45	Ins	Minuteman Bikeway
13	B1	The Hahvahd Tour		46	Ins	Charles River Bike Path
43	D6	Paddle Boston		52	Ins	North Point Park

SHOPS

6	B1	L. A. Burdick Handmade Chocolates		15	B1	Mint Julep
14	B1	The Coop		17	B2	Harvard Book Store
				47	Ins	Drinkwater's

HOTELS

| 4 | B1 | Charles Hotel | | 51 | Ins | Hotel Marlowe |
| 42 | D6 | The Kendall Hotel |

CAMBRIDGE

Kendall Square

Technology Square

Massachusetts Institute of Technology

Charles River

0   300 yds
0   300 m

DISTANCE ACROSS MAP
Approximate: 2.6mi or 4.2km

© MOON.COM

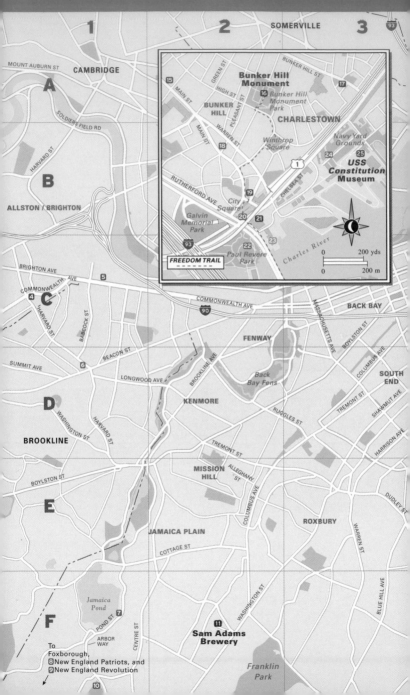

SOMERVILLE

MOUNT AUBURN ST

CAMBRIDGE

A

SOLDIERS FIELD RD

HARVARD ST

B

ALLSTON / BRIGHTON

BRIGHTON AVE

COMMONWEALTH AVE

HARVARD ST

BABCOCK ST

BEACON ST

SUMMIT AVE

C

COMMONWEALTH AVE

90

FENWAY

Back Bay Fens

LONGWOOD AVE

BROOKLINE AVE

BOYLSTON ST

KENMORE

D

WASHINGTON ST

HARVARD ST

BROOKLINE

TREMONT ST

RUGGLES ST

MASSACHUSETTS AVE

COLUMBUS AVE

TREMONT ST

SHAWMUT AVE

HARRISON AVE

SOUTH END

BOYLSTON ST

MISSION HILL

ALLEGHANY AVE

COLUMBUS AVE

E

JAMAICA PLAIN

COTTAGE ST

ROXBURY

WARREN ST

DUDLEY ST

BLUE HILL AVE

F

Jamaica Pond

7

POND ST

ARBOR WAY

CENTRE ST

WASHINGTON ST

11

Sam Adams Brewery

Franklin Park

To
Foxborough,
8 New England Patriots, and
9 New England Revolution

10

BOSTON STREET FINDER

MAIN ST

15

GREEN ST

HIGH ST

PLEASANT ST

BUNKER HILL ST

Bunker Hill Monument

16 Bunker Hill Monument Park

17

BUNKER HILL

MAIN ST

WARREN ST

18

CHARLESTOWN

Winthrop Square

Navy Yard Grounds

24

25

USS Constitution Museum

1

CHELSEA ST

RUTHERFORD AVE

19

City Square

Galvin Memorial Park

20

21

23

22

Paul Revere Park

FREEDOM TRAIL

Charles River

0   200 yds
0   200 m

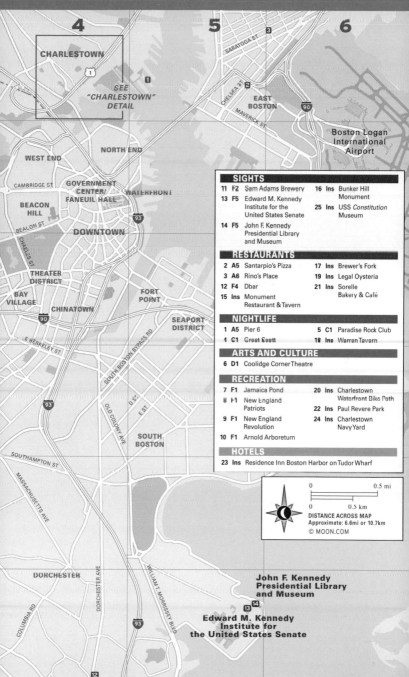

CHARLESTOWN

SEE "CHARLESTOWN" DETAIL

WEST END

NORTH END

CAMBRIDGE ST

GOVERNMENT CENTER/ FANEUIL HALL

WATERFRONT

BEACON HILL

BEACON ST

CHARLES ST

DOWNTOWN

THEATER DISTRICT

BAY VILLAGE

CHINATOWN

FORT POINT

E BERKELEY ST

SEAPORT DISTRICT

SOUTH BOSTON BYPASS RD

D ST

E ST

OLD COLONY AVE

SOUTH BOSTON

SOUTHAMPTON ST

MASSACHUSETTS AVE

DORCHESTER

DORCHESTER AVE

WILLIAM T. MORRISSEY BLVD

COLUMBIA RD

SARATOGA ST

CHELSEA ST

EAST BOSTON

MAVERICK ST

Boston Logan International Airport

SIGHTS

11	F2	Sam Adams Brewery	16	Ins	Bunker Hill Monument
13	F5	Edward M. Kennedy Institute for the United States Senate	25	Ins	USS *Constitution* Museum
14	F5	John F. Kennedy Presidential Library and Museum			

RESTAURANTS

2	A5	Santarpio's Pizza	17	Ins	Brewer's Fork
3	A6	Rino's Place	19	Ins	Legal Oysteria
12	F4	Dbar	21	Ins	Sorelle Bakery & Café
15	Ins	Monument Restaurant & Tavern			

NIGHTLIFE

1	A5	Pier 6	5	C1	Paradise Rock Club
4	C1	Great Scott	18	Ins	Warren Tavern

ARTS AND CULTURE

6	D1	Coolidge Corner Theatre

RECREATION

7	F1	Jamaica Pond	20	Ins	Charlestown Waterfront Bike Path
8	F1	New England Patriots	22	Ins	Paul Revere Park
9	F1	New England Revolution	24	Ins	Charlestown Navy Yard
10	F1	Arnold Arboretum			

HOTELS

23	Ins	Residence Inn Boston Harbor on Tudor Wharf

0 ——— 0.5 mi
0 ——— 0.5 km

DISTANCE ACROSS MAP
Approximate: 6.6mi or 10.7km

© MOON.COM

John F. Kennedy Presidential Library and Museum

Edward M. Kennedy Institute for the United States Senate

More from Moon east of the Mississippi

CHARLESTON & SAVANNAH

COASTAL MAINE
With Acadia National Park
HILARY NANGLE

FLORIDA KEYS
With Miami & the Everglades

MAINE
HILARY NANGLE

MICHIGAN
PAUL VACHON

NEW ENGLAND
JEN ROSE SMITH

NEW YORK STATE

NORTH CAROLINA
Walks in the Smoky Mountains National Park
JASON FRYE

RHODE ISLAND

TENNESSEE
MARGARET LITTMAN

VERMONT
JEN ROSE SMITH

VIRGINIA & MARYLAND
MICHAELA RIVA GAASERUD

MOON.COM
@MOONGUIDES

Road Trip Guides

City Guides

MORE FROM MOON

MOON
AMALFI COAST
With Capri, Naples & Pompeii
LAURA THAYER

MOON
BARCELONA & MADRID
JESSICA JONES

MOON
CROATIA & SLOVENIA
SHANN FOUNTAIN ALIPOUR

MOON
EDINBURGH, GLASGOW & THE ISLE OF SKYE
SALLY COFFEY

MOON
FRENCH RIVIERA: NICE, CANNES, MONACO & ST-TROPEZ
JON BRYANT

MOON
ICELAND
JENNA GOTTLIEB

MOON
IRELAND
CAMILLE DeANGELIS

MOON
MOROCCO

MOON
NORWAY
DAVID NIKEL

MOON
PORTUGAL
CARRIE-MARIE BRATLEY

MOON
PRAGUE, VIENNA & BUDAPEST
JENNIFER D. WALKER
AUBURN SCALLON

MOON
ROME, FLORENCE & VENICE
ALEXEI J. COHEN

GO BIG AND GO BEYOND!

OR TAKE THINGS ONE STEP AT A TIME

MOON ROAD TRIP GUIDES

Drive & Hike APPALACHIAN TRAIL
THE BEST TRAIL TOWNS, DAY HIKES, AND ROAD TRIPS IN BETWEEN
TIMOTHY MALCOLM

BLUE RIDGE PARKWAY Road Trip
INCLUDING SHENANDOAH & GREAT SMOKY MOUNTAINS NATIONAL PARKS
JASON FRYE

CALIFORNIA Road Trip
SAN FRANCISCO, YOSEMITE, LAS VEGAS, GRAND CANYON, LOS ANGELES, & THE PACIFIC COAST HIGHWAY
STUART THORNTON

NASHVILLE TO NEW ORLEANS Road Trip
NATCHEZ TRACE PARKWAY · MEMPHIS · TUPELO · MISSISSIPPI BLUES TRAIL
MARGARET LITTMAN

NEW ENGLAND Road Trip
BOSTON, ACADIA NATIONAL PARK, WHITE MOUNTAINS, BERKSHIRES, NEWPORT, AND CAPE COD
JEN ROSE SMITH

NORTHERN CALIFORNIA Road Trip
DRIVES ALONG THE COAST, REDWOODS, AND MOUNTAINS WITH THE BEST STOPS ALONG THE WAY
STUART THORNTON & KAYLA ANDERSON

OREGON TRAIL Road Trip
HISTORIC SITES, SMALL TOWNS, AND SCENIC LANDSCAPES ALONG THE LEGENDARY WESTWARD ROUTE
KATRINA EMERY

PACIFIC COAST HIGHWAY Road Trip
CALIFORNIA, OREGON & WASHINGTON
IAN ANDERSON

Drive & Hike PACIFIC CREST TRAIL
THE BEST TRAIL TOWNS, DAY HIKES, AND ROAD TRIPS IN BETWEEN
CAROLINE HINCHLIFF

Advice on where to sleep, eat, and explore

Detailed driving directions including mileage and drive times

Itineraries for a range of timelines

MOON
PACIFIC NORTHWEST
Road Trip
SEATTLE, VANCOUVER, VICTORIA, THE OLYMPIC PENINSULA, PORTLAND, THE OREGON COAST & MOUNT RAINIER
ALLISON WILLIAMS

MOON
ROUTE 66
Road Trip
JESSICA DUNHAM

MOON
SOUTH FLORIDA & THE KEYS
Road Trip
WITH MIAMI, WALT DISNEY WORLD, TAMPA & THE EVERGLADES
JASON FERGUSON

MOON
SOUTHWEST
Road Trip
LAS VEGAS, ZION & BRYCE, MONUMENT VALLEY, SANTA FE & TAOS, AND THE GRAND CANYON
TIM HULL

MOON
VANCOUVER & CANADIAN ROCKIES
Road Trip
VICTORIA, BANFF, JASPER, CALGARY, THE OKANAGAN, WHISTLER & THE SEA-TO-SKY HIGHWAY
CAROLYN B. HELLER

MOON
YELLOWSTONE TO GLACIER NATIONAL PARK
Road Trip
JACKSON HOLE, CODY, THE GRAND TETONS & THE ROCKY MOUNTAIN FRONT
CARTER G. WALKER

MOON BOSTON
Avalon Travel
Hachette Book Group
1700 Fourth Street
Berkeley, CA 94710, USA
www.moon.com

Editor: Kristi Mitsuda
Series Manager: Leah Gordon
Copy Editor: Deana Shields
Graphics Coordinator and Production Designer: Suzanne Albertson
Cover Design: Faceout Studios, Charles Brock
Interior Design: Megan Jones Design
Moon Logo: Tim McGrath
Map Editor: Albert Angulo
Cartographers: John Culp, Moon Street Cartography (Durango, CO)
Proofreaders: Samia Abbasi, Rosemarie Leenerts
Indexer: Rachel Kuhn

ISBN-13: 9781640498631

Printing History
1st Edition — 2018
2nd Edition — May 2020
5 4 3 2 1

Front cover photo: Harvard University rowing crew © Joe Sohm/VisionsofAmerica/Getty Images

Back cover photo: George Washington equestrian statue © Sean Pavone | Dreamstime.com

Printed in China by RR Donnelley